How You
THINK...
Determines
The Course
Of Your
LIFE

365 Devotions
For Renewing Your Mind

Also by Laura Mangin McDonald, MA LPC

———

Christian Insight for Life...for every day (2013)

How You THINK...

Determines The Course Of Your LIFE

365 Devotions For Renewing Your Mind

Laura Mangin McDonald, MA LPC

Christian Insight for Life

†

Requests for information and comments should be addressed to: Christian Insight for Life, P.O. Box 452796, Garland, TX 75045-2796

ISBN-13 978-1505880915
ISBN-10 1505880912

Cover Design: DeAnza Spangler
Author Photo: Bhurdphotography.com

Printed in the United States of America
www.christianinsightforlife.com

*"They will fight you, but they will fail.
For I am with you, and I will take care of you. I, the LORD,
have spoken!"*

JEREMIAH 1:19 (NLT)

PREFACE

Thank you for choosing this devotional. It will challenge how you think and deepen your relationship with God over the course of the next year. I can boldly make this promise because God's Word works and when we follow it...our lives work! I'm passionate about God's Word; it transformed my life and I've watched for years as it has transformed the lives of those I've worked with in my counseling practice! I loved God for years before I had revelation of His love for me, and that was because I didn't have my mind renewed with His truth! Until we embrace God's truth, we will seek from the hand of man what only God can deliver! And that's the purpose of this book: to give you a practical application for renewing your mind with God's truth, so you can know and be known by His love, and fulfill the plans He made for you long ago!

This devotional is based on three powerful truths that will enable you to be the authentic person God designed you to be! First, God is love. He chose, loved and purposed you; there's only one you in this world! You're designed by God to *add* meaning to this world, not to *find* your meaning in this world (EPH.2:10). Second, to gain insight into how much God loves you and to know how He will help you carry out His plans through you, you need to spend time with Him (PHIL.1:6). Third, how you think determines the course of your life. Renewing your mind with God's Word enables you to line up your thoughts with His, while demolishing the lies of the enemy that have worked their way into your identity (ROM.12:2). Meditate daily on these three truths, even on those days when you don't feel like doing it. Remember this: *what you feel doesn't change God's truth...but God's truth will change how you feel!*

Finally, every morning immediately be purposed in setting your mind on God's plans for you, *not* on God endorsing *your* agenda. Before you begin reading the devotional for the day, ask the Holy Spirit to guide you; remember, His role is to help you 24/7 to do all that God asks of you. God's Word works all the time, in every generation, in any kind of situation and with every person!

Blessings, friends!

Laura Mangin McDonald, MA LPC

Garland, Texas
December 2014

January 1

"But seek first his kingdom and his righteousness..."
MATT. 6:33

If we live for weekends, holidays and special occasion.... we won't enjoy life. If we keep others at arm's length, are unwilling to compromise, insist on being right, reject correction and refuse to apologize...we won't enjoy life. If we allow others to determine our thoughts, moods, actions, worth, value or purpose...we won't enjoy life. If we're stingy with money or possessions, give others our leftovers, love conditionally and withhold affection...we won't enjoy life. If we hold on to blame, unforgiveness, envy or bitterness, compare ourselves to others, are critical and negative, find it hard to laugh in general or at ourself...we won't enjoy life. If we're unwilling to admit weakness or defeat, deny insecurities, be vulnerable, claim to have all the answers, hold on to regret and guilt, allow little room for error, have difficulty asking for help and find it hard to forgive ourselves...we won't enjoy life.

When we seek God first, release our hurts to Jesus, trust the prompting of the Holy Spirit, renew our minds with the Word daily, believe that God supplies all our needs and that His strength is perfected in our weaknesses, pray about everything, cast our cares, believe the Word more than our feelings, walk by faith and not by sight, know God purposed and individually planned each of us long ago and that He will continue to do the good work He started in us until the day Jesus returns...then we will know the truth and the truth will set us free...*then* we will enjoy life.

MATT. 6:33; ISAIAH 61:1-3, 30:21; ROM. 12:2; PHIL. 4:7; 1 COR. 5:7; EPH. 2:10; PHIL. 1:6; JOHN 8:32

January 2

"My determined purpose is to know Him"
PHIL. 3:10

Jesus pulled up to my office one day and said, "Come on, we're going for a ride." I said, "Excuse me, Lord, I've got a lot of work to do, can this wait?" Jesus wanted to mess with my nice, neat and planned life. I felt I'd done my spiritual and emotional work-I'd let go of my guilt, hurt and anger, forgiven those I needed to and believed and confessed God's Word. But I was not taking any risks in the name of Jesus. I loved Him, but wasn't living a life totally committed to Him; I was very safe, orderly and predictable. These are good things, *unless* you hide behind them.

God had put some big dreams in my heart, but I dismissed them as my imagination; I'd entertain them for awhile and shelf them. Then Jesus pressed me on what I really believed: how do you know God will do the impossible unless you stand back and trust Him to? How do you know He uses foolish and weak things to confound the wise unless you're willing to look foolish and weak? How do you know the bold courage of the Holy Spirit is flowing through you, unless you're willing to do bold and courageous things? God's relentless love wouldn't allow me to settle - He confronted me: did I really love Him as I said? Was I allowing Him to work through me to make an impact? Was I more concerned about messing up and maybe missing Him than having a heart to follow Him, and would I choose safety over taking a risk in the name of love for Him?

Well, I got in with Jesus that day-I want to know and be known intimately by Him. Jesus said, *"Anyone who has faith in me will do what I have been doing and even greater things than these."* Will you lay down who you think you should be...so God can lead you into who He made you to be? Wake up, sleeper, lift your head, come out from behind your busy schedule, and the fears and lies you've believed for years; it's not about your *ability*...it's about your *availability* to serve as God has called and equipped you to.

You can't reach your destination without Jesus! Get in with Him; He knows the way, but get ready when you do, and buckle up, baby, because Jesus drives really fast!

LUKE 1:37; 1 COR. 1:27; 1 THESS. 1:5; JOHN 14:12-13; EPH. 2:10

January 3

"For I know the plans I have for you, declares the Lord..."
JER. 29:11

God has good plans for us. The only way we are eliminated is if we quit. God never promised easy...He promised victory! If we seek Him first He will bring us through every trial. Put your hope in His power, not your wisdom and understanding; then you won't be shocked when opposition shows up, discouragement chases you down, or when weariness overwhelms you!

God will supply all we need and then some. We can count on Him because He cannot lie; He keeps His promises. And, He's not a quitter, so...He's not quitting on us! He finishes what He starts - He will finish the good work He started in us long ago, until the day of Jesus' return. Will you agree with the good plans God has for you?

JER. 29:11; MATT. 6:33; PS. 34:19; 1 COR 2:5; HEB. 6:18; PHIL. 1;6, 4:19

January 4

"Don't be afraid; just believe..."
LUKE 9:50

Jairius' daughter was dead. No hope-don't bother Jesus. Even as he ran to Jesus begging Him to save his daughter, Jairus got the news : it's too late, don't bother asking. It won't make a difference.

What's broken and left for dead in your life? Sudden job loss, failed relationship, lost virginity, betrayal, rebellious child, foreclosure, financial ruin, grief so thick it suffocates you daily, death of a loved one, pain that consumes your very being? We look at devastation and it stares back as us-our world spins; how will we ever overcome...dear God, what will we do now? Shame plagues us; how can the pain ever stop gushing out of us? Where will we go from here? Jairus was told to stop asking because the girl was dead. When Jesus heard this, He said, *"Don't be afraid; just believe and she will be healed."* Jairus had to be in a daze - his only child dead. What would he do; how could he move on? He decided, while in the grip of grief, to listen to Jesus and follow Him.

Don't give up and stop asking Jesus for help when all you see is broken and dead. Keep praying, asking and following Jesus. When we're sinking in devastation and can't see a way out-hold on; Jesus is making a way for us, but we must follow Him. He is the Way, the Truth and the Life...of any dead situation we are experiencing. Jesus led Jairus' back to his home, where his dead daughter lay. Jesus told the people to "stop wailing." To overcome we must see and work through the eyes and strength of Jesus. He can bring life to any broken or dead situation we are facing. *We have got to trust His way of handling it.* Jesus overcame death! He is Life; let Him give life to your dead situation. Jesus ignored the laughter and snide comments of the naysayers. He took those He trusted, along with the girl's parents, to where she lay. He reached to her-her spirit returned and she got up. Let Jesus reach to you; don't be afraid, just believe. He will make a way for us; He is life to the death we are facing. He knows all about being broken and left for dead. He's overcome the world and He can help us overcome the broken and dead situations in our lives!

Luke 8:40-42, 49-56; John 14:6, 16:33

January 5

"Let your light shine before men..."
Matt. 5:16

Life *impacts* us; how we respond...*defines* us! Trials are a part of life - don't let them steal God's promises or become your identity. Take ownership of your life-repair what you've broken, return what you've stolen, stop blaming, quit wishing, take steps, make amends, finish what you've started, be real, stop faking, be a giver, stop being stingy; it's not your's anyway, keep your word, hold your words, forgive, let go of guilt, be full of joy, break off toxic relationships, speak life not death, receive grace, give grace...*be an overcomer!*

God promises to walk us through every trial we face, but He won't always make them disappear! We're more than conquerors because His Spirit lives in us. If God is for us, who can be against us? Don't waste another good day wishing or dreading. Will you take ownership of the life Jesus died to give you so God can pursue His plan through you?

ISAIAH 41:10; PHIL. 1:6; ROM. 8:31; JOHN 10:10; MATT. 5:16

January 6

"Do not be anxious about anything..."
PHIL. 4:6-7

Don't give up...discouragement wants to talk us out of believing God by entertaining "what ifs" - the situations we can't control. Ruminating on "what ifs" deafens our ability to hear the Holy Spirit's direction and forfeits the supernatural comfort He provides.

Instead of contemplating "what ifs," renew your mind with God's Word; output energy is the same, but one leads to death and the other...to *life!* God's peace guards our minds and hearts, and God is for you! These aren't just positive words-they are God's Words and they are full of *power!* Don't give up; hold on to God's Word.

PHIL. 4:6-7; GAL. 6:9; ROM. 8:31

January 7

"...he who began a good work in you will carry it on
to completion until the day of Christ Jesus."
PHIL. 1:6

Layers of life...a culmination of experiences and emotions. Some recall with joy, others with sorrow. Each layer tells a story...some we tuck in our hearts forever, others we want to completely forget. We get bogged down in the layers of life when we feel justified in our actions - the reasons we don't want to move forward. Some don't want to release their predictable routines; they feel safe and reason it's their option to move forward or not...so they forfeit their future, opting for the comfortable familiar. Others justify that they can't move forward; they're not able to shake off regret and shame so they watch reruns of "what I should have done and how things might be, if I would have..."

As Christians, we're to always be in forward motion and making a difference. Intensity can change according to the seasons of life, but the perpetual forward motion never stops. We're saved to fulfill the plans and purposes God called us for - we've got to see our lives from God's perspective. We're His children; we're equipped with specific skills and talents to do a job...yes, God loves us dearly and we're valuable to Him...so He gives us important jobs to carry out, to build up the body of believers. Every step has been ordered. He calls the end from the beginning. We're more than conquerors, not so we can sit on the sofa and complain about what's not right in our lives...but so we can *go out* and spread the Gospel, the good news; the same good news that saved us!

The layers of life...we go through them - some we like, others we don't...but none of them excuse us from not moving forward and carrying out the purposes God put in us!

PROV. 16:2; ROM. 8:37; EPH. 2:10; PHIL. 1:6; ISAIAH 46:10

January 8

"We live by faith, not by sight."
2 COR. 5:7

Focus and move forward...forever begins today-*right now*! Every step we take and each thought we have today is an investment in forever...because forever begins right *now*. Raise your expectations beyond what you can see or reason...you can't understand God's promises. We have to make a choice to believe them because He said so. Put your hope in His power...not your preconceived ideas and perceptions. The human mind cannot comprehend how God will deliver His promises, but many don't want to be let down-so they lower their expectations. God can't let us down because He keeps His promises!

Don't confuse your timeline with His delivery time; but, just so you know...His promises may take the slow train. Our preconceived notions will distort clarity in seeing God's truth. The human mind can't comprehend how, when, why, what and where God will do things. Those who believed and loved Jesus were distraught after His death...they had preconceived ideas of how God's promises would be fulfilled: "we hoped He was the One." Jesus asked His disciples after His resurrection, *"why are you troubled; why do doubts raise in your minds?"*

What preconceived notions are keeping you from believing that God will do what He has promised? Raise your expectations. Get focused and move forward...forever begins today. *Right now.* Are you ready?

1 COR. 2:5; 2 COR. 5:7; HEB. 12:27; ISAIAH 55:9; LUKE 24:21, 37; ROM. 12:2

January 9

*"He brought them out of darkness and the deepest gloom
and broke away their chains."*
PS. 107:14

You say it's hard to let go of the wrong that was imposed on you. You're right; it is. But do you believe it's easier to live in bondage to blame and unforgiveness? Blame keeps us chained to the wrong done to us. Until we release the blame into the hands of Jesus, we remain a prisoner in our own pain, and we forfeit the freedom Jesus offers us. There's a way that seems right in the mind and it leads to death, but those who seek God's truth are set free! You are free to chose...what do you believe?

JOHN 8:31; PS. 107:14

January 10

*"Blessed rather are those who hear the word
of God and obey it."*
LUKE 11:28

Debating God's truth...doesn't change His truth. Jesus lives in us...He goes where we go. He stays where we stay; He's alive is us! His power is in us to handle any impossible situation we face. *Jesus has overcome the world.* Our peace is in Him, not in what we hope works out. This is a truth; whether or not we choose to believe it, doesn't make it any less true.

God's promises are available to anyone who believes in Him; He doesn't discriminate. Many Christians become very confused when they consider whether to believe all of God's Word, or just parts of it. God's Word doesn't lie...it stands firm; there is no room for debate or modification. God's Word will not change. He keeps His promises. Blessed are those who hear the Word of God and obey it! *Believing God is a choice...not a feeling!* Believing is the key to accessing the promises, presence and power.

Don't ponder, debate and speculate. You will lose ground and become confused. Jesus is the Way, the Truth and the Life. Know His truth and be set free! He knows what you are facing this very second. Choose to believe that He will help you.

JOHN 8:32, 14:6, 16:33; ACTS 10:34; LUKE 11:28

January 11

"You are God's masterpiece..."
EPH. 2:10

Break up with self-defeat...foreverrrrr! If we really knew how much God loves us we would think and act differently and see ourselves as God sees us-fearfully and wonderfully made; His masterpieces. Knowing His confidence in us gives us the resources to overcome anything. Self-defeat wants to bind us in fear, anticipate let-downs, and be afraid of being passed-over, rejected and unfulfilled. Self-defeat is a liar...all the time.

There is no fear in God's love; dread does *not* exist. His love expels every trace of terror! Self-defeat taunts us, reminding us of past mistakes and insecurities. Lean into Jesus; His love isn't intimidated by our past mistakes and insecurities. Jesus didn't engage Satan in conversation; He responded only with Scripture. We're to do the same.

When self-defeat knocks on your door and wants to debate...slam the door! Renew your mind with the Word; speak it throughout the day; say what God says about you; keep the Word close to your eyes and always within reach. We will begin to think and act differently the more we say what God says about us, and the more revelation we will have of Him loving us.

Self-defeat is a coward. It cannot stand against the authentic power of God's love! Don't let self-defeat steal one more second...break up with self-defeat foreverrrrr!

PS. 139:15; EPH. 2:10; I JOHN 4:18; ROM. 12:2

January 12

"But thanks be to God, who always leads us in triumphal procession in Christ..."
ISAIAH 40:29

Life isn't fair; mistakes are made, people cheat, treat others harshly, let loved ones down, and bad things happen to good people. But our hope is in Christ-He promises to deliver us from each one. God's plans will not be stopped; He finishes what He starts and His Word will not return void. The burdens of life aren't on us-they're on Jesus, and He has deprived them of the power to harm us!

What a relief to know that all of the burdens we face are subjected to the power of Christ, Who lives in us! We can be certain that what happens to us doesn't define or determine our destiny. Thanks be to God, Who always leads us to triumph in Christ! God has good plans for you...will you trust Him?

2 COR. 2:14,15; PS. 34:19; JOHN 16:33; ISAIAH 55:11; JER. 29:11

January 13

"Now may the God of hope fill you with all joy and peace in believing, so that you will abound in hope by the power of the Holy Spirit."
ROM. 15:13

Believing God when despair consumes your being-when what you prayed and hoped for slips through your hands...how does one move forward when despair stares back at them? The answer is God's hope-His hope is full of power...the same power that raised Jesus from the dead! God's hope holds your mind and heart together enabling you to believe Him during the most hopeless times in life. His hope will give you hope again and bring you through this despair...will you let Him?

HEB. 6:19; EPH.3:18-20; ROM. 5:3-5, 15:13

January 14

"And my God will supply all your needs according to His glorious riches in Christ Jesus."
PHIL. 4:19

The human mind cannot process the harsh realities of life apart from the direction and comfort of the Holy Spirit. There is a fine line between being used up due to exhaustion during a difficult season, and being used up due to exhaustion from living life. The former is the result of pouring oneself out but *knowing with confidence* that God will supply all of your needs, and the latter is the result of pouring oneself out and wondering *if* God will supply what is needed. Will you let go and let God? He's got it all worked out!

PHIL. 4:19; MARK 11:22

January 15

"With the measure you use it will be measured to you..."
MARK 4:24

The measure of thought and study we give to the truth will be the measure of virtue and knowledge that comes back to us. And more will be given to you who hear...for him who has nothing even what he has will be taken away (SEE MARK 4:24-25). Get a good attitude...it determines the course of your life!

Truth is the operative word: many go through the motions of saying, giving and doing but their hearts aren't connected; outward actions are just outward actions. We're to be constantly renewed in the spirit of our mind-our attitude, lining it up with God's Word. Use what you've been given to the best of your ability, making the most of what God has placed in your hands. He says He will give you more. Don't believe the lie that you don't have anything to give or to use. God gives to each of us something to work with, and our attitude determines if we have the spiritual maturity to be trusted with more.

If we are griping about our current jobs, we're not ready for promotion. If we're trashing our current car, we're not ready to care for a new one. If we're not giving the first tenth of our income and being generous now with what we have, we won't give more when we have more. As Christians, we're guaranteed to achieve in God's design-His ways work all the time with all people, *when they submit their lives to Him.* That includes our attitude. It determines the course of our lives and what we're mature enough to handle. Will you submit your attitude today and live the life to which God has called you?

MARK 4:24; MATT. 23:25-28; EPH. 4:23

January 16

"The one who calls you is faithful, and he will do it."
I THESS. 5:24

Our confidence in God's Word is the assurance that He will get us on the other side of any trial in life, but we've got to cling to His Word! During any season of life we have to be purposed in renewing our mind with the Word for balanced living, but especially during difficult seasons, to mentally process the impossible realities we're facing. If a person begins to focus on her difficult season more than on renewing her mind with God's Word, she will begin to develop destructive thought patterns. These thought patterns cause a spiritual paralysis and interfere with the mind processing information. This leads to apathy and results in a disconnect.

God didn't design our mind to deal with the harsh realities of life apart from the direction and comfort of the Holy Spirit! There's a fine line between being used up due to exhaustion in being obedient to Christ, versus being used up due to exhaustion from living life. One is a result of pouring yourself out but *knowing* with confidence God will supply all your needs, and the other is pouring yourself out and *wondering* if God will supply what you need!

Cling to the Word...it's your confidence for life no matter what you face!

1 THESS. 5:24; ISAIAH 26:3; PS. 16:8; HEB. 12:1-3

January 17

"I will instruct you and teach you in the way you should go...:
PS. 32:8

God's truth has set you free...live like it! You may not always feel like it, but that doesn't negate it; *what you feel doesn't change God's truth, but God's truth will change...the way you feel!* We must know our weaknesses-the enemy does. It's where he attacks us because he knows it works. Listen closely: God doesn't invite us to be saved and then expect us to figure out how we are going to walk in the freedom He promises! He gives us the desire and power to follow Him, then instructs and teaches us in the way we should go, all the while giving counsel and keeping His loving eyes on us. God's truth has set you free...will you begin to live like it?

PS. 32:8; JOHN 8:32

January 18

*"... you will know the truth and
the truth will set you free."*
JOHN 8:31-32

Minimizing, ignoring or blaming something or someone for unresolved hurt keeps us chained to the experiences that have hurt us. Time passes; hurts don't. Unresolved hurts keep us from living in the present because we then live life through our past pain. Until the pain is resolved we are chained to the past. Hurt is as alive today as it was the day it happened, but it's not always identified because it has many layers of life on it.

Old hurt is misplaced and disguised as other issues and will manifest in relationships as disappointment, suspicion, and a need to prove one's worth. It can lead to anxiety, anger, depression and phobias. Old hurt lingers. It shows up as a vague emptiness that we can't put our finger on-an unidentified uneasiness or a general sense of feeing wrong. We may unknowingly attribute these feelings to other people, or even worse...believe the lie that that is all there is to life. Old hurt distorts perception-keeping the view of the present obscured.

Ask Jesus to search your heart and show you what you've not dealt with; get with a pastor, Bible-centered process group or Christian counselor if the old hurt continues to resurface. Jesus came to save us - bind up our wounds and bring us out of darkness! No job, person, status, relationship or good work can heal us...only Jesus can give back to us what was taken or given away and give us what we should have received.

Where the Spirit of the Lord is there is freedom! Will you make the decision to walk out the freedom promised to you, and fulfill the destiny God planned for you? Don't live one more day chained to the past!

PS. 139:24-25; ISAIAH 61:1; 2 COR. 3:17; PHIL. 1:6

January 19

"We have this hope as an anchor for the soul..."
HEB. 6:19

Putting our hope in what we're praying for instead of hoping in Who God is leads to grief; it's a subtle shift in thinking that wrecks us, because we have put a contingency on our relationship with God by hoping in what He will do versus Who He is! What we pray for changes. God's hope never changes. His hope is constant, steady and unshakable, and when we put our hope in Him...we are constant, steady and unshakable! God's hope allows us to rest in Him because He promises to supply all of our needs. God's hope gives a peace that surpasses human understanding, holds on when we cannot, and gives a confident view of what is to come. His hope never disappoints! Will you hold tight to God's hope...right now?

HEB. 6:19, 11:1; ROM. 5:3-5

January 20

"And my God will meet all your needs
according to his glorious riches in Christ Jesus."
PHIL. 4:19

The enemy is a roaring lion ready to discourage you by reminding you of your weaknesses and failures. The enemy's case is powerful because most of what he says is true-all of us have many weakness and failures. We can't correct our weaknesses apart from God, but with His strength, He will help us accomplish anything He needs us to do! His grace accepts everything about us while His truth is honest in what He will help us overcome. So when the enemy wants to get in your head and remind you of all the things you need to do and how grossly insufficient you are, immediately turn your thoughts to God's grace and truth and thank Him for enabling you to overcome! Do this every time the enemy condemns you and eventually you will redirect your thought patterns to respond without you even having to "think" about responding!

You can't correct yourself; doing so will take you into a pit of spiritual pride, which has you to think on thoughts like: don't ask for help or you will look weak, you will never overcome these problems, you should be further along in your Christian walk, etc. If a person persists in trying to correct his behaviors apart from God's grace and truth, her thoughts will default to self-loathing and apathy, which disrupt the growth process...and that's exactly the trap the enemy wants us in!

We've all been there, but we don't want to keep going back there! Focus daily on God's grace and truth; this mental exercise will strengthen you emotionally and spiritually. Don't entertain lies from the enemy. Will you agree with God that you are His masterpiece, created and purposed for His glory?

COL. 2:10-15; EPH. 2:10, 3:20; PHIL. 4:13

January 21

"His love endures forever."
PS. 136:1

If we've been hurt by someone who was supposed to love us, we will struggle believing those who have chosen to love us. Until we come to know the authentic love of Christ, hurt will distort our view of ourselves-believing that we somehow don't measure up and that we have to prove we're worth enough to be loved. *This is a lie; another person's approval or disapproval has nothing to do with our value!*

God says we are fearfully and wonderfully made-His masterpieces. He chose and loved us first. We are heirs of the King. These are God's truths; *they will never change and are not open for debate.* We must make a decision to believe that we are loved, chosen and adopted. Fear wants us to believe that we're less than because someone didn't love us like we thought they were supposed to. Don't entertain fear; each time it knocks on the door our your mind, immediately divert to God's truth: our identity is founded in God's love and His love never changes!

Until we have revelation of God's love we will continue to project our hurts onto Him by questioning if His love will fail like human love has for us. This unresolved hurt then overflows onto those who *do* love us. We must make a *decision* to believe we are loved even though we may not feel like it. Ask the Holy Spirit for revelation; He will help you. Don't take fear's bait. Stand firm on God's truth-He won't forsake us. His love never fails or gives up on us.

If someone didn't love you like they should have, that doesn't make you unloveable or prove that something's wrong with you-that makes something wrong with them! Will you believe God and and no longer let old hurt distort how you see? Where the Spirit of the Lord is there is freedom!

PS. 136:1, 139:14; EPH. 1:5, 1:11, 2:10; JOHN 3:16; ROM. 8:17; DEUT. 31:6

January 22

"I do believe; help me overcome my unbelief."
MARK 9:24

Where we end...Jesus begins-perfecting His power in our weaknesses, giving us what we don't have, and doing what we cannot. Apart from Him we can do nothing, and that really means *nothing*, including believing or having faith. Our part is to reach for what God promises, desiring to believe that He will give us everything we need to carry out what He asks of us.

Our tendency is to try to figure out how He will make things happen, but we cannot. When we do this we create doubt, because we're trying to apply human solutions to impossible situations...we're to believe God *can*, not figure out *how* He will! He will give us His hope to hold on to and help us with unbelief when we seek Him. This enables us to wait in the confidence that He will provide all we need! Will you put your faith in God's power and believe that He can help you?

MARK 9:24; 2 COR. 12:9; PHIL. 2:13, 4:13; JOHN 15:5; 1 COR. 2:5

January 23

"...and you have been given fullness in Christ"
COL. 2:10

Spending time in prayer is vital for our identity in Christ to be developed; our stability thrives on the intimacy we have with Him. Spending time in prayer isn't something we *have* to do; it's something we can do - it's a *privilege*. We need this time with Jesus to rise up and be who He says we are, and it's our time to praise, honor and thank Him, loving Him for Who He is. Praising Him...strengthens us!

Our Father God is the... I AM, the Alpha and the Omega, El Shaddai, Jehovah Jireh, Savior, Comforter, Protector, Provider, and Creator of the universe! He loves us; He lives in us and He knitted us together with His very own hands! He always has time for us...He approves of all of us, flooding us with His confidence-directing and correcting us, whispering dreams and ideas into our hearts, comforting and assuring us that He's got everything covered and that we don't need to be anxious or afraid.

Time spent with our Father is safe, intimate and validating; it's during this time that He shows us our value and worth-our authentic identity is found, and continually developed, in Him. When we go into the world we know who we are, not because of who we are, but because of Who we know we belong to; we are His! His confidence in us directs our steps.

Time with our Father: guard it and don't allow anything or anyone take you away from being alone with Him. Seek God, love Him with all your heart, receive His love...let Him be your Father; His love completes you! He will give you more than you could ever ask for or could even dream about. Spend time with Him...it's your privilege!

COL. 2:10; PS. 139:13; COL. 1:17. MATT. 6:33; EPH. 3:20

January 24

"I pray that from his glorious, unlimited resources he will empower you with inner strength through his Spirit."
Eph. 3:16

If you want to make a difference in this world...seek the One Who made it; to maximize your potential-go to the One Who put it in you! Your potential has a parameter-it comes to an end; *God has no end.* How your potential may be maximized by God depends on your willingness to completely rely on Him. Apart from God's love and direction, your potential maxes out in human effort. But humbly accepting God's love enables you to do all things He calls you to! Bottom line: your best isn't enough. Where your natural potential ends-God's supernatural ability begins! Embrace this truth consistently; it keeps you on the course to victory!

Over-thinking these truths will drown you in your own reasoning. Most don't move forward for fear of missing God, but a person can't miss God, *even if they're following Him!* God sees your heart; if you mess up, His mercy will cover you! And this is what believing is all about...walking by faith not by sight!

Eph. 1:19, 3:16 (NLT); 1 Cor. 1:25, 2:5; 2 Cor. 5:7

January 25

"My grace is sufficient for you..."
2 Cor. 12:9

Why are you searching your mind for an answer that only God has and only He can deliver? When you stop the search in your mind, you will be able to receive the comfort, confidence and guidance He gives you...*God's got this!*

Listen closely: your mind is about to burst and you're sleep deprived because you're trying to fix an impossible situation with a human solution. *Only God's provisions fix impossible situations.* Stop trying to do God's job...you will lose your mind. Rest in His sufficiency - His strength is perfected in your weakness. Apart from Him you can do nothing, and that really means nothing. But with Him you can do all things He strengthens you to do! And that includes empowering you with the desire to believe and trust that He's got everything figured out. Nothing is too big for God to handle, shocks Him, takes Him by surprise, or stumps His thinking. God doesn't need your help...He needs your trust so He can work through you.

2 COR. 12:9; JOHN 15:5; PHIL. 4:13; 1 COR. 2:5

January 26

"...where the Spirit of the Lord is, there is freedom."
2 COR. 3:17

If you believe your value in life is dependent on what you can or can't accomplish then you will feel accepted when you succeed and rejected when you fail. This belief leads to misery and places you in a perpetually agitated state because you're not defined by what you do or don't do...you're defined by "Who" lives in you and "what" He did for you!

We cannot save or change ourselves...if we could we wouldn't need a Savior! Are we so foolish, senseless and silly? Having begun our new spiritual lives...are we now reaching perfection by depending upon our own abilities? Then does He Who supplies us with His marvelous Holy Spirit and works powerfully and miraculously among us do so on...the grounds of "our doing," or on our believing in, adhering to, trusting in and relying on the message that we heard by faith?

God promises victory to every Christian; none is exempt, and there is no unique situation that His love cannot overcome. God only asks one thing and that is to believe in His Son, Jesus Christ. There's nothing we can do to earn or pay back what Jesus did for us other than to humbly receive it with unqualified assurance. This removes us from the salvation equation and gives full credit to Jesus Christ, our Savior and Lord! We can't earn the love Christ freely gives, nor can we achieve or take credit for His death on the cross or the power that raised Him from the dead. We got everything that is His the day we gave our life to Him.

When we embrace true humility, we take the focus off of us and put it on Christ. His Spirit living in us is our identity; we don't achieve an in identity in Christ...*it's given to us*! Will you stop focusing on what you can or can't do and freely accept all of God's love for you, so that you can walk in the freedom He promises you?

GAL. 3:2, 5; 2 COR. 5:17; JOHN 6:28-29, 8:31-32

January 27

"Do not let your hearts be troubled..."
JOHN 14:27

Are you already feeling agitated today? If so, you're looking at life through your strength, which lets the spirit of dread beat you up! Right now, remind yourself of this truth: Jesus gives His own peace; He bequeaths it to you from Him. We don't have to hope we can get it or try to find it...*it's ours*!

Don't let your heart be troubled or afraid; stop being agitated, disturbed, fearful, intimidated, cowardly and unsettled. Pull down that spirit of dread with the peace of Jesus *that lives in you*! If God is for you...who can be against you? Think on it and say it over and over and over. The more you think on and say it, the more you will believe it. You will know you're ready to move forward as you hold tight to this truth in your mind and profess it with your mouth!

ROM. 8:31; JOHN 14:27

January 28

"Consider it pure joy, my brothers,
whenever you face trials of many kinds..."
JAMES 1:2

Adversity will put to the test what we profess to believe about God and how we respond...and reveals where we stand. It exposes the false idols we've relied on, messes up the predictable routines that have stunted our development and purges pride we didn't even know existed. *Welcome this adversity* and know

God's love as never before; be known by Him in ways you've never imagined and open the door for the development of the authentic person He designed you to be.

Nobody looks forward to adversity, but it's required to grow in faith while gaining revelation of walking in the freedom God promises. You don't have to make a way for yourself-God has already done it! But you do have to agree with His truth and be willing to leave the comfort of the Christian fortress you've built and follow the unknown path God leads you down. When you accept the revelation that God is for you, has always loved you and wants you to rely completely on Him for all you need...then you will begin to let go of anxiety about being over-looked, not being good enough or not having what it takes.

Each time we face adversity we have an opportunity to lay down who we thank we should be and who we are trying to be, and become more of who God says we are...His masterpieces, who He created with His own hands to do the good works He planned specifically for each of us long ago!

What does your response to adversity reveal about you?

JAMES 1:2-8; JOHN 8:32; EPH. 2:10

January 29

"Those who look to him are radiant;
their faces are never covered with shame."
PS. 34:5

God's love overcomes...He will tell us who we belong to and who we are-that we are valued and loved. His love never changes because He never changes. In this, He's predictable and will never love us less no matter what we do. His love is a power that will ignite every neuron in our bodies because He *knows* every neuron in our bodies...He designed us!

Will you let God love you so you can know authentic love? You think you know love, but you've experienced counterfeit love. God's love doesn't harm, belittle or want you to beg and prove yourself worthy. His love accepts all of you-past, present and future. No person can make your pain go away, stop the scenes you replay in your mind continually, or still the voices of accusation, but... *God can and He will.* Call out to Him; He's mighty to save! His love completes you. You have worth despite what you've been told. They don't know, but God does. Will you let Him love you today?

You are not a left-over, side-lined or the last pick; you are a child of God! He chose you, knitted you together with His hands and He knows your name. Where the Spirit of the Lord is there is freedom. He is mighty to save; He will deliver you from all your fears; those who look to Him are radiant and their faces are never covered with shame! Will you let God love you today?

PS. 34:4; ZEPH. 3:17; ISAIAH 61:10; COL 2:10; 2 COR. 3:17

January 30

"He is before all things, and in him all things hold together."
COL. 1:17

If you're stressing about something, remind yourself how great is our God. He performs wonders that can't be fathomed, miracles that can't be counted, controls the clouds and makes lightning flash. He created the turquoise blue Caribbean, and the brilliant orange red of the setting sun. He existed before anything was, holds together all that is and reigns over the visible and the invisible. We cannot understand all that He does, but *we can choose to trust Who He is and what He does.*

Don't allow what you don't know to undermine your faith in the One Who does know. He's gentle, humble and kind, giving us rest for our souls. His yoke is easy and His burden light. Will you choose to focus on Him instead of what's stressing you?

COL. 1:16-17; MATT. 11:29-30

January 31

*"And I am sure of this, that he who began a good work in you
will bring it to completion at the day of Jesus Christ."*
PHIL. 1:6 (ESV)

A situation can consume, overwhelm and paralyze you for a period of time, but it doesn't have to determine your destiny. God *can and will* handle any situation you're up against. It's never too late for God to intervene...He owns time.

I've listened to many people over the years tell me of their situation...lost virginity at 13, learning disability, job stress, can't read, married four times, multiple abortions, chronic illness, DUIs, no education, depression and anxiety, no skills, high interest rates, abusive parents, friendless, job market frozen, numerous affairs, afraid, drug and alcohol abuse, eating disorder, prison, etc. God is not intimidated by any of these circumstances-*one touch of His hand*...give it to Him! He is for you; there's no one, nada, none or nothing bigger than our God. Don't allow the situation you are in to rob you of the plans God has for you!

JER. 29:11; ROM. 8:28; PS. 24:1

✝

February 1

"Lord, teach us to pray..."
LUKE 11:1

Jesus will escort us into the throne room of our Father anytime, day or night; we don't need an appointment or ever have to wait. Prayer doesn't have to be a long or loud, rehearsed or repeated; prayer pours out words from the inside of our hearts...at times inaudible groanings we cannot even understand. We can pray anytime, anywhere, anyplace. Prayer is an open door to the Father. It's a privilege...don't turn your back on it.

Prayer is a time during which our Father assures us that we've got what it takes because He's put everything we need in us; it's where we're certain He hears, understands and cares, where He nurtures, encourages and validates us. Prayer is a safe retreat where our Father comforts and guides us, reminding us that we're never alone because He's with us always! Prayer is a privilege-will you let Jesus escort you to the throne room?

LUKE 11:1; EPH. 6:18; 1 THESS. 5:17

February 2

"Rather, speaking the truth in love, we are to grow up in every way into him who is the head, into Christ,"
EPH. 4:15 (ESV)

Speaking truth...to those you love. It takes guts to speak God's truth to those you love who are in sin. Many ignore sin in loved ones for fear of pushing them away or into more sinful behavior. Listen closely: if you were powerful enough to push a person into sinful behavior...you would be powerful enough to *stop* their sinful behavior! God calls us to deliver the truth and He carries out the consequences of the truth. *Until sin is confronted in love-restoration can't take place!*

Avoiding difficult conversations leads to a shallow relationship; the mentality is, "as long as you don't bring up my wrong...we can get along!" *Truth* is the conduit and growth agent in healthy relationships; it's God's design. Without truth love can't grow and without love a relationship dies. Don't allow the enemy to intimidate you by placing a burden of ungodly and unrealistic expectations on you. The enemy will work through the person in sin to attempt to place the reason for their behavior back on you; don't engage in having to prove why they're wrong. Instead, assert why you won't allow their sinful behavior to place you in a compromised position-emotionally, physically, financially, professionally, spiritually, and so on. You can't change their behavior, but you *can* state what you will or will not do!

Confronting sin is an opportunity for restoration..."turning a sinner from the error of their ways will save them from death and cover over a multitude of sins!" (SEE JAMES 5:19-20). Ignoring a loved one's sin makes you a silent accomplice on their path of destruction! God's truth is the mortar that seals a healthy relationship; His model for love requires us to have the guts to require truth as the standard by which we live. Will you have the guts to speak God's truth in love to those you love? His love never fails us!

JAMES 1:22, 5:19-20; JOHN 8:31-32; EPH. 4:15 (ESV)

February 3

"But those who trust in the LORD will find new strength. They will soar high on wings like eagles. They will run and not grow weary. They will walk and not faint."
ISAIAH 40:31 (NLT)

Waiting on God is hard...but it's the only way for us to be developed and to determine our readiness for the next season God wants to take us into. So...how's your waiting coming along? Merely waiting for time to pass so we can put another day behind us doesn't qualify as waiting on God...that's just wasting time.

Waiting on God is a time of spiritual endurance, testing what we profess to believe, purging our pride and eradicating the false confidence we've acquired. Waiting on God is about us knowing that apart from Him we can do nothing. *It's what we do while in a season of little that determines what we will do in a season of more!* Faith sees what the mind cannot comprehend-believing God's promises despite the evidence in our hands. What we *see* doesn't determine our destiny...it's what we *believe*!

Waiting on God is a time to grow stronger. He will renew our strength and we will soar high on wings as eagles, run and not grow weary, walk and not be faint. If God says it, He means it; He doesn't lie. If we're doing all we are supposed to be doing, we can wait with confidence. If in doubt, ask God. He gives wisdom generously. This doesn't always make the wait any less painful, but it does promise that Jesus will never leave you and He will lead you through.

Keep your mind renewed with the Word, reach out and help others...it always takes the mind off of self. Make your wait count-you're closer than you think!

ISAIAH 40:31 (NLT); JAMES 1:2-8

February 4

"By faith we understand that the universe was formed at God's command,
so that what is seen was not made out of what was visible."
HEB. 11:3

Men tried to kill Him, Satan tried to tempt Him, and the world's lied about Him, but *nothing* can stop Him...His name is Jesus! Jesus, the Name above all names. He was before anything came to be, and will be until *forever*! He made everything you see and don't see, and nothing turns into something in His hands. His love makes dead come alive, turns ends into beginnings, impossibles into possibles, lost is found, broken is restored, darkness becomes light. He splashes bright rainbows across the skies, makes stars twinkle at night, has the sun to rise faithfully every morning, and paints it a brilliant orange every evening. My Redeemer lives! Doubt Him if you want to, but I never will; I must cling to His Word; my life depends on it!

His love is mighty to save...it can fix any broken part of your heart, give back what was taken, find what was lost, and give you what you never got! As surely as I stand today, I can be confident that I will be with Him forever! He answers to anyone who calls on His name...His name is Jesus! Call on Him and He will reach out to you. His love is big enough to handle anything you've done or anything done to you! Don't take my word-take His...it will change your life!

COL. 1:17; PHIL. 2:19; HEB. 11:3

February 5

"I have come that they may have life,
and have it to the full."
JOHN 10:10

Blame is a powerful emotion-it replays the wrongs done and keeps injustice fresh in our minds. Attempts to make the wrongs right have failed: the more we tried the more we failed. We cannot undo what's been done, but Jesus can! He is the Author and Finisher; He has no barriers. His love heals past, present and future.

Blame has no case against the power of Christ! He heals broken hearts and saves those crushed in spirit; He will give us beauty for ashes we've been carrying. His hope anchors our souls and hold on for us when we cannot. The realities of this life will cause many heartaches and hardships, but God promises to bring us through each one. When we can't see a way, take comfort; He's made a way...His Word is a lamp to our feet and a light to our path. We must acknowledge the reality of what we went through and then give our hurts to Jesus.

Seek the Lord; He will deliver you from all your fears. Those who look to Him are radiant; their faces are never covered with shame. Your hurts are real-Jesus knows this. Will you let Him in your heart and take Him to the places you were hurt so His love can heal you? He promises you an abundant life beyond your broken heart!

JOHN 10:10; PS. 34:4-5, 18, 115:109, 147:3; HEB. 6:19, 12:2; ISAIAH 61:3

February 6

"I pray also that the eyes of your heart may be enlightened..."
EPH. 1:18

Flood my heart with your light; help me receive the wisdom you offer me daily through your love. My faith is in You, Your Word and Your ability to reach me to make a difference in me. You have all the bases covered. I can move forward in Your confidence despite obvious barriers because of Your strength in me. I don't want to doubt You. Don't let me doubt, even when all looks to be against me in the natural.

Each day I will remind myself of Your love and promises...over and over and over; Your love covers, protects and gives me strength. Your love is tender, caring, never condemning-constantly renewing the eyes of my heart to fulfill the plans and destiny you gave me. Don't let me dismiss the fearless confidence You offer me constantly due to the feelings that sometimes overwhelm, flood and discourage me. Help me to remain steadfast, patient and to endure what you have called me to do, always remembering I'm a vessel for you, performing and fully accomplishing Your will so I can receive, carry away and enjoy to the full what You have promised! Faith looks crazy to those who cannot see...don't let their blurred vision interfere with what You have allowed me to see!

EPH.1:18; MARK 9:24; HEB. 10:35-36

February 7

"continue to live in him, rooted and built up in him..."
COL.2:7

Refuse to settle...if you've received Jesus Christ as your Lord and Savior; you are saved, so live like it! Don't dread on more day; lean your entire personality on Him - having absolute trust and confidence in His power, wisdom and goodness. Walk with Him; have roots [of your being] firmly and deeply planted, fixed and founded in Him (SEE COL. 2:7 AMP). Be continually built up in His confidence-this establishes your faith. Whatever God asks you to do He equips you to do! *You're equipped to the level you will trust Him.* Do it one step at a time; breathe, then do it again. It's hard, but not as hard as trying to do life your way.

Remain steadfast, patient, move forward, endure; don't throw away your confidence or forfeit your prize. Refuse to settle!

COL. 2:5-7 (AMP); HEB. 10:35-36

February 8

"See, I am about to do a new thing..."
ISAIAH 43:19 (NLT)

Have you been in the same season for a long time? Are you doing everything you know how to do but nothing is budging or opening up? You believe God's Word and profess it daily, but doubt is banging on the door of your mind and you're wearing down...you just want life to go back to normal again.

Listen closely: normal cannot satisfy or give you security; normal is here one day and gone the next. Your security is found only in God's sufficiency. When you let go of the false security of what you consider normal you can then rest in God's sufficiency. His strength empowers and makes you equal to anything; He infuses inner strength...you are self-sufficient (normal) in His sufficiency!

"For I am about to do something new. See, I have already begun! Do you not see it? I will make a pathway through the wilderness. I will create rivers in the dry wasteland" (ISAIAH 43:19 NLT). Don't forfeit moving forward because you won't let go of your idea of normal or underestimate what God is doing because you can't imagine how He will carry it out. Hold tight to God's hope; it never disappoints. You will see it if you don't give up on Him! Will you trust God and look forward so He can show you the future?

ISAIAH 43:19; 2 COR. 12:9; ROM. 5:5; 1 COR. 2:5

February 9

"For God did not give us a spirit of timidity..."
2 TIM. 1:7

Feeling fear and being fearful are two different things. Feeling fear is our built-in security system designed by God; it alerts us to danger. We seek Him when the alarm sounds-knowing that apart from Him the danger we face will certainly overtake us! Being fearful results when we struggle to believe God will provide; the more we reason it, the more fearful we become!

The crazy in all of this is ...we know we can't do anything about the situation we're facing unless God makes a way, but we still don't trust Him. The logic of this point is lost under layers of reasoning, which spikes the anxiety level and reduces the ability to focus. Get the picture?

We're all been there...but let's not stay there. Embrace the promise God gives us. He will never abandon us; nothing can snatch us from His hand. Next time your security system alerts you to danger...run to God. He's waiting to protect you!

2 TIM. 1:7; HEB. 13:5; ROM. 8:15; JOHN 10:28

February 10

"We have this hope as an anchor for the soul..."
HEB. 6:19

Thank you, Father, that we don't have to rely on our strength to overcome the opposition we face daily, to turn around impossibles we see, or rely on our hope in hopeless situations...because Jesus has already overcome the world and every impossible in it. His hope anchors us when this world depletes us! No devil in hell can steal, kill or destroy what Jesus died to give us..*unless* we release it to the enemy. God has given us authority over the enemy; *this is a truth, not a feeling*, so we must appropriate what we know...not what we feel.

We do not have the power to change others, but the Holy Spirit does. Our power is in our privilege of prayer-we can partner with our Father, the Creator of everything we see and cannot see, and agree with His promises to come to pass. We must ask God daily to help us believe when the path ahead is dismal and dark, knowing that His Word is a lamp to our path and a light to our feet! What He calls us to do, He will equip us to do.

We have to rest daily in God's provisions; seriously, like what other choice do we have? Jesus took it all: regrets of the past, fears in the present, and every unknown we will face in the future. Our confidence is in Him. Every time we come to the end we can be confident of the endless supply of the Savior's strength; He will do exceedingly, abundantly more than we could do or imagine. We must allow His strength to have full reign in us, by having faith...constantly. Will you let your Father love and care for you as He wants to so you can live the life He's purposed for you?

HEB. 6:19; JOHN 16:33; LUKE 9:1; 1; COL. 1:17; PS. 119:105; 2 COR. 12:9; EPH. 3:20; MARK 11:22

February 11

"You will keep in perfect peace him whose mind is steadfast..."
ISAIAH 26:3

Reasoning leads to insanity, but a mind that's steadfast in Him will be kept in perfect peace, because we trust in Him. God never sleeps, grows tired or runs out of ideas. There's nothing He cannot make or invent; He's never borrowed money or been unemployed, and we won't run out of time because...He owns time!

God loves you and will provide everything you need, so trust, rest and put all of your hope in Him; He anchors your soul! Will you make the decision today to have your mind take refuge in Him?

ISAIAH 26:3; EPH. 3:20; HEB. 6:19; PS. 46:1

February 12

"We are hedged in (pressed) on every side [troubled and oppressed in every way], but not cramped or crushed; we suffer embarrassments and are perplexed and unable to find a way out, but not driven to despair."
2 COR. 4:8 (AMP)

The long and hard seasons that deplete and fatigue us...are the very same ones that make us more than a conqueror! We can beg Jesus to remove these hard times, but He will probably move us through them instead. These seasons are the building blocks of our identities in Christ to be developed-the authentic person Christ designed.

Who can come against us if God is for us? Can anything separate us from His love? Is there a situation too big for Him, a hardship He can't handle, a hurt He's never dealt with? Nothing, nada, no one can come between Christ and us...ever! Don't run from this hard season-you would be running from the arms of Christ. He wants you to know He loves you and that His strength in you...makes you more than a conqueror!

2 Cor. 4:8; Rom. 8:31-39; 2 Cor. 4:7-9

February 13

"Then Christ will make his home in your
hearts as you trust him..."
Eph. 3:17 (nlt)

How deep is your love? Do you take everything to God, or just the big stuff? Do you plead with Him to help you land a job, but not talk to Him about how to organize your garage or keep your home in order? Do you ask for help in developing healthy relationships...making healthy food choices throughout the day? Do you think He cares about the new color you put in your hair or the new iPhone you want? I can tell you that, "yes," He does. *God cares about everything you care about.* He numbers every hair on your head, gave you a unique fingerprint and a unique plan for your life. He ordered every step of your life; He knows your name...God cares about every tiny detail of your life!

Maybe you were raised to not bother adults with small stuff..but our Father God reigns over all things, and that includes the small stuff. Many of us know this intellectually, but struggle with justifying if God really wants to know...but it's not our decision to justify. It's God's decision, and He says so...so it's so! Think about this...God wants a personal and intimate relationship with us. An intimate relationship is familiar, close, vulnerable, private...deep, because everything is shared, right? That's what God wants with us! He will stay up all night to talk with us if that what we want. How can you have an intimate relationship with God if you only take the big stuff to Him? The answer is...you can't! And, you know what else? Your intimacy with God is reflected in your intimacy with your loved ones. Do you only take the big stuff to those you love and handle the small stuff yourself because you don't want to "bother" them? To the extent we're open with God we will be open with those we love...because as we expose our hearts to God and see that He approves all of us, we are then able to open our hearts to those we love because we know we are approved. How deep is your love?

MATT. 6:33; JER. 29:11; COL. 1:17; EPH. 3:17 (NLT)

February 14
"...God is love."
I JOHN 4:8

Authentic love...comes from God who loved us first. Love is seen, love is secure, love believes God's promises, love is tireless, love is fierce and pushes back wrong, loves scales a wall to protect, love isn't afraid of criticism or rejection, love stands firm in adversity, love works though the night to provide, love perseveres when exhausted, love that's fabricated stinks, love may be hurt but is never destroyed, love waits and endures, never self-serving, love builds godly relationships, love holds on loosely, it doesn't control or manipulate, love seeks the Holy Spirit's direction, love doesn't choke, push, put down or force. love forgives and releases, but it never binds or compromises, love can't endorse sin, love moves in courage and knocks down Goliaths, love believes God in the middle of impossibles, love hears, speaks and walks in the Word with the confidence and boldness of Christ, loves relies on the authentic love that flows from the One Who authenticated love.

Holy, holy, holy, Lord God Almighty, Maker of heaven and earth...make sure your love is rooted in the One Who loved you first.

I JOHN 4:8; I COR. 13:4-8; 2 COR. 5:14-15

February 15

"Then you will know the truth,
and the truth will set you free."
JOHN 8:32

Give your mind a rest...prefer God's truth over what you're feeling! Inventory your thoughts hourly. Think about what you're thinking about; thoughts that don't line up with God's truth need to go. Let's say you're having thoughts of feeling insignificant, not valued by others or overwhelmed with a current situation. Your feelings are real but they don't change God's truth, so they need to be tossed out! If you allow them to stay, they will take root and become strongholds and shape the way you think. Likewise, the Word sets up strongholds of truth and shapes how you think! Will you prefer God's truth as your truth even though you don't always feel it to be the truth?

JOHN 8:32; ROM. 12:2; JOHN 8:31-32

February 16

"Fix your thoughts on what is true, and honorable,
and right and pure, and lovely, and admirable."
PHIL. 4:8 (NLT)

We are not designed to handle the demands of this world without God...we can do things Christ strengthens us to do. Going back in time or forward exhausts us-we're designed to live in the present. Entertaining potential situations deafens our ability to hear the Holy Spirit. He gives direction and comfort, but we can't hear Him when we're taking on demands in our mind! We have to focus on God's truth, which *renews* our mind. What we think about becomes our thoughts, which lead to actions.

We have constructed scenarios in our minds that have catapulted us weeks, months and years down the road. What's crazy about this thought process is...we didn't go anywhere and we're walking in situations that haven't come to pass; but in our minds they have! So even though you were still in the first 30 minutes of your day standing at the kitchen counter drinking a cup of coffee, you lived weeks, months and even years of potential trials. This is stress, the body reacting to demands it's not designed to handle apart from Christ. We're not designed to handle the demands of this world without God. We can do all things Christ strengthens us to do...not what we try to do apart from Him! Going back or forward in time exhausts us. We are designed to live in the present.

Write down the truth and speak it aloud throughout the day: "God's peace guards my mind and heart; He has good plans for me; I can do all things through Christ Who strengthens me; I am complete in Christ; where the Spirit of the Lord is there is freedom." These aren't just words, they are God's Words - His promises that stand forever, are full of power and that will save and transform your life! Don't give up. Renew your mind...God's got good plans for you!

PHIL.4:7-8; GAL. 6;9; JER. 29:11; COL. 2;10; 2 COR. 3:17; ISAIAH 40:8

February 17

" For we are God's handiwork, created in Christ Jesus
to do good works, which God prepared in advance
for us to do"
EPH. 2:10

People seek to be defined *by* the world...God seeks to define people *in* the world! We are God's own handiwork-His workmanship. He planned the paths we would take and prepared ahead of time that we should walk in them!

Don't be conformed by this world by selling out to man-made philosophies, intellectualism, peer pressure and human traditions. Instead be transformed and changed by the entire renewing of your mind, and doing away with anything that opposes God's truth, so that you will be in His perfect plans by doing the good works He planned for you. Will you give all of yourself to God and let Him define you in this world for His glory?

EPH. 2:10; COL. 2:8; ROM. 12:1-2

February 18

*"Now all glory to God, who is able, through his mighty power
at work within us, to accomplish infinitely more
than we might ask or think."*
EPH. 3:20 (NLT)

No breathing person is exempt from having issues-including
all Christians! God is not shocked by your behavior, doesn't
regret choosing you or being in a relationship with you, and
your issues don't overwhelm Him! Just breathe, get real and
bring your issues into His light so He can work through the
plans He made for you long ago! Your issues don't stop God's
plans...but you refusing to believe that He can bring them
about will. Renew your mind and agree with the power that's at
work within you!

EPH. 3:20 (NLT); ROM. 12:2

February 19

*"[For my determined purpose is] that I
may know Him..."*
PHIL 3:10 (AMP)

A road trip with Jesus...I had no idea it would go this long. Jesus never gave me a timeline and I didn't start out with one. I
just thought I would be back to my regular routine by now.
Jesus has taught me so much on this trip; for starters, He's
funny (you know He gave us laughter and the concept of hu-
mor). We're made to laugh...a lot. He's shown me how to enjoy
the ride while on the way to where I'm going. I've always been a
list-maker and a get-it-done kind of girl, but this road trip has
taught me how to make time for the scenery and relationships
along the way, versus just getting to my destination. I've most
cherished the intimate heart-to-heart talks with Him. Every
day He wants to know what I see, then He will tell me what He
sees.

We've spent time talking about real humility; my complete reliance on His strength. For me to accomplish anything or overcome challenges, I must receive His love; it's big enough to take
on my regrets, mistakes, hurts, fears... His love has given me the

strength to agree with His forgiveness of me for the despicable things I've done, as well as forgive others for the wrongs they've done to me, *but I have to let go and hand them to Him*. He asks that I agree with His truth; apart from Him I can do nothing...but with Him I can do all things. He's not impressed with my superhero actions; His power is perfected in my weaknesses-not when I try to do things that are impossible without Him.

I've learned about the power and boldness of the Holy Spirit. It's the only way to have the courage to do what God asks; we just don't have that kind of boldness on our own. Every time I get to the point of thinking that I just can't take another un-known day, Jesus wows me to speechlessness with His love. He fills me with an undeniable sense of hope that can only come from Him, and that washes away the doubt and discourage-ment that had trapped me. He shows me a glimpse of the fu-ture and reminds me that He purposed me long ago to do the good works He planned, and that He will complete what He started in me! My determined purpose is to know Jesus...what about you?

PHIL 3:10 (AMP); PS. 126:2; JOHN 15:5; 2 COR. 12:9; PHIL. 1:6, 4:13; EPH. 2:10

February 20

"For God is working in you, giving you the desire and the power to do what pleases Him."
PHIL. 2:13 (NLT)

God's love makes us right! Our plans are in vain until we em-brace what God wants to accomplish through us. He wants us to know how much He loves and approves us - which includes all of our failures, regrets, mistakes, poor choices, weaknesses and current sins. We don't have the power to manage our be-havior, let go of our past or conquer sin...but God's love does! Jesus took it all at the cross to remove what we cannot. Our part is to agree with what He did for us at the cross. It is done! But...until we believe this truth, what He did won't have the powerful impact it should.

God's love and approval at work within us gives us the desire and the power to do what pleases Him. We must know that God sees us as right *in His righteousness* even when we do wrong. If not, pride will convince us to make ourselves right, but we will only feel more wrong. God corrects us to make us right..not wrong. If we take our sin to Him it will lose it's power in us. What we keep from Him...keeps it's power. Working harder won't make us feel right, it will only frustrate us and usually return us to the behaviors we despise in ourselves. Only God's love makes us right! He is the Vine and we are the branches; if we remain in Him and He in us, we will bear much fruit. Apart from Him we can do nothing. Will you lay down your plans to make yourself right in God's eyes and receive His love and approval?

PHIL. 1:6, 2:13 (NLT); ROM. 10:3; JOHN 15:5

February 21

*"Therefore God exalted them to the highest place and
gave them the name that is above every name."*
PHIL. 2:9

Jesus never messes up...His plans are perfect. He fixes what was broken, restores what was lost, straightens our paths, makes the blind see and the deaf hear; He makes something from nothing, heals the hurting, binds up the wounds of the bro-kenhearted, gives hope to the hopeless; He shows ups when others don't, holds us when others won't, reveals what others can't.

He has no barriers. He's unstoppable-the Name above all names...*Jesus*! His love completes us. He is the way, the truth and the life. Will you let Jesus love, approve and accept all of you today?

PHIL. 2:9; ISAIAH 61:1-3; COL. 1:16; HEB. 6:19; JOHN 14:6, 16:13

February 22

*"You will not have to fight this battle. Take up your positions;
stand firm and see the deliverance the LORD will give you..."*
2 CHRON. 20:17

Some days we just get tired. We're beat up. We feel as though we are failures - fake Christians; we don't want to be kind, caring or understanding. We don't feel like being mature or taking the higher road or believing we have what it takes. We just want to fall out on the floor and have a ginormous fit...and sometimes we do just that!

But then we regroup, get a grip, get back up and fix our eyes back on Jesus! The good news is that the battle has been won; it's done...over! Jesus took it all! Let this truth encourage you when you've reached the end of yourself and cannot take any more. Jesus is your Helper, Strong Tower, Rock, Deliverer, Refuge, Strength, Shield, Salvation and Stronghold-everything you need to get through the battle *that's been won for you*! If God is for you, who can be against you? The battle is not yours-it's God's. Though you will have to face the battle God will fight it on your behalf. God's power works best in our weaknesses; His grace is sufficient.

Remember this the next time you're tired and beat up: God's got it; it's done...over! But, you must go through the battle to claim the victory. Get your eyes back on Jesus so you can!

2 CHRON. 12:9, 20:17; HEB. 12:2; PS. 18:2; ROM. 8:31

February 23

*"It is for freedom that Christ has set us free. Stand firm, then, and do not let
yourselves be burdened again by a yoke of slavery."*
GAL. 5:1

Until we address our hurts we are chained to our past. Addressing hurt is uncomfortable; it takes work. Many ignore hurts, reasoning that time has passed and nothing can be done. It's true that time has passed...*but the hurt hasn't*. An unresolved hurt is as alive today as it was the day it happened, but because it has many layers of life, it's not always recognized, which leads us to believe that we are over it. Many of us struggle accepting that someone we trusted hurt us, because, really, it makes the hurt all the worse. But until *all of the hurt* is brought into the light...all of the person cannot heal. Minimizing and dismissing the reality of what happened keeps us tied to the experience and unable to live in the present because we view life from our past pain. Will you take Jesus to all of the parts of your broken heart and let His love begin to heal you?

GAL. 5:1; ISAIAH 61:1 (NLT); HEB. 6:19

February 24

*"Consider it pure joy, my brothers and sisters,
whenever you face trials of many kinds..."*
JAMES 1:2

Embrace the wait...don't waste it. Waiting on God is a time to be productive. Use this time wisely. Waiting isn't merely counting down days; it's building up stamina, endurance and character.

God doesn't make us wait because He's mad at us. It's because He loves us and wants us to be equipped to go into our next season! Our greatest lesson is to know He approves and loves us. He's our source for everything we need. We know this and we believe it, but God wants us to *embrace* it. Every new season calls for bigger believing. We never arrive until we see Jesus face-to-face! God's ways won't adhere to the world's ways, which have conditioned us. The more we believe God, the more He will ask us to believe. This increases our faith, which enables us to be better equipped as we move forward to where He has called us. But most of all, it's to experience His deep love for us! The bigger the risk in obedience, the bigger the miracle. Embrace the wait...don't waste it!

JAMES 1:2

February 25

*"Then you will know the truth,
and the truth will set you free."*
JOHN 8:32

The middle part of believing - where we will be turned inside out and come to know the love of Jesus like never before. The only way to know...is to go through, where we leave our familiar and move into the unknown, new season. It's where God will do a work in us. We are confronted with His truth and find that it will set us free...*if we embrace it*! We will come against a barrage of doubt, our insecurities confronted, beliefs challenged and pride purged. We will be uncomfortable, uncertain and unsettled. Our former predictable schedules gone, and false confidence knocked out from under us, leaving us with a sense of awkwardness.

The middle is longer than we ever plan, and we will endure more than we ever imagine! The middle is vital for God to develop our character, knowing that nothing satisfies or completes us apart from His love. We discover that we don't know nearly what we thought we did...raw and vulnerable brings revelation from the Holy Spirit, which is exactly the reason these times are crucial for character development.

The middle gives us confidence in who we are in Christ-we will know where we stand with God. He will sustain, comfort and encourage us...every one of His promises is true; we are His masterpieces, created to do the good works He planned long ago. Emotions come and go, but He never changes. We stay connected to Him because He supplies everything we need and we trust Him because of Who He is; we don't have to know what He will do to believe that He has good plans for us. We know His voice, we're never alone...*never*. When we get into the new season, we will be ready not because we are there...but because we know our Father and that He loves and approves of us! Our confidence is in Him...exclusively!

JOHN 8:32, 10:14-15; COL. 2:10; EPH. 2:10, 3:20; JER. 29:11

February 26

*"...and forgive us our sins,
as we have forgiven those who sin against us.."*
MATT. 6:12 (NLT)

People we love will offend us, and mostly we're able to quickly forgive and move on. But, then, some offenses are like bullet wounds to the heart that knock us down, and we're left drowning in a pool of blood. *Forgiveness* is God's promise that we can heal and move on from the heart wounds inflicted by those we love.

Listen closely: forgiveness does not dismiss the harm done, but it allows God's hands to skillfully and tenderly remove the bullet of offense lodged in your heart, while making room for His love to heal the wound from the inside out. Forgiveness is God's gift to us to potentially restore relationships. Although that's not always possible, we can confidently stand on His promise that forgiveness enables us to completely heal from the wounds inflicted by loved ones. Will you let God heal all the parts of your wounded heart today?

PROV. 20:2; ROM. 12:18

February 27

"...the mind controlled by the Spirit is life and peace."
ROM. 8:6

A conversation with God...lesson on fear. Fear will scream silently in your mind throughout the day: you missed it, someone took your spot, you won't get that chance again; work harder, maybe you can make up for lost time; don't trust and you won't get hurt; don't count on anyone, don't ask for help or you will look weak and incompetent; God is upset with you; you don't matter, they're using you; that idea is selfish; you lost your temper again; nothing is going to change.

Know this: fear's only ploy is to create panic, which drowns out hearing My voice. Listen closely: I've got it. You didn't miss anything. I have no barriers to providing for you-My love transcends time; the past, present and future have no hold on Me. I own time! Don't drown in fear's lies or try to resolve conflicts that are beyond you; the mind of the flesh leads to death, but the mind controlled by the Spirit is life and peace.

Look at the world through My Word; it's a lamp to your feet and a light to your path. My Word cannot be separated from Me...to profess to be a Christian but to think like the world will mess you up...really. Accept Me, renew your mind with the Word and then you will hear My voice. You do know I've ordered each of your steps, right? You were planned by Me, you don't have to feel this to believe this, but as you believe it, you will feel it. Know this: I've always loved you...but I desire for you to love Me, too. I want to spend time with you each day. I want an intimate relationship with you; even though I never leave you, sometimes you forget. Call out to Me, anytime, any place; I will answer. Let My love satisfy you...now rest child; I've got everything covered.

ROM 8:6, 35-39, 12:2; EPH. 2:10; PS. 37:23, 119:105, 139:13; COL. 1:17; REV. 1:8

February 28

"Call to me and I will answer you..."
JER. 33:3

When live overwhelms you...God is with you! Call out to Him; He always answers. When you're afraid, put your trust in Him. His truth will set you free. He is for you - nothing and no one can come against you. His hope anchors your soul, firms and secure. Delight yourself in Him and He will give you the desires of your heart. His Word is a light to your path and a lamp to your feet. His love never fails.

Call out to Him and He will deliver you from all of your fears. Those who look to Him are radiant, their faces are never covered with shame. He will make your righteousness shine like the dawn and the justice of your cause like the noonday sun. Will you give God the things in life that are overwhelming you?

JER. 29:12, 33:3; JOHN 8:32; HEB. 6:19; PS. 34:4-5, 37:6, 56:3, 119:105; 136:1

February 29

"Let us not become weary in doing good, for at the
proper time we will reap a harvest if we do not give up."
GAL. 6:9

Some seasons are a blur...tired is an understatement. We seek the Lord and we're doing all we know to do, yet discouragement and doubt press on every side. We are working hard, but don't see any results from our hard work. Just keep moving; this season is not in vain. God doesn't waste pain. Listen closely: God is always faithful. But we don't always see His faithfulness...until He reveals the finished product. Let us not become weary in doing good, for at the proper time we will reap a harvest if we do not give up. God will bring to completion the good work He started long ago!

Commit all you do to the Lord; trust Him and He will do this...make your righteousness shine like the dawn and the justice of your cause like the noonday sun! Don't give up, friend; God won't give up on you!

GAL. 6:9; PHIL. 1:6; PS. 37:5-6

†

March 1

"This means that anyone who belongs to Christ has
become a new person. The old life is gone; a new life has begun"
2 COR. 5:17 (NLT)

You've agreed with wrong for so long that you believe it's who you are. Listen closely: wrong was done to you...*that doesn't make you wrong and it's not who you are!* You are a child of the Most High King, Jehovah Jireh, El Shaddai, God Almighty. Receive your inheritance! Spend time with Christ daily and He will tell you who you are. Read the Word; it's your roadmap for life. Ask God to search your heart for anything that isn't in agreement with His Word, profess the Word aloud over your life and the lives of those you love, praise and worship His Holy

Name, thank Him that He is alive in you...because the truth has set you free!

Jesus has overcome every wrong done to you in your past, present and future. This is a promise; God's truth, but you must decide if you believe it. God's promises are only powerful to the one who believes. So you say that it's hard to let go of wrong; you're right, it is. Ask yourself this: is it easier to live in spiritual poverty? By holding on to wrongs, you choose to forfeit the freedom Jesus died to give you. A man's ways seem right, but in the end lead to death, but a mind controlled by the Spirit is life and peace (SEE PROV. 14:12). There is no wrong that is bigger than God's love. Will you make a decision today to live the life Christ died to give you, and rely on the power that raised Him from the dead, which enables you to walk out this life?

1 COR 5:17; JOHN 6:29, 8:32; PROV. 14:12; ROM. 8:6

March 2

"Have faith in God..."
MARK 11:22

Walking in victory requires a quick and consistent response to the lies of the enemy. Don't let his lies linger in your mind; they twist and distort God's truth. The enemy challenges your beliefs from a human perspective, which can't discern spiritual truths from the Holy Spirit. This leads to desperate thinking, which overwhelms the mind then manifests in anxiety, insecurity, and, ultimately, disaster. A man's ways seem right but lead to death (SEE PROV. 14:12).

Go after each lie; replace each with God's Word. Rest in His confidence and He will make a way for you each time. You don't have to know *how* God will provide...to believe that He *will* provide! God's Word works; it won't return void. Will you let go of the lies in your mind, no matter how real they may feel, renew your mind with God's Word, and expect the promises He's made to you?

MARK 11:22; PROV. 3:5-6, 14:12

March 3

*"Let the praises of God be in their mouths,
and a sharp sword in their hands..."*
Ps. 149:6

We live in a changing world, but have an unchanging God; our faith is based on what we *know* to be true, *not* what we see and feel. We can be certain God is with us despite the uncertainty we are going through. It's critical that we keep our thoughts on His Word; thinking what is pure, right, noble and lovely. Speak God's truth over and over and over; God's Word will supernaturally lift us up from what tries to pull us down. God's Word is a sword-use it to fight daily battles!

To add or take away from God's truth is flirting with disaster, and will cause confusion in our minds. Don't drown in the grandeur of self and try to do life your way...you will forfeit God's promises! Will you see God, know His truth, speak His Word, then execute it and walk in it to carry out the plans He made long ago?

Ps. 149:6; Eph. 2:10; Col. 2:8; John 16:33

March 4

*"Ask and it will be given to you; seek and you will find;
knock and the door will be opened to you."*
Matt. 7:7

God never trades even...give Him what *you* have and He will give you what *He* has. It's an uneven trade every time. God can and will always give more...but that's His nature! He's a huge giver; He will generously provide all you need and more...with plenty left over to share with others.

Doing the math won't get you the answer, but having faith will! So give God your first, best and all the rest. Trust Him with everything: every loved one, those who oppose you, financial situations, talents, direction in life, expectations, medical diagnosis, etc.

Don't hold anything back. It's an uneven trade every time, with God giving you far more than you could ever give Him.

EPH. 3:20; 2 COR. 9:8; MARK 11:22; PROV. 3:9-10; MATT. 7:7

March 5

"Now to him who is able to do immeasurably more than all we ask or imagine..."
EPH.3:20

Don't forfeit the fire...it's where you meet Jesus! "Fires" are those dire situations in life where we have to choose what seems radial or rational; we're faced with going into the fire and trusting God, or justifying why we cannot. These fires test what we profess to believe...then reveal where we stand. I have forfeited some fires in the past because I relied on my reasoning instead of God's truth, and thus cheated myself out of God's best for me. I regret now that I doubted that Jesus would be there for me. Since then I have doubted, but instead of leaning into my own understanding, I ask Jesus to help me with my unbelief (SEE MARK 9:24). I don't want to miss Jesus again; I'm in awe of the depth of His relentless love.

I really do not have words to express how my faith has grown in the fires of life, but I know with certainty that I can count on Him to meet me every time. What fires are you avoiding? Job concerns, relationship issues, marriage problems, parenting conflicts, unhealthy friendships, character development, general life dilemmas, or...your relationship with Jesus? Forfeiting the fire threatens our livelihood and jeopardizes our integrity...both keep us from knowing God will be with you. What God calls us to, He will bring us through. Going in the fire and coming through has nothing to do with our abilities, but everything to do with the abilities of Who we believe in! Will you let God show you...you can believe in Him?

EPH. 3:20; DAN. 3:16-27; PS. 34:4-5

March 6

*"My grace is all you need. My power
works best in weakness.' So now I am glad to boast about
my weaknesses, so that the power of Christ can work through me."*
2 COR. 12:9 (NLT)

The truth will set you free...but you have to know it and believe it. The issues we continue to ignore keep us from moving forward and fulfilling the desires God has placed in our hearts. We may be dissatisfied, angry and silently bitter about our lives, but nothing will change until we allow God's grace to change the way we live. Stop pretending to be ok, speaking "Christian-ese," and going through the motions of looking right. Only Jesus can make us right; we can't do anything apart from Him. We are still going to mess up, but that doesn't make us a mess up! Release pride, let go of the denial you've been packing around for years; the Holy Spirit will help you-if you will let Him. Face the truth; stop blaming situations and people for the reasons why you are not doing what God put in your heart.

God's truth exposes the things that keep us in denial; expect to be uncomfortable. The truth hurts, but it also sets us free to walk out the destiny God planned for us! Will you let the truth set you free...so you can get on with the plans God has for you?

2 COR. 12:9 (NLT); JOHN 8:32, 15:5; PHIL. 1:6

March 7

*"Lean on, trust in, and be confident in the Lord with all your
heart and mind and do not rely on your own insight
or understanding."*
PROV. 3:5 (AMP)

In this world you will encounter bad, wrong and unfair things; no person is exempt. Preparation, planning and prayer may help reduce the occurrences, but don't eliminate the reality-these things happen to everyone. Some of them are imposed on us and others we bring on ourselves, but the answer for overcoming either is always the same: Jesus Christ! He came to save, heal and bind up wounds of all those who call on His name. God knitted together every human with His own hands, designing them to fulfill the destiny He planned long ago. Despite the obviously fallen world we live in, we are promised a hope that soothes our soul, a joy that overflows, and a peace that surpasses human understanding.

So, how do we have this hope, joy and peace God promises? I'll tell you: it begins with your thoughts, which are housed in your mind. Seek God in your mind-dialogue with Him and thank Him for His promises to care for you, and His power through you to believe Him. Believing God is the greatest gift you will ever give yourself, because it impacts *every* person you love, and generations to come. Will you trust in the Lord with all your heart today?

PROV. 3:5-6(NLT); JOHN 15:11, 16:33; HEB. 6:19; I COR. 2:5; ROM 8:6

ᑐMarch 8

"What shall we say about such wonderful things as these? If God is for us, who can ever be against us?"
ROM. 8:31 (NLT)

The long and hard seasons that deplete and fatigue you...are the very same ones that make you more than a conqueror. You can beg Jesus to remove these hard times, but He's more likely to get you through them. These seasons are the building blocks for your identity in Christ-the authentic you. You're pressed, pushed and purged of most of your comforts...the earthly securities and things you cling to more than Christ. When these things are threatened-you're threatened because they're grafted into your identity; you believe without them you won't make it.

It's only when the props are taken away, the back-ups removed and the comforts that made you feel approved, good enough and important are gone...that you find Jesus. It's when you're out of resources, no plan B, and you *choose* to believe or to go crazy. Jesus is waiting for you to get to get to the end-so He can begin. This is how you become more than a conqueror. A conqueror doesn't gain merit based on who or what they conquer, but an authentic conqueror knows their strength comes from Jesus-the One Who chose and justified them.

Who can come against you if God is for you, can anything separate you from His love, is a situation too big for Him, a hardship He can't handle, a hurt He's never heard of? Nothing, nada, no one can come between Christ and you- *ever*! Don't run from this hard season-you'd be running from the arms of Christ. He wants you to know He loves you. His strength in you...makes you more than a conqueror!

ROM. 8:31-39 (NLT); HEB. 12:26-28; PS. 118:6

March 9

"Humanly speaking it is impossible.
But with God everything is possible."
MATT. 19:26 (NLT)

It's time...to break up with doubt! Doubt's agenda is to steal your dreams, lie about God's promises and torment your mind. He poses as being concerned and speaks in partial truths, which are lies by omission. He baits you with partial truths to confuse you and cause you to doubt your walk with Christ. He begins questioning the dreams God put in your heart: "are you sure you heard God correctly; you don't want to believe something that's not true or make something up, do you?" Then he moves on to your understanding of scripture: "yes, God promises good plans and gives you the desires of your heart, but maybe you want too much; aren't you a little self-serving?" Finally, he has you examine your life as a whole: "have you really made a difference? Is God pleased with you, or have you disappointed Him so many times He cannot possibly use you?"

Listen closely: we are to use our mind to reason, calculate and project probable outcomes...but our reasoning must *always* be submitted to God's truth. If not, we reason ourselves into doubt! Will you break up with doubt...today?

MATT. 6:33, 19:26 (NLT); EPH. 2:10; PHIL. 1:6; 1 PET. 5:8

March 10

*"The mind governed by the flesh is death,
but the mind governed by the spirit is life and peace."*
ROM. 8:6

Are you trapped inside your head? You're feeling desperate because you're losing perspective. Desperation is anchored in fear. Fear is from the enemy; he attacks our thoughts to create distortions and oppose God's truth. When this happens our perspective skews our view of the truth, and our thoughts become distorted. *Our perception is our reality*...what we perceive is what we believe. When this happens we feel kind of crazy because we know God's truth, but we also fee hopeless. We feel bad for feeling hopeless, because we say that we should know...then guilt floods us. We're trapped inside of our own heads! The enemy has us where he wants us: desperate, confused and guilty.

A mind focused on emotions leads to death. A mind focused on the Spirit leads to life and peace. Where the Spirit of the Lord is there is freedom (SEE 2 COR. 3:17). Don't settle; we feel it's impossible to turn our minds around, and it is...apart from Christ. Apart from Him we can do nothing, but we can do all things when He strengthens us (SEE JOHN 15:5; PHIL. 4:13). He will strengthen us to His truth; His power is perfected in our weaknesses. Our feelings will change, our thoughts may become distorted, and our hope will fail at times, but our Father God will never change. His Word is true all of the time. And, most of all...He will never fail us! God won't quit on you...so don't you quit on Him.

ROM. 8:6 (NLT); 2 COR. 3:17, 12:9; LUKE 1:37; JOHN 8:32, 15:5; PHIL. 1:6, 4:13

March 11

*"Now faith is being sure of what we hope for
and certain of what we do not see."*
HEB. 11:1

What a relief to know that our faith can see what our minds cannot comprehend...being confident in God's promises despite a lack of evidence in our hands. For our hope is in our

Savior and what is to come, *not* in what we can see. Our Savior will deliver every one of the promises He's made to us; we can be confident in this because He cannot lie! He has given us the keys to the Kingdom and a measure of faith to see! Are you choosing to believe, using your keys and faith to see the promises God has made to you and to me?

HEB. 11:1; 2 COR. 5:17; MATT. 16:19; ROM. 12:3

March 12

"And God will generously provide all you need..."
2 COR. 9:8

You're toiling in your efforts and exerting your strength to achieve what you believe will satisfy you while you plead with God to give you just these few things you're asking for. You say that you don't understand why God is withholding your modest requests when He could easily provide for you. I'll tell you why...for starters, God doesn't enable us to live in the spiritual poverty that many are willing to settle for. If a child of His insists on it, He will continue to allow them to encounter circumstances that will return their heart to Him. Next, He wants us to live the abundant life Jesus died to give us-far beyond what your mind can imagine, but it requires that we let our plans die. Dying to self allows the power of God to pour through us; it's called His grace; where we end, He begins!

Finally, we just don't know what we don't know. God purposed us to do good works long ago, but we have to put our hope in Him, not in people, situations and circumstances. We're living like junkies, desperately looking for a fix and willing to do about anything for relief because we cannot see beyond the desperation of the moment! God knows this and He's not giving up on us, so we must not give up on Him! He will see us through this if we will let Him.

Listen closely: nothing gives us relief like the love of God; all else pales in comparison. When we renew our minds with God's truth and embrace His grace, we will know that He is for us and not against us, and that His truth will set us free to be the authentic people He designed us to be! Will you put your hope in God, instead of the hand of man?

2 COR. 9:8, 12:9; ROM. 8:31

March 13

"I have filled him with the Spirit of God, giving him
great wisdom, ability, and expertise in all kinds of crafts."
EX. 31:3 (NLT)

If you believe that Holy Spirit whispered that it's time for you to leave a season...then you need to get going! It's scary leaving a season, but disobedience will forfeit the next season that God is calling you to, and poison the one you're trying to stay in. Doubt whispers that you're a quitter, and you do feel as though you are giving up, but what you're giving up is *your* plans in exchange for *God's* plans!

God's Word is your confidence to move forward. Where He calls you He will keep you, and where He keeps you...you will thrive. There is nothing holy about staying when God says *"go"*! Move forward in faith. God wants to show you some new things...are you ready?

EX. 31;3; ISAIAH 43:19

March 14

"So do not fear..."
ISAIAH 41:10

Do you completely trust God to bring you through hard seasons? If you *mostly* trust Him, you are not *completely* trusting and you will become anxious. Anxiety develops in the mind when an outcome is uncertain; this is God's design. It is our internal alarm signaling danger; the alarm goes off when we feel unsafe. If our alarm is working correctly, we run to God when we're afraid, confident that He will provide. We cause a malfunction when the alarm goes off and we try to take on the burden independent of Him, or if we only partially trust Him. To correct the error, we renew our minds with His truth: He is with us, will provide whatever we need, and bring us through the crisis.

As followers of Christ, our outcome is certain. God says not to be afraid or dismayed; He will uphold and strengthen us. Believing God doesn't require that we know *how* He will deliver, but it does require that we believe He *will* deliver. Otherwise, we forfeit the comfort His promises give. If you struggle believing, ask the Holy Spirit to help you; He is your Helper and Comforter, and He will give you revelation! Only by faith can you believe God's promises, and only the Holy Spirit can give you the faith to believe.

Which brings us full circle: we're not exempt from hardships, but we are promised that God will bring us through each one. Will you believe God to bring you though?

PS. 34:19; ISAIAH 41:10; HEB. 11:1; PHIL. 2:13, 4:19; ROM. 12:2; EPH 2:8, 3:20

March 15

*"For God is working in you giving you the
desire ad the power to do what pleases him."*
PHIL. 2:13 (NLT)

Do you find yourself having the same problems over and over? Don't settle and accept this as just a way of life. The good news is that you are the common denominator and God gives wisdom generously without finding fault. You can expect God's wisdom to lovingly give you correction and direction.

God asks one thing from us when we seek Him, and that is that we believe in the One He sent...not just believe in His existence, but believe that He loves us and will abundantly provide all we need-more than we can dare imagine! God wants us to boldly approach Him and to confidently expect an answer. But, be careful to not reduce His answers to those of mere human wisdom by placing it alongside opinions from others or in the mix with your own reasoning. God calls this "double-minded" thinking, and He says not to expect to receive anything from Him (SEE JAMES 1:2-8).

If you find yourself being double-minded, immediately ask God for forgiveness and for help with unbelief. He will, and, remember, He gives wisdom generously without finding fault. You do not have to grope through life. God has promised *abundant* life, despite many trials. Make a decision to believe this promise. He will help you. Will you let Him?

PHIL. 2;13 (NLT); JAMES 1:2-8; PROV. 3:5-6; JOHN 6:29; EPH. 3:20

March 16

"And my God will meet all your needs according to his
glorious riches in Christ Jesus."
PHIL. 4:19

Stop trying to do God's job-you will lose your mind; you're trying to fix impossible situations with human solutions! God strengthens you to do all things He calls you to do...*not* what you call yourself to do *then* call on God to strengthen you! Trying to do God's job leads to an unsettled, anxious and agitated mind.

God will meet all your needs and give you peace that surpasses all human understanding, and God will bless you at all times and in all situations. Now, will you breathe, rest in God, and move forward with all the things He calls you to do?

PHIL. 4:13, 19; 2 COR. 9:8

March 17

"I can do everything through him
who gives me strength."
PHIL. 4:13

Who God calls, He equips. Not in your own strength, but in God's strength, for it's God Who is constantly at work in you, energizing and creating in you the power and desire, both to will and work for His good pleasure, satisfaction and delight. God won't ask something of you that He won't carry out through you. Maybe others have, but He won't. But, he *does* need your trust and cooperation to work through you. You have strength for all things in Christ, Who infuses inner strength into you. Know the Word, know God, know His truth; it's your lifeline, to be grasped tightly through each adversity. Many evils confront the righteous and God delivers him in each one. Don't be naïve...obedience doesn't exempt you from trials, but it does promise God's provision to come through each!

Keep your mind on God's truth; speak it and keep it in your heart. When doubt hits, come against it with the Word. Do this day in and day out-focusing, purposing, and determining to know Him. And, then, you will reach the full potential that God designed you to fulfill through the plans He made long ago.

PHIL. 2:14, 4:13 (NLT); JOHN 8:31-32; PS. 34:19; EPH. 2:10

March 18

*"We have this hope as an anchor for our soul,
firm and secure."*
HEB. 6:19

Putting your hope in what you're praying *for* instead of Who you're praying *to* leads to grief; it's a subtle shift in thinking that wrecks us, because we've put a contingency on our relationship with God by hoping in what He will do versus Who we know Him to be! What we pray for changes, but God's hope never does; His hope is constant, steady and unshakeable. When we put our hope in Him...*we* are constant, steady and unshakeable!

God's hope allows us to rest in Him because He promises to supply all of our needs. God's hope gives a peace that surpasses all human understanding, holds on when we cannot, and gives a confident view of what is to come! His hope never disappoints. Will you hold tight to God's hope...right now?

HEB. 6:19, 11:1; ROM. 5:3-5

March 19

"And God will supply all your needs ..."
PHIL. 4:19

In JOHN 6:5, Jesus asked Phillip for a human solution to an impossible situation: feeding 5,000 men, plus their families, even though there wasn't enough food available. Jesus did this to test Phillip's faith. Getting nothing from Phillip and the others, Jesus took a ridiculously insignificant amount of food and gave thanks to the Father for His provision. Every person had more than enough, and 12 baskets of food were left over!

God is able to bless us abundantly in all things. Whatever we release into the hand of Jesus will be offered up to the Father; He takes our not-enough and turns it into an exponential potential...more than enough! This is God's promise, but sadly fear wins in the minds of many due to their own reasoning convincing them to rely on their abilities instead of God's power. This belief forfeits God's laws of harvest.

It's not the amount we have...it's how much of the amount we're willing to release into Jesus' hands and then *believe* that God will make something out of it. Don't hold back giving what you have and forfeit God's provisions. Are you facing an impossible situation as was Phillip? Will you give what you have to the Lord and watch Him make something from nothing?

PHIL 4:19; JOHN 6:6; 2 COR. 9:8

March 20

"But when the spirit of truth comes, he will
guide you in all truth..."
JOHN 16:13 (NLT)

God has planned every second of your life to make a difference in this world, but you've got to agree with who God says you are so that you can walk out each one. God made you with His own hands; you are His masterpiece, whether or not you believe it. There's nothing about you that's shocking to God. He's been with you during every hardship, knows each mistake you've made, is fully aware of your shortcomings, and loves you!

God wants you to know how much He loves you so you can rest in His provisions, and move forward with the life He planned for you! Fulfilling God's plans require a switch in focus from what you can or cannot do, to what God will do through you. Your ongoing attempts to correct your negative behaviors both frustrate and lead to failure because apart from the guidance and direction of the Holy Spirit your efforts are short-lived. It's the very reason many start the race with such vigor only to drop out exhausted, angry and cynical. They moved forward only partially relying on the Holy Spirit, either by not renewing their mind with God's truth and not relying on the Spirit for daily revelation, or they believed they should be beyond certain failures or above asking for help throughout the day. None of us can walk in the victory God promises unless we're constantly seeking the truth and revelation of the Spirit!

If you will begin to renew your mind with God's Word and ask the Spirit for revelation, He will guide you in all truth; the truth that sets you free! Your focus will change from trying to be free *from* things to being free *in* Christ, and to who you are because of Him and what He wants you to do in this world! Are you open to receiving the truth?

EPH. 2:10; JOHN 14:26, 16:13-14; I COR. 2:5

March 21

*"I did this so you would trust not in human wisdom
but in the power of God."*
I COR. 2:5 (NLT)

If you're feeling discouraged or overwhelmed, let this truth give you hope: hardships and heartaches are inevitable in life, no person is exempt, but...every person is promised a way out! The Lord's angel camps around His loyal followers and delivers them; He pays attention and hears their cries for help. He saves them from all of their troubles! He's near to the brokenhearted and delivers those who are discouraged.

Save yourself much grief in life; accept that you will not always know the "why" of many situations, but you can be comforted in knowing Who is always with you! Put your hope in God's power-not your wisdom. Memorize God's Word; speak it aloud daily, put your eyes on it and listen to it. God's Word is your anchor. It will comfort you and save your mind from bursting into a million pieces during every heartache and hardship. The Lord promises to comfort you. Will you let Him?

1 COR. 2:5 (NLT); PS. 34:7, 15-19

March 22

"I have told you these things, so that in me you may have peace. In this world you will have trouble. But take heart! I have overcome the world."
JOHN 16:33

What tries to kill you...will actually catapult you into the destiny God planned for you long ago! Line up your view of you with God's truth-He says you are His masterpiece, more than a conqueror, an overcomer, fearfully and wonderfully made, blessed, chosen, and a loved child of God! These are truths that never change, unlike your view of you, which changes constantly according to how you're *feeling* on any given day. Push into God's truth's when life hurts, when loved ones leave, medical conditions change, a child breaks your heart, you're cheated on, gossiped about, passed over, let down, lied to, rejected, violated, and isolated. You still matter - God says so!

His hope will anchor you. Any thought that doesn't line up with God's truth must go. Renew your mind with His truth all day long! Talk to yourself with God's truth, profess it, write it down. The Truth is supernatural; it will change the chemistry of your brain, lifting the heaviness from your mind!

PS. 139:14; EPH. 1:3, 2:10; ROM. 8:37; COL. 3:12; 1 JOHN 3:1

March 23

"...be made new in the attitude of your mind."
EPH. 4:23

You're no longer managing this mess...it's managing you, and it's almost managed to do you in! Deception is dominating your thoughts; renew your mind with God's Word so He can help you. This mess doesn't have a chance against the power of Christ. His Spirit lives in *you*, and He promises to bring you through the mess, but you have to put your hope in His power-not human wisdom.

You do this by renewing your mind constantly throughout the day...being made new in the attitude of your mind. "*I called out to the Lord and He answered me; He delivered me from all my fears; those who look to Him are radiant...their faces are never covered with shame!*" ((SEE PS. 34.4-5)

EPH. 4:23; PS. 43:4-5; 1 COR:2:5

March 24

"But blessed are those who trust in the LORD
and have made the word their hope and confidence."
JER. 17:7 (NLT)

It's how we act in the places we don't want to be that determines how long we need to be there. Our faith grows when we're in places we don't want to be. Believing is easy when all is going as planned, people we love are getting along and following Jesus, the home sold as predicted, raise and bonus money came through, doctor's report was good, slow sales picked up, hard work and commitment are recognized, etc. But the kind of believing that walks us through every trial is the believing that holds fast when we see no way out and our world is crumbling. That's the kind of believing that no devil in hell can ever steal! But that kind of believing isn't developed just because we say we believe; we have to be *tried and tested* to get to there.

It's believing God during the unknown and uncomfortable that leads to unwaivering faith! It's where we finally realize that we never had any control to begin with; we just relied on a lot of familiar routines, comforts and predictable schedules. It's where we're honest, mad, sad and crying, laying before the Lord and holding nothing back...asking Him how we are supposed to get through!

It's in these places that God gets us exactly where He wants us; a place of being raw and real with Him, and that leads us to trust His truth...the truth that sets us free! Embrace these times and trials. They cannot be avoided, but we never fail either...we either grow and develop or we stay there until we cooperate. Will you cooperate with the Lord and let Him grow your faith?

JER. 17:7 (NLT); JOHN 8:32; PROV. 3:4-5

March 25

"But blessed are your eyes because they see,
and your ears because they hear."
MATT. 13:16

How to keep it together when life is falling apart...

1) Trust God's Word more than you trust what you're feeling and seeing (JOHN 16:33).
2) Make a decision to believe that God will provide what you need, despite how impossible things seem to be (PHIL. 4:19).
3) Let go of what you don't understand and cling to God's truth in all you do; He will show you the way to go (PROV. 3:5-6).

Blessed are those who have not seen and yet have believed (JOHN 20:29). No verdict given by man is final; only God's Word is final (ISAIAH 55:11)! When life is falling apart put your hope in God; He holds on for you when you can't (HEB 6:19).

JOHN 16:33, 20:29; PHIL. 4:19; PROV. 3:5-6; ISAIAH 55:11; HEB. 6:19

March 26

"And his hope will not lead to disappointment..."
ROM. 5:5 (NLT)

Hold tight to God's hope...right now in the second you're in, then hope in Him the next second, and so on.... Situations lined up early this morning with the intent to cover you in discouragement. They didn't have to work too hard; you were already weighted down with a bunch of yesterday's discouragement. It's just that today you're on the brink of going under because you're beyond exhausted! You've prayed, boldly professed God's promises, fasted, rebuked every demon you can think of, and enlisted the prayers of family, friends and all of your Facebook friends! All of these things are good and viable means to elicit help, but if your hope is in an outcome rather than in God, you've forfeited the hope He promises.

Listen: putting your hope in what you're praying for instead of hoping in Who God is will always lead to grief...because your hope is contingent upon prayers being answered versus the hope that sustains you. God's hope promises to satisfy you, but not always your requests. He answers prayers, of course, but not always in the way we what them answered...because His ways are higher and better than ours.

God's hope gives us a peace that surpasses human understanding, holds on for us when we cannot, and gives us a confident expectation of what is to come. His hope never disappoints! Will you take hold of God's hope...right now?

ROM 5:3-5(NLT); HEB. 6:19, 11:1

March 27

"Give your burdens to the Lord..."
PS. 55:22 (NLT)

God will fix what you're facing in a mighty way if you will get out of the way. Are you holding on to a situation...trying to save or revive it, consumed with thinking about it? Does it weigh you down, wake you up at night, give you headaches, stiff neck and an upset stomach, determine if you do or don't spend money?

Many say they believe that God can do anything, but they don't give Him much of a chance to prove it. Our interference delays God's intervention. When you get out of the way...God has room to make a way! Stay in the Word and speak and renew your mind with it throughout the day, seek Christ constantly, listen to your thoughts, be careful of the words you speak and examine how you spend your time, who you hang out with, what you watch on TV and listen to on your iPod. This will keep you doing your part while God does His part. God loves you and is waiting to fix what you're facing in a mighty way, but you must get out of His way. Will you...so He can?

Ps. 55:22 (NLT); ROM. 12:2; MATT. 6:33

March 28

"I sought the LORD, and he answered me;
he delivered me from all my fears."
Ps. 34:4

Some trials in life intend to steal, kill and destroy your hope by imposing a darkness in your mind. Your mind is pushed to the edge and takes you under unless you breathe-then breathe again, and again. You cannot overcome these kinds of trials apart from the constant love of Jesus flowing through you; call out to Him! He will show up in the middle of the emotional insanity you're going through and be with you every step, *if* you remain in Him.

I would have been declared emotionally dead if I had not clung to he love of Jesus during trials such as these. His love revived me, saved me, and gave me hope when I had none! Whatever is too much for you to bear, whatever you've given up on, whatever is trying to steal, kill or destroy you..the love of Jesus is the answer!

Acknowledge the reality of what you're going though then put your hope in Jesus; His hope holds on for you when you cannot. The eyes of the Lord are on the righteous, His ears attentive to their cries. He's close to the brokenhearted and saves those crushed in spirit! The love of Jesus is bigger than the trials intending to steal, kill and destroy your hope. Believe, breathe, then do it again. You will eventually get through whats trying to steal, kill and destroy you.

PS. 34:4, 15, 17, 18 (NSV); JOHN 6:29, 10:10; HEB. 6:19

March 29

"Trust in the LORD with all your heart;
do not depend on your own understanding."
PROV. 3:5 (NLT)

Come out...take off your grave clothes! Make a decision about the trial you're going through; it's not the end of you! The Spirit of the Lord lives in you and He will lead you in all truth. Stop going through the motions, checking off the to-do list, speaking "Christian-ese" just to get another day behind you. You've settled for just getting by and Jesus doesn't just get by; He's overcome and you have, too, because the Holy Spirit lives in you! Jesus is calling your name, asking you to come out, take off the grave clothes! Trust Him to help; He will get you to the other side of this. Your part is to believe and speak His truth...but you haven't been speaking His truth with boldness because you're afraid to hope for more than He might deliver.

Listen: you've got to distinguish between hoping in God, versus hoping in *what He will deliver*. His promises and His ways are perfect. Put your hope in Him...not man's wisdom. Empty yourself of the fears that dug your emotional grave, purge what you've been denying, holding back, minimizing, trying to prove, pushing down. Cry a river and grieve over what was lost, stolen or never given. Grief validates what you're feeling; it says that you matter and makes room for God's hope to fill you. People who cannot grieve will stay stuck in their pain. But you don't have to; your hope is in Him. Jesus is calling you to come out and take off your grave clothes! Will you?

PROV. 3:5-6 (NLT), 14:12; JOHN 11:43-44

March 30

*"Don't copy the behavior and customs of this world,
but let God transform you into a new person..."*
ROM. 12:2 (NLT)

God promises us victory in His Word. His truth sets us free and literally transforms our life! Our part is to renew our mind with the Word; if we do not, we will drift into worldly thinking and living, and forfeit the victory promised. Our conscience has to be calibrated to the Word, purposely lined up with it or it will do what it believes is right; a man's ways seem right to him but lead to death (SEE PROV. 14:12). It is a subtle reasoning process that leads one thought at a time into deception; the intent isn't to reject God's truth, but a mind not purposed on God's Word will default to opposing God's Word.

The Word is counter-intuitive to the mind: we don't naturally want to forgive those who've harmed us, love somebody who's unloving, give when our means are limited, or believe before we see. We have to seek the Word constantly to stay on course. Thoughts that don't line up have to be tossed out immediately! Opposing thoughts allowed to linger become part of your thought patterns, which lead to action that opposes God's good plans for your life.

No one has it all together, and God doesn't expect that, but He *does* desire that we seek Him so His grace can cover us when we do mess up! When you do mess up, don't turn away from God; His intimate love is the fuel that sustains you when you cannot see how you can do what He asks. When depleted, tired and weary, His Word is your anchor. Don't throw away your victory. Will you calibrate your conscience to His truth and live the transformed life He promised?

ROM 12:2 (NLT); JOHN 8:32; PROV. 14:12; HEB. 6:, 10:35; I COR. 15:57

March 31

*"You will keep in perfect peace him whose mind is
steadfast, because he trusts in you."*
Isaiah 26:3

Trust God...His peace will guard you heart.. You've been violated and experienced many let-downs in life. You were robbed, but...are you going to allow the past to rob you of your present and your future? God didn't rob you; others did, so don't hold a grudge against Him. Your emotions are distorting and separating you from His truth and love. God will set you free from your bondage of past pain. He will restore what was stolen, given away or never received, giving it all back and more, but you will never know this truth...*unless you trust Him.*

Following God doesn't exempt you from pain, but it does promise He will bring you through! You will have more heartbreak and hurt in the future, but God will soothe you through each episode. God is in control over what you see and do not see; He holds creation together in His hands. Faith isn't based on what you see God do, it's based on Who you believe He is! Will you trust Him and let His peace guard your heart?

Isaiah 26:3; Jer. 27:7; Phil. 4:7; Col. 1:16-17

†

April 1

"Don't worry about anything; instead, pray about everything."
Phil 4:6 (NLT)

Despite the despair that's inevitable in life, we're promised hope that soothes our souls, joy that overflows, and peace that surpasses human understanding. These are God's promises. Many ponder, debate and speculate meaning, validity, reliability and application but, at the end of the day, that doesn't make His promises any less true! Replace your reasoning with praying...tell God what you need and thank Him for all that He has done. This is the process for renewing your mind constantly. Will you do this so you can live the life that God has promised to you?

PHIL 4:6-7 (NLT); ROM. 12:2

April 2

*"Therefore do not throw away your confidence
which has a great reward."*
HEB. 10:35 (ESV)

Keep pushing, friend; you're being pressed on every side...another day of being purposed for Christ. You're tired and want to give up, but you know what God put in your heart. Yet, doubt mocks your efforts and you question if you're making it all up. One battle after another...does it ever stop? No; the battles do not stop, but Jesus said to keep moving forward and we will reap a harvest if we don't give up. Our confidence is in God's Word; He's not a quitter and He won't quit on you!

Press, push, keep going...your work is eternity-driven! The last battle before each win is always the toughest, and it is also where our character is developed and perseverance is birthed. Anyone can begin to run, but it's those who endure who are richly rewarded and receive God's promises; His hope holds on for us! Keep going, your work is making a difference.

I sought the Lord and He answered me; He delivered me from all my fears. Those who look to Him are radiant and their faces are never covered with shame (SEE PS. 34:4-5). Commit what you do to the Lord and trust Him, and He will make your righteousness shine like the dawn and the justice of your cause...like the noonday sun (SEE PS. 37:5-6). Will you keep pushing and let God pursue His plans through you?

HEB. 10:35-36 (ESV); PS. 34:4-5, 37:5-6

April 3

"For we are God's masterpiece. He created us anew in Christ Jesus, so we can do the good things he planned for us long ago."
EPH. 2:10 (NLT)

You are God's masterpiece, crafted together by His hands to carry out His specific plans for you in His Kingdom. He is committed to your development and will work with you through your entire life in order for you to reach the full potential He planned.

If you will trust Him when you don't understand, know that apart from Him you can do nothing, and embrace His correction...you can be fully used by God. Rejecting any of these will eliminate you from your complete call. God will sculpt, shape, press, squeeze, delay, detour, test, add to, withhold, tear down, and take away things so that you will become mature, complete and lack for nothing. Embrace these trials; they test your faith, build your endurance and develop the perseverance that produce His hope in you.

Ask God for insight and wisdom. He gives it generously without finding fault. God's correction makes you right, not wrong! He loves you and is committed to you. He will never give up on you...you're His masterpiece! Will you make the same commitment to God and never give up on Him?

EPH. 2:10 (NLT); PS. 91:16; PHIL. 1:6; JAMES 1:2-5

April 4

"All his days his work is pain and grief; even at night his mind does not rest."
ECC. 2:23

Save yourself a lifetime of frustration, fatigue and failure; seek God first. Nothing else really matters until you do. Know the Word so you can stand firm when the enemy whispers lies that you don't have what it takes. It's crucial to renew your mind daily with the Word, or the enemy will make a mess of your mind and your life!

Are you ready to stop working harder to gain ground and begin to completely trust God with the life He planned for you, using the strengths and qualities He purposed in you? I pray that you will not allow deception to convince you to do life your way one more day...it doesn't work.

ECC. 2:23; ROM. 12:2; MATT. 6:33

April 5

"We had hoped He was the Messiah -
it's been three days since He went away..."
LUKE 24:21

Jesus...He knows what you need, can give you what you don't have and get you were you need to be. He carried the burdens of your life to the cross and wiped out the power of each one of them. But He didn't stop there; He went on to fight hell and won-then on the third day He was raised from the dead! Jesus' loved ones watched as He was hanged on the cross and died. Their hope faded before them as they witnessed Jesus take His last breath; they forgot the promise He made to them: " *I have to go but I will send a Helper to be with you always.*"

When the plan didn't go as they anticipated...they lost hope in their mind because they couldn't see or reason how, and they forgot about what was promised. They were watching through their human wisdom and forgetting the power of God working on their behalf. They relied on what they could see...not on Who they professed to believe. Human reasoning pushed them into despair. Have you allowed your reasoning to push you into despair based on what you can see?

I COR. 2:5; LUKE 24:21; JOHN 14:-6

April 6

"For the LORD gives wisdom, and from his mouth
come knowledge and understanding."
PROV. 2:6

Relationships in life: some we pick and enjoy, others w're placed in and they require much effort. Some come easy and other are just plain hard. Some energize, while others drain. Some are close and others far apart. Some are honest and others aren't. Some we keep for a lifetime, but others have to be severed from our lives. God will help us with each one. He offers wisdom, knowledge and understanding in our relationships. His truth is our guide. If we're not hearing His wisdom, we're probably too busy dialoging with our thoughts and listening to our feelings.

Until we prefer God's wisdom, knowledge and understanding to our feelings we will not hear His guidance for our relationships. Our feelings change and can give us neither the objectivity nor the stability and truth that God reveals. God's ways can feel uncomfortable, unnatural and require unwanted work, but if we are sincere in wanting to do things His way, He will give us desire and power to carry out what He instructs us to do.

God's help is forfeited when feelings are given preference over God's truth. A man's ways seem right, but lead to death (SEE PROV. 14:12). God will give you wisdom without finding fault. Will you accept and apply His wisdom to your life and relationships?

PROV. 2:6, 14:2; PHIL. 2:13

April 7

"For God is working in you giving you the
desire and the power to do what pleases him."
PHIL. 2:13 (NLT)

Are you doing what's comfortable for you...in the name of Jesus? If you opt for comfort over the unknown you will reason yourself out of God's good plans. Don't be mistaken: following Christ will turn you inside-out; it's an often uncomfortable, unknown and sometimes almost unbearable journey, but it leads to the authentic you. You will work hard and be tired, but it's a tired that pleases God and develops you, unlike labor done in vain that leads to dead ends. Are you allowing safe and predicable to dictate your walk with Christ? Do you say that you love Him, but know that you're not totally living for Him? How do you know God uses the weak and foolish to confound the wise unless you're willing to look weak and foolish. How do you know that the boldness of the Holy Spirit will flow through you unless you risk being bold?

Don't settle...nothing compares to knowing God's love and living the life He planned for you. Do the work God designed you to do in this world for His glory! His love enables you to rest in His sufficiency. You're approved so you no longer feel compelled to prove. You're valuable because you *belong to* Him, not because of what you *do for* Him. But you won't know this until you walk out what you profess to believe about Him! Will you accept all of the love that God has for you, and walk out the authentic life He planned for you?

PHIL 2:13 (NLT); EX. 31:3

April 8

*"I praise you because I am fearfully and
wonderfully made..."*
PS. 139:14

If someone didn't love you as they were *supposed* to...that doesn't make you unloveable. No one has the power to determine that you are unloveable, because God chose you in advance to fulfill His purposes. If you've been hurt by someone who was *supposed* to love you...you will have a hard time believing those who have *chosen* to love you. God's love will help you heal from this rejection; He restores the brokenhearted and binds up their wounds. Think on this truth every day because you are fearfully and wonderfully made!

Hope in Him all day long. His hope will never disappoint. Do not let another person determine your value...only Jesus has that authority, and He says that *you are approved*! You must decide if you will accept His truth. I called out to the Lord and He answered me; He delivered me from all my fears. Those who look to Him are radiant, their faces are never covered with shame (SEE PS. 34:4). Call out to the Lord; He will answer you...because He loves you!

PS. 34:4-5, 139:4-5; ISAIAH 61:1-3; EPH. 1:5, 11

April 9

*"But God chose what is foolish in the world to shame the wise;
God chose what is weak in the world to shame the strong."*
1 Cor. 1:27 (esv)

Jesus is calling...will you answer? He calls for every person to come after Him; He wants to be your Guide. Few follow for fear of leaving their familiar, sadly forfeiting the future God planned for them. Following Jesus requires going against norms, conventional ways and the popular vote. God likes to create shock value to confound the wise. He will ask you to carry out ridiculous, radical and impossible tasks so there's no doubt but that it's Him. He laughs as the naysayers stare with mouths open. Following Jesus can bring isolation, resistance and ridicule. This is the fire you must go through to know He's your source, supplying all you need to accomplish your mission.

Be confident in His ability flowing through you-the work He began in you. He will continue to perfect you up until the day of His return! You know in your mind that what God has asked of you is impossible; that's why you have to completely rely on His ability. Opposition, doubt and discouragement will come at you daily, wanting you to justify your cause. *Don't engage.* It's a ploy to create confusion and distract you from hearing the Holy Spirit. Focus and listen; move forward even when you see no physical evidence. Your evidence is Who you believe in and the words spoken to your heart. Hold on to these words tightly; cling to them when you're discouraged and weary! God put this call in you to use you...not to prove you. He will make your righteousness shine like the dawn and the justice of your cause like the noonday sun! Jesus is calling...will you answer?

1 Cor. 1:27 (esv); Phil. 1:6; Ps. 37:6

April 10

"He heals the brokenhearted and binds up their wounds."
Ps. 147:3

What a relief to know that God's love is bigger than human love; that we do not have to be bound to the wounds of other people! He restores what was lost, stolen or given away. He gives us the love that we should have received and heals the parts of our hearts that were violated, broken and deceived. He makes up for all the hugs never received, the "thank-yous" never given, all the "you matters" never heard-all of the 'nevers" that never should have happened.

God doesn't dismiss or overlook any hurts. His love is bigger than any wound imposed on you or that you may have imposed on another. God's love is bigger, and can fix, correct and make new what human love cannot! Will you let His big love heal all of you?

PS. 147:3; ISAIAH 61:1-3; DEUT. 30:1-3

April 11

*"Search me, O God, and know my heart! Try me
and know my thoughts."*
PS. 139:23 (ESV)

If you find yourself consistently agitated with someone, usually it's because they have something you want, stir up an unresolved issue, or they're having the boldness and courage to go after a dream such as one God has encouraged you to pursue, but which you've resisted out of fear. Ask the Holy Spirit to search what's going on in your heart and to give you revelation regarding the reason for your irritation with this person.

The bottom line is this: no person has the power to make you feel something, but their behavior can "irritate" an issue in you that you've not dealt with. Don't dumb-down your response and dismiss it. The Holy Spirit will give you insight if you're willing to receive it. Don't cheat yourself out of the wisdom He will give you by minimizing your feelings as, "I just don't like them, that all." That's *not* all; there's more to it and you won't know until you look into your heart with the Holy Spirit's wisdom.

PS. 139:23 (ESV); JOHN 14:26; PROV. 14:8

April 12

"We demolish arguments and every pretension that sets itself up against the knowledge of God..."
2 COR. 10:5

Release the ashes-the wrongs done to you. Wrong things were done to you, but you are not wrong. Let go of the memories that chain you to the past and what you believe about yourself because of what someone did or said to you. God loves you! You're His masterpiece! Allow His love to soothe you, and His Word to cleanse your wounds. Stop looking to others to make you okay; you will be disappointed each time. Others cannot heal you-only Jesus can. Stop the replaying of lies in your mind that tell you that you are a mistake, left over or not good enough. Replace these lies in your mind with God's truth: you are His masterpiece, God's workmanship, more than a conqueror, loved, cherished, and chosen! Say these truths day in and day out and you will eventually begin to agree with them. These are God's promises -will you choose to believe them?

2 COR. 10:5; PS. 147:3; EPH. 2:10

April 13

"...let the Spirit renew your thoughts and attitudes."
EPH. 4:23 (NLT)

Jesus has no agenda, other than to unconditionally love all of us, but we are often uncomfortable receiving love with no conditions attached. We've learned that love has to be earned. You cannot *earn* God's love: He loved us before you ever knew Him. He chose you and tenderly knitted you together with His hands; you're His masterpiece. Lift your head and look up. Your Father is smiling and He desires for you to know how much you are loved by Him! God's love for you isn't measured by what you've done or where you've been: He loves you because that is what He does...*God is love*!

Will you make a *decision* to believe God even though you don't *feel* it? Will you allow the Holy Spirit to heal your spirit and help you renew your mind every day with God's love? Some days and, sometimes, in whole seasons, you will have to say

God's truth over and over and over, but you will eventually believe the truth if you don't give up on God. He will never give up on you!

EPH 4:23 (NLT); GAL. 6:9; JOHN 14:26; EPH. 4:23

April 14

"Be made new in the attitude of your minds."
EPH. 4:23

Dear child: I want you to know that I do not expect you to have it all together...I've asked you to give Me all you have and I will help you put it all together. Remain in Me and I will remain in you. This is my partnership with you, and My commitment to you: I will continue to bring to completion the good works I started in you long ago! You're My masterpiece. I created you because I loved you first, but also to make a difference in this world. You are fearfully and wonderfully made because My love lives in you: apart from My love you can do nothing, but with My love you can do all things I've asked of you!

When you sin, do not turn away from Me; turn *toward* Me, so I can help you. Repenting leads to freedom in Me. I never condemn you and I will give you wisdom generously-even when you make deliberate and foolish choices. You have to know that nothing is too big for My love! Are you ready to give Me all you have so I can help you put it all together?

EPH. 4:23; EPH. 2:10; PHIL. 1:6; ACTS 3:19

April 15

"And hope does not disappoint..."
ROM. 5:5

Don't grope in the dark any longer and hope that you will find your way. Jesus made a way for you! Let Him love all of you; don't hold anything back. What you bring in the light loses it's power. Put your hope in Him when grief comes like a robber in the night. His hope holds tight to the truth for you. He will make a way when you cannot see a way. No one can believe for you: that's why it's called a *personal* relationship. Life is hard, but Jesus is Lord and He's overcome this world. He's deprived it of the power to harm you! This is His promise, but a promise is only powerful if it's believed...do you believe?

ROM 5:5, 8; JOHN 16:33; HEB. 6:19; PS. 25:5

April 16

*"...for you know that the testing of your faith
produces steadfastness."*
JAMES 1:3 (ESV)

The testing of your faith challenges what you profess to believe about God; and, how you respond...reveals where you stand. This testing exposes the false idols you've relied on, messes up the predictable routines that have stunted your development, and purges pride you didn't even know existed! Welcome this testing and you will know God's love like never before, be known by Him in ways you never imagined, and the door will be opened for the development of the authentic person God designed you to be.

Rejecting this testing forfeits the growth required to move into the next season God is calling you into. Take the test and take the next step! God is with you until the end!

JAMES 1:3 (ESV); PHIL. 1:6; PROV. 1:5

April 17

*"For we are his workmanship, created in Christ Jesus
for good works, which God prepared beforehand,
that we should walk in them."*
EPH. 2:10 (ESV)

Nobody looks forward to adversity, but it's required to grow in faith while gaining revelation of walking in the freedom God promises. You don't have to make a way for yourself-God has already done it! But, you *do* have to agree with His truth and be willing to leave the comfort of the Christian fortress you've built and follow the unknown path God is leading you down. When you accept the revelation that God is for you, has always loved you and wants you to rely completely on Him for all you need...then you will begin to let go of anxiety about being over-looked, not being good enough, or not having what it takes!

Each time you face adversity, you have an opportunity to lay down who you think you should be and who you are trying to be, and become more of who God says you are-His master-piece, who He created with His own hands to do the good works He planned *specifically for you* long ago! What does your response to adversity reveal about you?

EPH. 2:10 (ESV); JAMES 1:2-8; JOHN 8:32

April 18

*"And I am sure of this, that he who began a good work in you
will bring it to completion at the day of Jesus Christ."*
PHIL. 1:6 (ESV)

Nothing can overtake you because God is with you and holding your hand. Before the truth can set you free you must *know* the truth! God's truth is for you to overcome...taking you from where you are to where He wants you to be, to fulfill the plans He made for you long ago. This is His promise to you, but you must first believe it. Until God's promises are believed in your mind...they won't be walked out in your life!

God will help you believe-just ask Him. Are you ready to leave where you are in your mind so God can take you to where He wants you to be?

PHIL. 1:6 (ESV); JOHN 8:32; ISAIAH 41:10

April 19

"The LORD your God is with you, the Mighty Warrior who saves."
ZEPH. 3:17

Make a decision to walk by faith-not by sight. Expectations are determined on the inside of you, *not* the circumstances sur-rounding you! Life is cruel and unfair many times, but you can have a confident expectation, being sure of what you hope for and certain of what you don't see! Jesus has overcome this world-this is a truth, *despite* what your eyes see. Expect Him to walk you through the circumstances you're facing!

The joy of the Lord is your strength-His joy completes you. He supplies all your needs-abundantly...more than you dare imagine. Expectations aren't determined by your ability-what you can or can't *do*. They're determined by what you *believe*! What do you believe? It determines what you expect.

HEB. 11:1; ZEPH. 3:17; COL. 1:17; 2 COR. 5:7; NEH. 8:10; JOHN 15:11; EPH. 3;20

April 20

*"The LORD is close to the brokenhearted
and saves those who are crushed in spirit."*
PS. 34:18

Jesus heals...what was lost, stolen, or given away. He tenderly restores every broken part of your heart, replaces your hurt with His love, and your depravity with His dignity. Trade in your fears, mistakes and uncertainties for His boldness, correction and future. No person, achievement, or financial security can replace what's missing in you, but...Jesus can, and He will! He heals broken hearts, binds up wounds and will release you from being a prisoner to your own pain. Will you give Jesus every part of you, so He can heal every part of you? Then you will know the truth and the truth will set you free!

PS. 34:18, 147: 3; ISAIAH 61:1-3; JOHN 8:32

April 21

*"Don't act thoughtlessly, but understand
what the Lord wants you to do."*
EPH. 5:17 (NLT)

Don't deny reality...but don't deny God's truth, either! God's truth is your lifeline for every trial: unemployment, illness, delayed dreams, failed relationships, grief, insufficient funds, anger, foreclosure, addictions, family secrets, guilt, broken hearts, false accusations, rejection...and anything else that has ever been or will be!

God's truth is that He will never leave you, so do not be afraid. He holds together all you see and do not see, has good plans, is for you and not against you, supplies all of your needs, and gives you the strength to become more than a conqueror. Your part is to trust and to have faith constantly.

Hold tight to God's truth; don't allow doubt to rob you and conform your thoughts to worldly thinking. The Holy Spirit will guide you. Keep His truth on your lips, in front of your eyes, speak and listen to it, and only place your hope in God! God's truth is your lifeline in every trial...will you take hold of it?

EPH. 5:17 (NLT); ROM. 12:2; MARK 11:22; JOHN 15:7; PS. 46:10

April 22

"Then you will know the truth, and the truth will set you free."
JOHN 8:32

Doubt's agenda is to steal, kill and destroy the truth God promises. He poses as being concerned, but he speaks only in partial truths. It is deception! He begins by questioning the dreams that God has placed in your heart. Next, He moves on to your understanding of Scripture. Then, he has you to examine your life as a whole: have you really made a difference? Is God pleased with you? Finally, he questions what you believe about your loved ones.

You've been praying for a long time with no answers in sight; in fact, things appear to be worse. You conclude that your situation is impossible. This is a partial truth. The complete truth is that...with men this is impossible, but that all things are possible with God! So, yes, your situation may be impossible for you, but not with God! Write down JOHN 8:32 and put it several places where you can see it, then say it aloud. It's a promise over whatever you are facing. Be on guard; doubt will come at you with partial truths to steal, kill and destroy the rich and satisfying life God has promised! Don't be deceived by doubt-know God's truth, and it *will* set you free!

JOHN 8:32, 10:10; MATT. 19:26

April 23

"My grace is sufficient for you,
for my power is made perfect in weakness."
2 COR. 12:9

We know God's grace enables us to move through any given day, but it's during extreme seasons of fatigue that we cling to His grace, knowing that it's a lifeline giving us the mental and spiritual clarity we need to overcome! God's supernatural sufficiencies interlock with our human insufficiencies and enable us to carry out what would be otherwise humanly impossible.

God promises this clarity to all Christians who seek Him and renew their minds with His truth. Renewing our minds is an ongoing process that never stops-we have to read, speak, write, meditate on, discuss and pray God's Word. God's Word is our confidence, and promises to not just get us by, but to *overcome and move through* every difficult season. Will you rely on God's Word to enable your stability for daily living, but especially during seasons of extreme fatigue?

2 COR. 12:9-10; PHIL. 2:13

April 24

"For I can do everything through Christ,c who gives me strength. "
PHIL. 4:13 (NLT)

Are you tired of having the same struggles over and over? You've tried your best to work through them only to experience some victory, then default to failure mode, and the cycle repeats. You've stopped asking for prayer; you're just too embarrassed. You love Jesus with all your heart, you're doing what you know to do, but you're at the end of yourself.

As hopeless as this sounds, it's a great place to be! When I say this in counseling sessions, my clients think I'm crazy, but I explain that...crazy is trying to do ourself what only the Holy Spirit can do. People confuse not giving up with trying to push through life's struggles in their strength.

God never asked us to do life independent of His strength. Tap into the source of all power today!

PHIL. 4:13 (NLT); COL. 1:11; EPH. 3:19-20

April 25

"But take heart, because I have overcome the world."
JOHN 16:33 (NLT)

Listen closely: God designed us to rely on Him for everything. His strength is perfected in our weakness; this is His grace. Grace is the power of God released through us to meet our needs and to do what we cannot do. Grace gives us the ability to exceed our own ability! You've done all the things you need to do except the main thing that you need to do: embrace the reality that apart from God's grace you will continue to fail!

You've been trying to free yourself from these struggles, believing that if you could just master them, you would then experience freedom. This will never work because we don't experience freedom when we're free *from* something-we experience freedom *in* Christ...in His truth! Knowing His truth won't exempt us from failing occasionally, but it does promise that His grace will meet us in the middle of every failure and pull us out! No person is exempt from struggles, nor can anyone overcome them independent of God's grace. He will never give up on you; He's committed until the end...will you commit to receive His grace until the end?

2 COR. 12:9-10; PHIL. 1:6, 2:13; JOHN 16:33 (NLT)

April 26

"Love the LORD your God with all your heart and with all your soul and with all your strength."
DEUT. 6:5

Seek to connect with the Lord based on His promises-*not* your problems. Problems change...His promises don't. You will cheat yourself out of experiencing the greatest promise ever made to you if you only seek the Lord to handle your problems. God cares about your problems, but He cares much more about you knowing His love and you loving Him. And when you know His love and are known by Him...you will be confident He will handle every one your problems!

God wants you to know how far, wide, tall, deep, huge, absolutely ginormous His love is for you; nothing, nothing, nothing comes before His love for you. He delights in you, He chose the color of your eyes, the texture of your hair, and the gap in your front teeth...He made you from His love. You are part of Him; you are His child! He will never let go of your hand; this is His promise to you. When you know the power of His love...your problems lose their power! Renew your mind with His promises every day-they will sustain you during the hard times, hold on for you during the hopeless times and give you a peace that surpasses all understanding every day of your life! Don't pass on knowing the greatest promise that will ever be made to you... God loves you!

DEUT. 6:5; EPH. 3:16-21; 1 JOHN 4:19; PS. 37:4, 43:4

April 27

"I have said these things to you, that in me you may have peace. In the world you will have tribulation. But take heart; I have overcome the world."
JOHN 16:33 (ESV)

Life is unfair; people cheat and bad things happen. Don't give your sanity away trying to figure out things you cannot control. Put your faith in God's power...not human wisdom. Following Jesus doesn't exempt us from trials, but He does promise to bring us through each one! Don't let the "why" take your eyes off of the "Who." He will love, comfort and never leave you!

JOHN 16:33 (ESV); 2 COR. 2:5; PS. 34:19

April 28

"I sought the Lord, and he answered me;
he delivered me from all my fears.
Those who look to him are radiant;
their faces are never covered with shame."
PS. 34:4-5

Believing is not a *feeling* you feel...believing is a *decision* you make! Believing is based on Who God is, not on whether you understand everything about Him. Many have a hard time with this truth and lose direction in life, slowly fading into disbelief. Their belief is based only on what they can understand.

When I committed my life to Christ, I made the decision to believe, but I didn't completely trust Him. I was honest and told God that I wanted to believe, but I was scared to trust Him. Then God sent His help-mercy and grace, to do a work in me. My Father God met me where I was. I was doubting...I sought Him and He answered me. God delivered me from all my fears.

God made a way for me. Jesus says to ask and it will be given, seek and you will find, knock and the door will be opened (SEE MATT. 7:7). God meets us where we are; we must decide if we will believe Him when He does meet us...this is how we strengthen our faith daily. Will you put your faith in God today?

PS. 34:4-5; MARK 9:24; MATT. 7:7

April 29

"See to it that no one takes you captive through hollow and deceptive
philosophy, which depends on human tradition and the elemental
spiritual forces of this world rather than on Christ."
COL. 2:8

See to it that no one takes you captive through hollow or deceptive philosophy, which depends on human tradition and the basic principles of this world. Don't be wise in your own eyes; seek God. This will bring health to your body and nourishment to your bones. Renew your mind with the truth to stay balanced in daily living.

83

You flirt with disaster when you entertain teachings that credit humanity. Many want to believe some of God's truth, then mix it with other beliefs. Jesus is the *only* way, truth and life (SEE JOHN 14:6). No person is to add to or take away from God's truth. If they do, they shut the door on His presence and promised protection of peace in their minds and hearts. Don't drown in the grandeur of self-deception and forfeit the peace of God's presence that is available to you. Turn, repent and run to Him. He will refresh you like the spring rains that water the earth. (SEE HOSEA 6:3).

COL. 2:8; ROM. 12:2; HOSEA. 6:3

April 30

"Then you will know the truth, and the truth will set you free."
JOHN 8:32

Debating God's truth doesn't change it. Every person who accepts Jesus as his or her Lord and Savior has access to His promises. Whether they believe in and walk out His Word will determine if they live out His promises. God doesn't lie; many want to debate His Word as if it's open for modification. It's not.

Don't ponder, debate or speculate. You will lose ground and become confused. Blessed are those who hear the Word and obey it! *Believing God is a choice, not a feeling!* Walk by faith, not by sight. This is how we spiritually strengthen our believing muscles. Jesus said He's deprived the world of the power to harm you; He's conquered it for you. This gives you courage during trials, knowing you don't have to figure this life out because Jesus has!

Believe and let Jesus Christ flow His power through you to accomplish the good plans God called you to long ago. Agree with God; give Him an opportunity to finish the good work He started in you and bring it to completion. Jesus knows what you're facing this very second. Chose to believe that He's got you covered. Don't debate, speculate or ponder one more second! Will you believe Him and be blessed?

JOHN 8:31-32; PHIL. 1:6; 2 COR. 5:7

✝

May 1

"And we know that God causes everything to work together for the good of those who love God and are called according to his purpose for them."
ROM. 8:28 (NLT)

God likes a good mess...He turns each one into a great message! God uses what you give Him. Don't dismiss your mess because you don't see how He can use it. God can make nothing into something, and He will make your mess into a message for His glory! God can and will make something of your mess...will you let Him?

ROM. 8:28 (NLT); EPH. 3:19-20

May 2

"But you belong to God, my dear children. You have already won a victory over those people, because the Spirit who lives in you is greater than the spirit who lives in the world."
1 JOHN 4:4 (NLT)

The power of Christ in you is far greater than the problems staring back at you! See what you're facing through the power of Christ. Don't rely on your understanding; it will steal the promises of God! Move forward with the confident assurance of God's promise: if God is for you, Who can be against you! You don't have to know *how* God will follow through on His promises to you...to believe that He *will* keep His promises to you! God's power is greater than any problem you will face. Will you chose to believe?

1 JOHN 4:4; PROV. 3:5-6

May 3

"For to be carnally minded is death;
but to be spiritually minded is life and peace."
ROM. 8:6 (KJV)

You must calibrate your conscience to the Word daily; if not, your conscience will do what it believes is right: there is a way that seems right in the mind, but its end leads to death. A conscience not submitted to the Word results in subtle reasoning that leads you one thought at a time down the path of deception. Your intent isn't to reject God's truth, but a mind that's not submitted to the Word daily will default to doubting or opposing God's truth.

The blood of Jesus has made us "right" with God by faith; this is God's promise but we won't live like it unless we renew our mind with His Word. Commit your conscience to the Lord, preferring His truth over what you're feeling. Do this as a daily exercise to strengthen your trust muscles. The more you trust the Lord the more you allow His boldness to flow through you and carry out the plans He made for you long ago!

ROM. 5:1, 8:6 (KJV), 12;2

May 4

"Every place that the sole of your foot will tread upon I have given to you,
just as I promised to Moses."
JOSHUA 1:3 (ESV)

Leave your "Christian comfort zone"...to experience God's best for your life. Every person in Bible who experienced God's best had to step out of his or her comfort zone and into the unknown. This required them to release all their familiar, comfortable and predictable places and things, and walk into the "un:" the unfamiliar, uncomfortable, and unknown. This is the only way God can take us through the crash course of "trusting Him." It's only when we've been stripped of everything we cling to, so that we can only cling to Him...and finally know Him and be known by Him that we can then trust Him to lead us to...where we've never been before!

Are you willing to experience God's best for you?

JOSHUA 1:3 (KJV); PROV. 3:5-6; PHIL. 3:10

May 5
""I will repay you for the years the locusts have eaten..."
JOEL 2:25

You have a life beyond your broken heart. God promises that He will heal your broken heart and bind up your wounds. But if you blame another person for where you are in life...you're giving them the power to determine where you *stay* in life.

Maybe your childhood was stolen by someone you trusted, a parent withheld love, you were bullied in school, false accusations led to a job loss, a promising business deal went wrong depleting your savings, a best friend told your secret. Blame is a powerful emotion because it focuses on the reality of what happened to you and keeps your wounds open...then it punches you with the lie that your destiny has been stolen.

If you believe this lie, you will focus on the injustice, knowing that you cannot undo what's been done. It's true you can't...but Jesus can - He's the Author and Finisher, He has no barriers. He is unstoppable! His Word will not return void; His love heals the past, present, and future! Your hurt is valid. Blame reminds you of the events with accuracy, but blame has no case against the power of Christ! He heals broken hearts and saves those crushed in spirit. He will give you beauty for the ashes you have been carrying. His hope anchors your soul and holds on for you when you cannot. The realities of life will cause many heartaches and hardships, but God promises to bring you through each one and to restore you. Your part is to release wrongs to Him so that He can...will you?

JOEL 2:25; PS. 34:18, 115:109, 147:3; HEB. 12:2; ISAIAH 61:1-3

May 6

"Stay alert! Watch out for your great enemy, the devil. He prowls around like a roaring lion, looking for someone to devour."
I PETER 5:8

Your greatest strengths are your greatest weaknesses. God gives you strengths to carry out His plans in the Kingdom and glorify Him, but if you're not submitting your greatest strengths to His authority, then you're fair game for the enemy to undermine your greatest strengths, turning them into your greatest weaknesses!

You can do all things through Christ Who strengths you...not what you choose to do to strengthen yourself, then pray for God to endorse. Apart from Christ your strengths become your weaknesses. You might be sincere in doing good, not becoming weary and believing the harvest will come, but you will just about kill yourself if Christ isn't flowing His strength through you!

Deception masquerades as Christian excellence...encouraging you to keep going for the glory of God, but God is *not* glorified if you're carrying out your plans instead of His! It's a subtle trap many fall into - they are sincere, but sincerely wrong.

I PET. 5:8; PHIL. 4:13; EPH. 3:16; LUKE 4:3

May 7

"He will make your righteous reward shine like the dawn, your vindication like the noonday sun."
PS. 37:6

Doubt is a dream-killer and has every intent of killing the dreams God put in your heart. Doubt begins to steal from you by asking how long ago it was that God put the dream in your heart, and, if you've done everything He's asked of you...why the long wait? You agree; it's been a long time; you're tired. Then doubt subtly injects you with reasoning that kills your hope: did you misunderstand or exaggerate a little? If so, no big deal, but doubt keeps picking at you. Don't keep giving life to something you cannot see. You agree; you'd be foolish. You begin to feel embarrassed and silly-hurt mixed with anger. You promise you'll not get your hope up like this again. You're exactly where doubt wants you...giving up hope and the dream God in your heart.

If you don't have hope, you don't have a future. If you don't have a future, you don't have hope - a vicious cycle going nowhere. Put your hope in God, not in what you see. Commit your ways to Him, trust Him and He will make your righteousness shine like the dawn and the justice of your cause like the noonday sun! Don't give up hope...you have a dream to carry out; the season is near-you're so close. Keep moving!

PS. 37:5-6; HEB. 6:19; GAL. 6:9

May 8

"Then the LORD replied: "Write down the revelation and make it plain on tablets so that a herald may run with it."
HAB. 2:2

This journey is not to discourage you...it's to prepare you! To sustain it, write the vision down plainly and look at it daily so you see it coming and going. Most importantly, remember why you do what you do; the vision is God's truth being carried out through you but the burden to *prove* it isn't on you - that's God's job! Agreeing with and carrying out His Word ignites the vision...writing it down and looking at it daily keeps the flame burning!

Some days doubt and weariness overshadow the vision-that's okay, it happens. Just keep your eyes on Jesus...His grace is sufficient and He will give you rest, and the exact word of encouragement you need to keep moving. Laying your life down to follow Jesus will be by far the most difficult thing you've ever done, but it will bring by far the greatest freedom you've ever experienced.

Don't throw away your confidence. It will be richly rewarded. Keep the vision in front of you!

The journey is not to discourage you...it's to *prepare* you so when you have done the will of God...you will receive what He has promised!

HAB. 2:2; HEB. 10:35-36; GAL. 6:9

May 9

"Bless the LORD, O my soul:
and all that is within me, bless his holy name."
PS. 103:1 (KJV)

Without Jesus I surely would have lost my mind by now! Jesus is my hope and His Word is my confidence...walking by faith is my certainty, even when I cannot see a way. I do feel fear, and the only way I can overcome is to count on Jesus, Who has overcome! Even then I still need His help to have faith in Him daily. When I feel alone, I'm not because His truth trumps what I feel - He will never leave or fail me.

Some seasons bring a heaviness on my heart and a fatigue that gnaws on my bones. But, His promises keep me looking ahead! I *won't* forfeit the destiny I'm promised and I *will* embrace the hope and joy Jesus gives daily on this journey. I've got to guard my heart above all else, for out of it flow the issues of life (SEE PROV. 4:23). Daily I ask for help to purge my selfish desires, and to want a relationship with Jesus more than I want anything else. I lack nothing, not because I've got it all together, but because the love of Jesus provides me with all I need. I don't focus on what I'm not...I focus on Who He is! Jesus is more than enough, He supplies all of my needs. He is my Jehovah Jireh! Jesus is my hope and His Word is my confidence! And He is yours, too. Will you let Him be?

PS. 103:1 (KJV); PS. 139:23; PROV. 4:23

May 10

"Peace I leave with you; my peace I give to you.
Not as the world gives do I give to you.
Let not your hearts be troubled, neither let them be afraid."
JOHN 14:27 (ESV)

Relief doesn't come when the *burden* changes...it comes when your *perspective* changes. When you release to Jesus the burden you're facing, you move it off of you and into His hands. This allows you to experience the peace He promises because you're no longer trying to manage an impossible situation. Your hope is no longer tethered to the burden that was causing feelings of hopelessness. Now you're tethered to Jesus...who never fails you! Will you change your perspective today and experience the peace Jesus promises you?

JOHN 14:1, 27 (ESV); HEB. 6:19

May 11

"Make you perfect in every good work to do his will, working in you that which is well pleasing in his sight, through Jesus Christ; to whom be glory for ever and ever. Amen."
HEB. 13:21 (KJV)

Let's be real: we all struggle and some days do us in. But, we have everything we need to reach our full potential-it's God's design! Whatever He asks of us...He equips us to do! *God Who is all the while effectually at work in us energizing and creating in us the power and desire both to will and to work for His good pleasure and satisfaction and delight* (SEE PHIL 2:13).

God won't ask something of you that He will not enable you to do. Maybe others in your life have, but He will not. God empowers you to be ready for anything and equal to anything through Him, Who infuses inner strength. You are self-sufficient in Christ's sufficiency! You have what it takes, but you must use what you've been given, and then you will be given more.

Post Scripture on your phone and write verses on index cards or sticky notes, and put them everywhere! I carry them in my purse, and if I'm in the middle of the grocery store and feel a wave of discouragement sweep over me, I stop right there and pull out a Scripture to remind me of God's truth...He never changes, although my feelings do; I count on Him to be with me until the very end. Will you count on Him, too?

HEB. 13:2 (KJV); PHIL. 4:13; MARK 4:24-2

May 12

"He brought them out of darkness, the utter darkness,
and broke away their chains."
PS. 107:14

Will you let Jesus break the chains that have been on your family for generations? Many dismiss old hurts, reasoning that they will pass with time and nothing can be done about them. Time passes...hurts don't. An unresolved hurt is as alive today as the day it happened, but it's not always recognized because it has many layers of life on it. A person is chained to the hurt imposed by another person until he or she is healed. Perspective is obscured because they see and hear life through their past pain. Hurt is insidious; although it's in the past, it impacts every aspect of a person's life and perpetuates through every generation until it is stopped.

Don't throw away the life that Jesus died to give you. Release the hurt to Him. There is a way that seems right in the mind, but in the end leads to death (SEE PROV. 14:12). Only Jesus can heal you; you cannot heal yourself, nor can you heal from what you will not bring into His light. Jesus came to save, bind up our wounds, free us from captivity, and bring us out of darkness! Until you let the love of Jesus heal you...you're left in darkness, a prisoner in your own life and a captive in your own hurt. Will you release your hurt to Jesus and let Him break the chains that have been in your family for generations?

PS. 107:14, 139:23-24; ISAIAH 61:1; PROV. 14:12; 2 COR. 3:17; JOHN 10:10

May 13

*"Patient endurance is what you need now, so that you will continue to do
God's will. Then you will receive all that he has promised."*
HEB. 10:36 (NLT)

Get a revelation of your privileges...God's Word is alive in you.
Nothing can overcome you! Jesus Christ lives in you; He's overcome the world and so have you. You will have trials, but don't
allow them to make you weary and throw away your confidence. Persevere, so when you have done the will of God you
will receive what He has promised! Rest in God; you're not
alone in this fight...unless you try to reason and do things your
way. Many days you will not "feel" like you've overcome, but
that doesn't negate the truth that you *have*, because the Overcomer lives in you!

God's Word is your confidence for everything and anything you
need in life. Line up every thought with the Word. Thoughts
that do not line up have to go! You are never left to your own
limited abilities, unless you choose to go your own way. If
you've been doing life your way, repent and turn to God. He's
waiting. His love will refresh you and His Word is a lamp to
your feet and a light to your path (SEE PS. 119:105). Get a revelation of your privileges...then *apply* them to your daily life, because you are an overcomer!

HEB. 4:12, 10:36 (NLT); JOHN 16:33; MATT. 1:28; ACTS 3:19; PS. 119:105

May 14

*"I pray that from his glorious, unlimited resources he will empower you
with inner strength through his Spirit."*
HEB. 3:16 (NLT)

God will carry out His cause through you, but it's up to you if
you will let Him. Don't ever think that He can't use you for His
purpose...His hands knitted you together for His purpose!
Don't be discouraged when you're rejected, passed over or ex-
cluded, test scores report moderate to low range and don't meet
criteria, aptitude assessments reflect poor results, personalty
inventories show no matches, and phone calls and emails
aren't returned. God still has good plans! If you're following

God with all your heart, you're on course. He doesn't miss anything. Nothing obstructs His view. He will find you anywhere-darkest night, biggest fire and deepest waters. God's with you; you matter, you count, you're valued, and His grace is sufficient for you! This truth enables you to persevere through adversity and to carry out the call He's put in you!

Don't put your hope in man's wisdom. Put it in God's power! God's plans, evaluations and responses are the only ones that matter because He's in charge of all we see and don't see. His verdict is final. There's nothing too big or too inconsequential for Him to consider. His love is bigger than anything you are facing, and He can make something from nothing.

No verdict given by man is final; only God's Word is! Stay on course; don't be discouraged when others imply that you don't have what it takes. God says that you do, and that's the only verdict that counts. He will bring you through this. Will you trust Him to?

EPH. 3:16, 18 (NLT); COL. 2:10

May 15

"Seek the Kingdom of God above all else,
and he will give you everything you need."
LUKE 12:31 (NLT)

God knows everything about you and He's not surprised at all. There's nothing you're dealing with or need to overcome that's too much for God. Your worst mistake, biggest regret, most painful memory, unresolved issues, financial dilemma, mental or medical diagnosis, or very unique situation-none of these things are too much for God! He can handle your situation; the question is: will you let Him?

Over the years in counseling sessions people have told me that they prayed, but God didn't answer. A closer look revealed that they "prayed" a lot about how they wanted God to handle their situation, but never trusted Him to actually take it! Until we release our situation, He can't help us.

God gives us the freedom to live life the way we want to, but when we do, we are responsible for managing our situations. Living life God's way promises His protection and provision. He's planned every second of your life to include wrongs, mistakes and rebellion. He turns each one around for His glory, for those who love Him. God's got it all worked out for you...will you trust Him to help you in your situation?

LUKE 12:31 (NLT); PS. 127:2; JOHN 14:27

May 16

"Your word is a lamp for my feet, a light on my path."
PS. 119:105

We know God's grace enables us to move through any given day, but it's during seasons of extreme fatigue that we cling to His grace, knowing it's the lifeline that gives us the mental and spiritual clarity to overcome! God's supernatural sufficiencies interlock with our human insufficiencies and enable us to carry out what would otherwise be humanly impossible!

God promises this clarity to every Christian who seeks Him! Renewing our mind is an ongoing process that never stops. We have to read, speak, write, meditate on, discuss and pray God's Word. God's Word is our confidence, and through it, we are promised to not just get by but to *overcome* and move through every difficult day we face! Will you rely on God's Word to fight the good fight of faith for you?

JOHN 15:5, 16:33; PS. 34:19, 119:105; ROM. 8:11, 12:2; 2 COR. 12:9

May 17

"Humble yourselves before the Lord, and he will lift you up."
JAMES 4:10

Let's be real...the race God is calling us to is grueling. You will be exhausted many days and might consider giving up at times; maybe you already have. No person is exempt from the mental or emotional fatigue; it's a sign to rest and be restored. Many try to be a superhero and push past their fatigue, but there's nothing holy about moving forward in your own strength Humble yourself before God. Ask Him if there is any pride in your desire to please Him. Pride deceives us into believing we're somehow being holy when in fact we're really being prideful. Don't try to be a superhero; it doesn't glorify God and He's not impressed. Plus, it takes the focus off of Him!

Will you get real with God so you can run the race as He planned it for you?

JAMES 4:10; PHIL. 3:14; PROV. 11:12

' May 18

"He existed before anything else, and he holds all creation together."
COL. 1:17 (NLT)

God's Word trumps all things. Don't fret or be anxious about anything - it doesn't matter how lost, useless, long ago it happened, far away, impossible to comprehend, hopeless, dead, broken, angry, bitter, jealous or envious it is...God's Word trumps all things. He existed before all things and in Him all things consist, cohere and are held together. He knows your name, every single thought you've had, are having or will have. He's the Alpha and Omega-He speaks and nothing becomes something...taking shape and form! Holy sees, Holy knows and Holy does!

Will you trust God to walk you where you can't see to go? You know in your heart you're not where you're suppose to be, but you don't know how to get to where God wants you to be...He wants to show you but you must begin to trust Him-line up the thoughts in your mind with the truth in the Word and submit to the leading of the Spirit to give you counsel and guide you. God's Word trumps all things...will you trust Him to show you?

1 PET. 5:7; PS. 139:5; COL. 1:17

May 19

"To those who listen to my teaching, more understanding will be given, and they will have an abundance of knowledge. But for those who are not listening, even what little understanding they have will be taken away from them."
MATT. 13:12 (NLT)

Don't focus on trying not to be anxious; that will just make you *more* anxious. To eliminate a behavior, you don't try to stop doing it...you *replace it*. Renewing the mind is just that: replacing thoughts that oppose God's truth; this is a reactive correction that tosses out thoughts that oppose God's Word.

Eventually you work your way into a proactive correction that regenerates thoughts based on truth and keeps out opposing thoughts. And that's how you eliminate anxious thoughts! It's a mental exercise to be used daily for generating thoughts that are in agreement with God. This doesn't mean you won't be sideswiped by anxious thoughts, but you will know the response to working through those anxious thoughts. You will become better at it the more you do it! Use what you have and you will be given more; choose not to use what you've been given and even what you have will be taken.

Be proactive in the renewing of your mind and God will give you more understanding!

MATT. 13:12 (NLT); EPH. 4:23; JAMES 4:6

May 20

"For our earthly fathers disciplined us for a few years, doing the best they knew how. But God's discipline is always good for us, so that we might share in his holiness."
HEB. 12:10 (NLT)

If you're open to God's correction, you will walk out the plans God purposed for you long ago. God's correction makes you right-He will sculpt, shape, press, squeeze, add on, take away, build up and tear down your behaviors. This is how He tests your faith, which builds the character that develops endurance, and it's endurance that unleashes the spiritual stamina to stay on course!

Spiritual stamina is required to endure and overcome the inevitable battles that just get bigger down the road. But you don't have to be afraid or anxious because God's correction empowers you with His strength to move through them! God's correction makes you right...not wrong. Will you embrace His correction so He can achieve His plans through you?

HEB 12:10-13; ROM 5:3-5

May 21

"I press on toward the goal to win the prize
for which God has called me heavenward in Christ Jesus."
PHIL. 3:14

You are God's people and you're called to the race of life. The enemy wants you to believe that you don't have what it takes to run, but he's a liar, liar, pants-on-fire! God made you *for* the race; you *have* what it takes to win. Focus on your run and don't compare yourself with others. God only wants to talk to you about *your* progress. Persevere and move through the obstacles of hurt, rejection, lies, grief, fear, unfairness, loneliness, sadness, fatigue, disappointment, offenses and unknowns. Each one draws you closer to Christ, and His power is made perfect in your weaknesses. Independent of Him you won't make it!

When what you see doesn't line up with what you expected, don't drop out of the race...put your hope in God's power. Not your reasoning. God will bring to completion what He started in you, and this race isn't over until you go to heaven. If you're breathing, you're expected to run. Do life with other Christians who will be honest with you; real friends challenge where you are in the race, not to judge, but to hold you accountable. God purposed and approved you; don't let anyone tell you otherwise. The Spirit of God lives in you...enough said!

You are God's people. He planned this race long ago, *and it's won!* The question is...will you keep running?

PHIL 1:6, 3:14; GAL. 6:4

May 22

"And now, dear brothers and sisters, one final thing. Fix your thoughts on what is true, and honorable, and right, and pure, and lovely, and admirable. Think about things that are excellent and worthy of praise."
PHIL. 4:8 (NLT)

Your emotions will wage war with God's Word daily-no person is exempt. Walking in the freedom God promises is hard, but God's equipped you to overcome hard; it's His promise made to every believer! It's done one thought, one breath, one step and one day at a time, and *only* the Holy Spirit can give you the grace needed each day to do it. Your part is to fix your thoughts on the Word and daily condition your mind in the mental exercise of preferring God's truth over what you're feeling, seeing and hearing. This is a proactive approach which trains and strengthens your mind in advance to be positioned in the truth so when your emotions wage war on your mind...you are ready and able to press back with God's truth!

This is a hard process and the Holy Spirit will give you the grace to execute it-*if you rely on Him*. Will you throw out every thought that opposes God's truth to live in the freedom He promises you? Emancipate, liberate and celebrate...you are free-so live like it!

PS. 32:8; ROM. 12:2; PHIL. 4:8 (NLT)

May 23

"Don't copy the behavior and customs of this world, but let God transform you into a new person by changing the way you think. Then you will learn to know God's will for you, which is good and pleasing and perfect."
ROM. 12:2 (NLT)

Are you conforming or transforming? To conform is to comply with the socially acceptable conventions-pressure to behave to standards. To transform is to make a thorough or dramatic change in form, appearance and character. Don't conform to the patterns of this world, but be transformed by the renewing of our mind. Renewing your mind is not merely replacing negative thoughts with positive thoughts-*it's replacing the lies of conformity with the truth of God's Word*!

Check yourself....are you allowing God's truth to transform you? Do your talk and your walk line up? If you profess the Word, but walk with the world, you will be divided in your beliefs and eventually be ripped apart in your mind and unstable in all you do! Be transformed in your mind. Constantly renew the attitude of your mind with God's Word, reject the lies of conformity and you will be on course for the good plans God made long ago!

ROM. 12:2; EPH. 4:23, 5:17

May 24

"You can identify them by their fruit, that is, by the way they act."
MATT. 7:16 (NLT)

There are many counterfeits in the world masquerading as being from God. But, just because a person or a situation appears godly, doesn't mean that he or it is. If you will listen, the Holy Spirit will caution you if a situation or a person isn't genuine. Expect the enemy to counter the caution and accuse you of being a critical spirit, or judgmental, for believing something to be wrong.

A fish on a person's car, a Bible in a person's hand, and shouts of "Amen!" don't make them a Christian, any more than having high-end kitchen appliances and 500 cookbooks will make someone a gourmet cook. Watch the walk and taste the food...by their fruit you will recognize them.

MATT. 7:16

May 25

"Enter his gates with thanksgiving and his courts with praise;
give thanks to him and praise his name."
PS. 100:4

Do you pray to thrive...or just survive? The enemy's purpose is to steal, kill and destroy; Jesus came so we could have an abundant live and thrive-not just survive (SEE JOHN 10:10). Do you pray with confidence based on what God promises in His Word? Do you pray with less boldness when facing impossible situations by decreasing your expectations? Do you approach God with the same confidence during hard times as you do during good times - always thanking and praising Him?

Don't fall into the trap of wondering where Jesus is when the situation gets worse; He's with you. Remember, He lives in you. Jesus has overcome, so pray with fervent boldness, thanking and praising God for His provision. The enemy wants you to believe God has washed His hands of you, that you didn't follow His directives, or that you missed Him because you messed up. The enemy will tell you anything to get you to believe that the burden is on you...but it's not. The burden to prove everything is on God, and He's already proven it all: He is before all things and holds them all together in His hands!

Your burden is to believe Him. When you believe God you can pray boldly. It won't matter how impossible the situation appears. You will will know with confidence that He's got your situation in the palm of His hand. Continue to thank and praise Him for taking care of everything. Don't entertain lies of the enemy; turn away when he whispers to you that you're running out of chances. *You don't rely on chances*...you rely on promises. Thanks be to God, Who gives us victory by making us conquerors through our Lord Jesus Christ. Have faith in Him constantly! Pray to thrive...not just survive!

JOHN 10:10; PS. 100:4; 1 COR. 15:57; MARK 11:22

May 26

"Pay careful attention to your own work,
for then you will get the satisfaction of a job well done,
and you won't need to compare yourself to anyone else."
GAL. 6:4 (NLT)

Be inspired *by*...but don't compare *to*. Each person is to compare their ability only against their own ability-then they can take pride in what they've accomplished. Some get more-others get less; the number doesn't indicate value or level of success...the success indicator is how you *use* what's been given to you. God holds you responsible for what He calls you to...not how you compare to what another person is called to do.

Comparing is a contest you're guaranteed to lose; resulting in feelings of inferiority or superiority that lead to jealous and resentful or arrogant and presumptuous behavior. It's not what you have...it's how you use what you have! Be free and be you-where the Spirit of the Lord is, there is freedom! Are you walking in the freedom God's given you to carry out what He's called you to do?

GAL 6:4; 1 COR 3:8; 1PET. 4:10

May 27

*"Then you will know which way to go,
since you have never been this way before."*
JOSHUA 3:4

What is your Jordan? The Jordan River had to be crossed to enjoy and experience the Promised Land. It had been 40 years...God gave specific instructions for the crossing. Has God given you specific instructions for crossing your Jordan? You know in our heart it's what you're supposed to do. You reason that it's not a good time: the water level is too high, the current is swift, and now you're doubting that you even heard God correctly. You're certain that all of the preparations have led to now; it's harvest season...the time to reap what you've sown. You look across the Jordan and see where God wants you to be; He said that it's yours, but you must possess it!

All your fears are accurate; you cannot do this, but...God can. He has the *ability*; He needs your *availability*. God doesn't amuse Himself by wringing you out to see how tough you are. He wrings the "I" out of you to make room for Him.

The only way you're going to cross your Jordan is by His strength. Stop wasting time on "if you can or can't." You can't, but God will if you let Him. But...you won't know He will until you step into the river. When you step in, the waters will roll back and the ground will be dry. God told the Israelites to keep a distance from the Ark of the Covenant so they could see the way to go, as He knew they had not been that way before. God's tenderness is evident. He knows many of the things He asks of us are impossible, He knows we want to please Him, and He knows we struggle with fear. But if we will trust Him, He will go before us and make a way.

No one can convince you to trust God; the more bold steps you take the more trust you gain and the more your relationship deepens. I pray you will cross your Jordan and fulfill the plans God has for you. Your life will be full and complete if you will trust God to lead you across...will you let Him?

JOSHUA 3:4; GAL. 6:9; JER. 29:1; PROV. 3:5-6

May 28

"For you have need of endurance, so that when you have done the will of God you may receive what is promised."
HEB. 10:36 (ESV)

Focus on the truth, not what you feel; be cognizant of the thought patterns in your mind that lead you into excessive reasoning that opposes God's truth. Don't allow these thoughts to linger or they will begin to build barriers in your mind and obscure your view of the truth! Reasoning will lure you one thought at a time off the course God has called you to, but you won't know it because you're deceived. That's the thing about deception...it deceives the one it's entrapped!

Throw off anything that hinders you or sin that binds you from seeing what God sees for you! Make your relationship with Him first above everything-guard, treasure and hold tight to it, loving Him with all your heart, mind and soul because He will hold onto to you and never let go! Jesus has cleared a path. God's Word is your fuel and His Spirit will guide you on the course God's called you to...focus on this truth-not what you feel!

HEB. 10:36; LUKE 21:19; ROM. 12:12

May 29

"Then Jesus said, "Come to me, all of you who are weary and carry heavy burdens, and I will give you rest."
MATT 11:28

God's got your back! He's planned every day of your life. He's reliable and keeps His promises. He's never overslept, missed a meeting, had a hard time staying awake, difficulty articulating His thoughts or expressing Himself, been too sick to attend an event, missed a flight, been stuck in snow, had to borrow money or been out of a job...He's certain, confident, caring, funny, beyond brilliant! His yoke is light, His joy completes you and He will do far more than you dare ask!

Keep your mind on these truths-it is your daily lifeline. Profess the Word, listen to and sing it and post it all over your home-on your refrigerator, garage door, laundry room, bathroom mirror and the toilet paper dispenser...then you will be reminded that God's got your back!

MATT. 11:28-30; JOHN 15:11; EPH. 3:20

May 30

"My grace is all you need. My power works best in weakness."
2 COR. 12:9 (NLT)

Where your strength ends...God's begins; your best isn't enough. This is a hard statement to accept, but it's true. God will meet you at the end of your best every time, if you rely on His strength every time! His ability connects to the end of your inability-His sufficiency picks up where your sufficiency ends and His power is made perfect in your weakness! Will you embrace this truth so God can release the good works He planned long ago through you?

2 COR 12:9-10; EPH 2:10

May 31

"Have not I commanded thee? Be strong and of a good courage;
be not afraid, neither be thou dismayed: for the LORD thy God is with thee
whithersoever thou goest."
JOSHUA 1:9 (KJV)

God will work through the opportunity He gives you-not the one He gives to someone else. Throughout life, God will strategically place you in different roles to carry out specific purposes. Don't compare what you do to another person's calling, or you will devalue your role and risk removing yourself from being used by God.

Your value isn't defined by what you do; it's defined by Who you belong to. Knowing you belong gives you the freedom to be comfortable with opportunities presented to you. Circumstances will change throughout life but...God's love and value for you will not. Embrace what God gives you...and He will give you more!

MARK 4:24; JOSHUA 1:9 (KJV); 2 CHRON. 15:7

June 1

"And he is not served by human hands, as if he needed anything. Rather, he
himself gives everyone life and breath and everything else."
ACTS 17:25

God Himself breathes His life into you to give you a hope and a future. His love soothes your mind-bringing it into proper focus of His truth. He tenderly pours His love into every hurting area of your heart; continuing until the wounds find relief, finally overflowing into your spirit and refreshing you...giving you the stamina needed to move forward with His confidence.

Will you factor in His presence in all you do and know how crazy in love your Father is with you...then let His ability move through you to handle your inability?

Take a risk...trust Him. I guarantee it will work...because He said so and He never breaks a promise.

Acts 17:25; Jer. 31:25; Isaiah 44:3 (ESV)

June 2

"We demolish arguments and every pretension that sets itself up against the knowledge of God, and we take captive every thought to make it obedient to Christ."
2 Cor 10:15

Stay on course...consistency and commitment are the keys to this victory! Recall what Jesus whispered to your heart: this journey is to equip you...not discourage you. Doubt mocks your efforts and calls out your past mistakes, while questioning your understanding-did you hear correctly, do you think they meant that, are you sure? Remember that doubt wants you to give up before you get there-then tell you that you are a failure for not moving forward! Learn from mistakes...but don't let them paralyze you and stop you from pursuing what God's calling you to do.

You're being bombarded by mental distractions...because you're so close! Keep moving-you're carrying out God's mission; your due season is close. Learn from mistakes...but don't let them paralyze and stop you from pursuing what God is calling you to do. Keep moving, recalling what Jesus whispered to your heart!

2 Cor. 10:15; Isaiah 40:31; Gal. 6:9

June 3

"When pride comes, disgrace follows, but with humility comes wisdom."
Prov. 11:12

Pride lies...it wants you to believe you're above being offended-especially if it's a small offense and that you should easily dismiss it because you know the Word and you've got a strong walk. Listen closely: *a strong walk is only as strong as it is dependent on God!* The only way to remain strong in your walk is to depend on God for everything...to include working through small offenses! Bottom line-what you release to God is dealt with in His strength-what you keep from Him is dealt with in your strength. Who's strength will you depend on?

PROV. 11:12; JOHN 15:5; PHIL. 4:13

June 4

"Blessed are all who take refuge in him."
PS. 2:12 (ESV)

It's scary to trust God when you've been hurt by others you trusted. His love won't feel comfortable at first-you're guarded because of your past hurt. Listen carefully: your past hurt is giving you a skewed view of God. He's the only One Who can heal your hurt. Until you trust Him you won't be able to heal...because only His love can heal you.

I know it's scary to trust God; I've been where you are, but I'll tell you it's the greatest risk I've ever taken and His love completely healed and changed my life...it will yours too! It's your decision-God will never force you like others have.

PS. 2:12 (ESV), 18:2-3, 56:3-4; PROV. 3:5-8

June 5

"For am I now seeking the approval of man, or of God?
Or am I trying to please man? If I were still trying to please man, I would
not be a servant of Christ."
GAL. 1:10 (ESV)

How many times have you not moved forward because you weren't clear if the idea in your mind was from God or you? The only way to trust God is to step out and trust what you believe you heard in your spirit.

Until you have a revelation that God's love for you is greater than your mistakes, you will not trust if you're hearing Him or not. The enemy will plant seeds of doubt in your mind....that you might miss God, that your up against impossible odds or that your thoughts are grandiose! Family and friends may question your certainty-not to discourage you, but to challenge your thinking. Then some of them may impose their own fears on you, which *is* discouraging. This is the very reason you have to cling tight to what God speaks to your heart then trust the power of the Holy Spirit to intercede for you. Understand that each time you trust God, the enemy will attack your mind with doubt, but don't give him a foothold!

We build trust in hearing God by moving ahead when we're afraid. Doing so empowers us to trust the promptings we hear from the Holy Spirit. This enables us to move forward and believe God will provide despite the obvious barriers we have to move through! To be used by God, your focus has to on pleasing Him above being approved by others. Are you ready?

Gal. 1:10 (esv); 1 Thess. 2:4; Prov. 29:25

June 6

"...and are justified by his grace as a gift, through the redemption that is in Christ Jesus."
Rom. 3:24 (esv)

Your willpower doesn't work, but grace does. You can't deliver yourself...but Jesus can. Your willpower motivates you to begin, but it's Jesus' power that sustains you to continue on to completion! If we depend on human willpower alone then we deny the power of the cross!

Daily, seek the Lord instead of seeking to overcome; your intentions are sincere and seem right, but put the focus on your external performance instead of the internal power of the Holy Spirit...it's the power that happens on the inside that changes your life! You overcome nothing apart from Him, but with Him you can do all things He calls you to do! If we could save ourselves we wouldn't need a Savior!

Rom. 3:24 (esv); Acts 1:8; 1 Cor. 15:57

June 7

"Is there anything too hard for the LORD?"
GEN. 18:14 (NLT)

Praise Him in everything. He's given you everything you will ever need. It's called the Trinity...God the Father, Son and Holy Spirt! God reigns over all you see and don't see-His hands hold this world together. Jesus took on hell and won, and has gone before you to make a way, and the Holy Spirit lives in you; He's your compass, directing your path and giving you the power to do what God asks of you!

Is there anything too hard for God to do, overcome, get a hold of or let go of, move on with, lay down or forgive? Nothing is too hard for Him...*nor for you*-because His Spirit lives in you! Many have accepted Christ as their Savior; they know their spirit is saved, but they have not made Christ their Lord, which rules their mind and determines their course in life!

Make Christ your Lord and you will then walk in the power and freedom that was given to you at salvation. Your spirit was saved, but your mind wasn't...your mind has to be renewed with God's promises *every day*! Where the Spirit of the Lord is-there is freedom!

If you're not renewing your mind with God's truth, you will feel afraid and anxious, but focusing on thanking God keeps you connected to His promises, which are His provisions to care for you!

2 COR 3:17; GEN. 18:14 (NLT)

June 8

"...that the man of God may be complete, equipped for every good work."
2 TIM 3:17 (ESV)

Grace and truth are your BFFs...make sure you know them and hang out with them constantly! They are God's gift to you. Grace accepts everything about you, and truth is honest about where you are-they work in tandem over the course of your life to lead you in the plans God made for you long ago!

Until you accept grace and truth, you will be inconsistent in doing what God asks of you, which takes you off the course He planned for you long ago! This inconsistency results in frustration and creates a failure mentality in your thinking and leads you to believe you can't do what God asks of you! Don't believe this lie! God would never ask us to do something unless He equipped us to carry it out. That's why grace and truth are your BFF - they keep you on course. But you must embrace them *with no conditions attached*-they are gifts from God to enable you to walk in His confidence every day.

Will you start hanging out with grace and truth every day...read the Word and know what God says about them? They will transform your mind and change the way you live!

2 Tim. 3:17 (ESV); 1 John 2:21; Eph. 1:6-8 (ESV)

June 9

""I do believe, but help me overcome my unbelief!"
Mark 9:24 (NLT)

Don't let doubt rob you of God's promises; ask Him to help you overcome your unbelief. Stand on what you *know* to be true...not what you *feel* to be true. God's truth says that Jesus will do exceedingly, abundantly more than you could ever imagine, according to the power that's at work within you. That power is the Holy Spirit. The day you accepted Jesus Christ as your Savior, He saved your spirit and came to live in you. The Holy Spirit gives you the power to carry out anything God asks of you...He is the power that's at work within you!

Eph. 3:20; Mark 9:24 (NLT)

June 10

"I am the Good Shepherd; and I know
and recognize My own, and My own know
and recognize Me"
JOHN 10:14 (AMP)

God loves you and wants you to walk in the Kingdom plans He made for you long ago. He will continue to carry out the good work He started in you until Jesus Christ returns! You have to be on guard, reasoning is a roaring lion waiting to devour God's truth in your mind.

Be ready to counter the attacks he uses over and over. He goes after your Achilles Heel - your weak spots. He studies you and knows all your areas of frustration, trigger points, things that defeat you, etc. To counter the attacks be spiritually prepared and conditioned. Keep your mind on God's truth and seek Him first in all you do...He won't let you miss Him. One more thing: you are never alone to figure all of this out. Remember that the Holy Spirit lives in you and gives you discernment 24/7. Just ask for His help. Are you ready to get on with God's plans?

1 PET. 5:8; JOHN 10:14 (AMP); PS. 86:3

June 11

"This hope is a strong and trustworthy anchor for our souls."
HEB. 6:19 (NLT)

God's promises are true. Many ponder, debate and speculate meaning, validity and reliability, but at the end of the day, God's promises are no less true. When we desire to trust God, He meets us at our trust level, giving us what we need to increase faith. Many reject His truth and map out their own plans to prevent or overcome the inevitable dangers in life; they are convinced their ways are right. They put their faith in human wisdom over God's power. They are deceived, and the thing about deception is that it deceives the one who entertains it. The human mind is finite; apart from the direction of the Holy Spirit, the mind will come to the end of itself.

God reigns over the universe and holds it together in His hands; no human mind, regardless of its brilliance, can master God's domain. But anyone who trusts in and accepts Jesus as her Lord and Savior is promised to have all her needs met-beyond what they could ever imagine! In this world you will have many trials. God will help you...will you let Him make a way for you?

JOHN 15:11, 16:33,HEB. 6:19 (NLT); PROV. 3:5-6

June 12

"But if from there you seek the LORD your God, you will find him if you seek him with all your heart and with all your soul."
DEUT. 4:29

You will not experience the full life God wants to show you by sitting on your sofa and playing it safe. Many will miss out on most of God's promises in life because they are playing it safe in life. They fear that if they follow God they might mess up or make mistakes. The reality is...they *will* mess up and make mistakes, because that's how we learn. None of us are born with an astonishing ability to discern God's voice. As with anything, we learn and become skilled. We have to practice, take risks, make mistakes, then do it all again! As we move forward we get better.

The promise we have in taking risks to follow God is that He promises to stay with us until the day we see Jesus face-to-face! Along the way God honors and redeems our steps because our hearts are correct in following Him!

DEUT. 4:29; MATT. 6:33, 7:7-8; LUKE 12:29, 31

June 13

"For we live by believing and not by seeing."
2 COR. 5:7 (NLT)

Many miss life because they are waiting on God to deliver on a promise. Don't let this happen to you. Make your mind up: you don't have to know *how* God will make things work to know that He *will* make things work. He provides exceedingly more than we dare imagine, delivers us from every trouble and will never leave us, yet none of us are exempt from the trials and troubles along the way.

Having made up your mind enables you to "free up space" in you thoughts to be more focused in walking by faith and not by sight. Every waiting period is an opportunity to become stronger in your faith because your focus is more on Scripture and thanking God for His provisions. Sadly, many waste this time by getting stuck on "why" and "when." This only prolongs their wait because it reveals a lack of spiritual maturity, and thus their ability to move into the next season. Make your wait count so you will be ready to go when God is ready to take you into the next season.

2 COR. 5:7 (NLT); I COR. 15:58; JAMES 5:7

June 14

"The Spirit of the LORD will rest on him-- the Spirit of wisdom and of understanding, the Spirit of counsel and of might, the Spirit of the knowledge and fear of the LORD..."
ISAIAH 11:2

What you think about determines the course of your life. In your mind you will never consistently rise above your circumstances unless your mind is submitted to God's Word. The mind relies on reasoning and emotions to navigate your worldly course. If your day is going smoothly, your mind will give you a good report. But, if something upsetting happens, your mind then gives you a negative report...and so goes a fluctuating mind that keeps a person on an emotional roller coaster.

Some people can be positive in their mind, relying on their own strength until they experience a devastating situation. As Christians we can submit our minds to God's truth and be confident that He will give us wisdom, understanding, strength and knowledge in all circumstances. God's truth keeps our minds stable in an unstable world.

ISAIAH 11:2; ROM 8:2-7; PS. 139:1

June 15

"No, despite all these things, overwhelming victory is ours through Christ, who loved us."
ROM. 8:37 (NLT)

Are you being pressed, pushed and purged of many of our comforts...the earthly security and things that we cling to more than we do to Christ. When these things are threatened we're threatened because they are grafted onto our identities. We believe that without them we cannot make it. But it's only when the props are taken away, the backups removed and the comforts that made us feel approved, good enough and important are gone, that's when we find Jesus, and His love, security and promises.

It's when we're out of resources with no back-up plan and we must choose to believe or go crazy! Jesus is waiting for us to get to the end of ourselves so He can begin. This is how we become more than conquerors. A conqueror doesn't gain merit based on who or what she conquerors, but a conqueror knows that her strength comes from Jesus, the One Who chose and justified her! Nothing can separate you from His love...move forward; you are a conqueror!

2 COR. 4:8; ROM. 8:31-39 (NLT); 2 COR. 4:7-9

June 16

"Stay alert! Watch out for your great enemy, the devil. He prowls around like a roaring lion, looking for someone to devour."
1 PETER 5:8 (NLT)

Unresolved feelings of rejection will steal, kill and destroy your hope...you're unable to live in the present because you're living life through past hurt. When you feel dismissed in a situation-feelings of rejection begin to overwhelm you. You pray and try to fight off the feelings, but the more you fight...the more dismissed you feel! Then anger begins to scream on the inside of you while your heart sobs with a pain you can't even describe. You just can't understand why this person would treat you this way. Logic tells you that you're overreacting, but your feelings are smothering you.

Be careful...you've fallen into a pit; the enemy is like a roaring lion and will devour you at this point. Run to Jesus-He will help you! You're experiencing two separate issues: 1) your feelings are hurt because you feel disregarded and disposed of, and 2) unresolved shame is distorting your perception. It's a huge vacuum inside of you-screaming that you don't matter, you're not valued and people dismiss you. You're aware that your feelings are hurt, but you don't realize that rejection is fueling the emotions of intense hurt mixed with anger. Rejection distorts your perception...keeping the view of your present obscured. Until rejection is flushed out with the love of Jesus, it will continue to control you. Let Jesus have it-He will go to work and won't stop, *but He needs your cooperation*. Let Him love all of you and *expect* Him to heal you!

The enemy wants to convince you that others are causing this pain...they're not. You're chained to your rejection and only the love of Jesus can restore you. Don't let rejection take what Jesus died to give you. Jesus will cut the chains of rejection and heal you with His love...will you let Him?

1 PETER 5:8; JOHN 10:10, 14:23; JER 29:11

June 17

*"The Spirit of the Sovereign LORD is upon me, for the LORD has
anointed me to bring good news to the poor. He has sent me to comfort
the brokenhearted and to proclaim that captives will be released and
prisoners will be freed."*
ISAIAH 61:1 (NLT)

Jesus came to save and heal us, to bind up our wounds, free us from captivity and bring us out of darkness. Bring your hurts into the light and acknowledge who hurt you; give them into the hands of Jesus; release what they did to you. Many believe that forgiving is dismissing the harm done, but forgiving means that you will no longer carry the harm in your heart.

When we verbally give the release, forgiving the person who caused us harm, we allow Jesus to emotionally remove the chains that kept us bound to that person and the hurt imposed.

Next, we give Jesus all the hurt we've been carrying, emptying ourselves of it, purging every last drop. We will be flooded with emotion from all those years of denying, holding back, minimizing, trying to prove that we were good enough, and holding back tears.

This is grief - the recognition of what was lost, stolen or never given. Grief validates what we have experienced; it says we matter and what happened to us mattered. Then the love of Jesus will come in like a flood, filling up every part of us, especially the parts that carried the hurt. Until His love floods us, we're left in the darkness, prisoners of our own pain-captives in our hurt. Will you let Jesus love and heal you today?

GAL. 5:1; ISAIAH 61:1 (NLT); HEB. 6:19

June 18

"Come to me, all who labor and are heavy laden, and I will give you rest."
MATT. 11:28 (ESV)

You don't have to live with this hurt any longer, but you will as long as you continue to carry hurt in your heart. Admitting that unresolved hurt is a problem in your life is the first step to freedom, followed by asking the Holy Spirit for help. Asking for help is a sign of strength, not weakness-what you bring in the light...loses it's power! *But if you keep it-you've got to manage it!*

I implore you, don't live a life of spiritual poverty because you don't want to address your unresolved hurt! God will give you the desire and power to do what you need to do in order to heal-just ask Him...He gives wisdom generously! Know the truth and the truth will set you free-this is God's promise.

It's true: times passes...hurts don't, but you don't have to live this way one more day! Will you let the love of Jesus heal you?

JOHN 10:10, 8:32; LUKE 4:18; 2 COR. 3:17; JER. 29:11; PHIL. 2:13

June 19

"Blessed be the God and Father of our Lord Jesus Christ! According to his great mercy, he has caused us to be born again to a living hope through the resurrection of Jesus Christ from the dead,"
1 PETER 1:3 (ESV)

Grief is a painful process, but the Lord will love and give you the help needed to move through it. Remain in Him and He will remain in you; He will provide all you need-more than you ever imagined...*if* you will put your hope in Him alone. He is your living hope; He will never let go of you-so don't ever let go of Him! Trust Him with all your heart, soul, mind and strength. Your dream is dead...*but your hope isn't!* God will place a new dream in your heart. Will you rest and put your hope in Him and let His love comfort you until He does?

1 PETER 1:3 (ESV); JER. 24:7 (ESV); 1 TIM. 4:10 (ESV)

June 20

"Blessed by the LORD, Who bears our burdens and carries us day by day, even the God Who is our salvation!"
PS. 68:19 (AMP)

We're not designed to handle the burdens of this world without God, but we *can* do all things Christ strengthens us to do (SEE PHIL. 4:13). Going back or forward in time exhausts us. We're designed to live in the present. Entertaining potential situations deafens our ability to hear the Holy Spirit; He gives us direction and comfort, but we can't hear Him when we're trying to handle burdens on our own. We have to focus on God's truth, which lifts us up from underneath our burdens.

PS. 68:19 (AMP); PS. 25:5; GEN. 49:18

June 21

"Don't you realize that in a race everyone runs, but only one person gets the prize? So run to win!"
I COR. 9:24 (NLT)

Believing God takes effort-a deliberate taking hold of the Word in your mind and pressing through adversity. This kind of strength doesn't come from you...it comes from the Holy Spirit Who lives in you! Following Jesus is a full time job requiring you to be cognizant of staying on course even when it seems hopeless in the natural. But, if you will desire direction and actively listen for the Holy Spirit, you will hear Him...because it is God's design!

The Holy Spirit's role of living in you is to glorify God, and He does this by equipping you with a supernatural power to carry out the plans of God! Isn't that a relief? The burden of proof isn't on you, your part is to execute the truth by being a vessel for God during your time on this earth.

Your time and investment in believing God far exceeds your wildest dreams or anything you dare imagine! Likewise, inconsistency and unbelief on your part forfeit the good works God planned for you long ago. Don't allow the thoughts that oppose God's truth to forfeit the course He's called you to and to perpetuate into future generations! Be deliberate and take hold of the Word, and press through adversity...God is with you in every breath and every step!

I COR. 9:24 (NLT); PS. 28:8 (NSV); PS. 43:3

June 22

"May the God of hope fill you with all joy and peace as you trust in him, so that you may overflow with hope by the power of the Holy Spirit."
ROM. 15:13

Life is full of uncertainty; this is a reality. No matter how much we plan we can't be certain our plans will come to fruition. God tells us to not let this reality discourage us because His truth trumps reality! He promises we can live a rich and satisfying life being certain, courageous and confident despite the reality of life's uncertainty...if we will put our hope in Him alone!

When we put our hope in God versus people, situations and outcomes we can expect to live this satisfying life God speaks of. This doesn't exempt us from experiencing uncertainty, which includes grief, loss, heartache and gut-wrenching emotions, but God promises to bring us through these times! Our part is to believe He will and use the tools He gives us, which are: memorizing scripture, speaking it out loud throughout the day, putting our eyes on it, and asking Jesus to help us overcome unbelief. We have to be deliberate in making these things part of our day during the hard *and* good times...this routine is our spiritual arsenal for the ongoing battles in life, and it's how we to stay on the course God's called us to! Will you commit to the course God's called you to?

1 COR. 9:26 (AMP); ROM. 15:13; COL. 1:5

June 23

"Restore to me the joy of your salvation and grant me a willing spirit, to sustain me."
PS. 51:12

Unresolved shame sets up thought patterns in the mind that skew a person's perception of the world...life is lived through past pain. Shame poisons the mind, heart and core being, resulting in a person not liking who they are. Their view of themselves is projected onto their family and future generations until it is stopped. Shame is the same as the reproach God addresses in JOSHUA 5:9: *"Today I have rolled away the reproach of Egypt from you."*

Before the Israelites could walk in the victory God promised, they had to be circumcised-the reproach that was imposed on them had to be rolled back before they could conquer and occupy Jericho, the first city in the Promised Land. The reproach was the shame imposed on them while in Egypt; it wasn't fair. God never promises things are fair, but He *does* promise He will bring us out from under what unfair things did to us! This means we have to endure pain to overcome the pain initially imposed on us...this is a choice and sadly many get stuck in the unfair aspect and never receive the healing God offers.

The circumcision the Israelites endured was a physically painful process involving being cut in one of the most sensitive areas of the body, and that would also require time to heal as well. This rolling away of reproach is likened to how we heal from any kind of emotional pain that's been imposed on us... although we do not have to endure a physical circumcision, the emotional rolling away is just as painful. We have to open up and be cut in sensitive areas, cutting off parts of us: the lies we've believed, negative thinking patterns and behaviors developed from those thought patterns.

Healing is never an easy process, but until we heal we can't walk in the victory God promises us. God never leaves us to figure all this out. He is with us every step and promises to see us through until the end! Will you let God roll the reproach of shame off of you so that you can live the life He's promised you?

Ps. 30:10; 51:12; 54:5; 1 Sam. 2:1 (NLT)

June 24

"[Now] we have this [hope] as a sure and steadfast anchor of the soul..."
Heb. 6:19 (AMP)

Acknowledging hurts, surrendering them to Jesus, forgiving those who imposed the hurts, then grieving, is the only way to move on from offenses in life and heal as God promises. If we refuse this process, we will go through life with wounds on our hearts, never experiencing the full promises of God. We will impose our hurt on others and always feel cheated because only Jesus can give back what's been taken or given away, or give to us what others cannot. He promises hope - an anchor for our souls, firm and secure. Where the Spirit of the Lord is, there is freedom!

Isaiah 61:1 (NLT); Heb. 6:19; 2 Cor. 3:17

June 25

"Give your burdens to the LORD, and he will take care of you. He will not permit the godly to slip and fall."
PS. 55:22 (NLT)

You have constructed scenarios in your mind that have catapulted you weeks, months and years down the road. What's crazy about this thought process is...you didn't go anywhere and you're walking in situations that haven't come to pass, but in your mind they have. So, even though you are still in the first 30 minutes of your day, you have lived through years of potential trials! This is the enemy hijacking your imagination! Our imaginations are to be used in faith, to see what God sees...*faith sees what the mind cannot comprehend.*

Entertaining these potential situations deafens our ability to hear the Holy Spirit. He gives direction and comfort, but we cannot hear him when our imagination is being hijacked. We have to focus on God's truth, which renews our mind. What we think on is where we go in our mind.

Each time your thoughts try to lead you down the runway of destruction...turn away and look to Jesus. He's waiting to lead you back to His truth! Remember: He has overcome this world. Cast all of your cares on Him.

PS. 55:22 (NLT), 68:19; PROV. 16:3

June 26

"In your relationships with one another, have the same mindset as Christ Jesus"
PHIL. 2:5

Relationship boundaries-a healthy relationship keeps balance. Coming together doesn't mean you leave who you are behind to join the new relationship, forget the former people who loved you before you fell in love, or trade out your interests in favor of loving this new person. These are red flags that will lead to disaster later. Value yourself enough to keep your relationship before the Lord-asking Him if this relationship is being led by Him.

God's planned your future-don't forfeit it. Talk with mature friends who are not afraid to speak God's truth to you in love, then take it to heart. Finally, seek a Spirit-filled Christian counselor who can encourage and challenge you to be the person God's called you to be-he or she will explain patterns and help you connect the dots. Agree with God's plans for your life-His ways work and when we follow Him...our lives work!

PROV. 3:5-6; PHIL. 2:5; 2 COR. 6:14

June 27

"Fixing our eyes on Jesus, the pioneer and perfecter of faith."
HEB. 12:2

Blame keeps you chained to the harm done to you while robbing you of the future, because you keep looking at the past! Blame is powerful-it focuses on the reality of the wrongs done to you. When blame reminds you of the past and that you can't undo what's been done, remind yourself: it's true you can't...but Jesus can!

He's the Author and the Finisher, He has no barriers-He's unstoppable. His Word will not return void. Time has no impact on Him because He owns it! Acknowledge what happened, give all your hurt and disappointment to Him, then trust He will guide you on how to proceed. Don't get stuck on when, how or if God's going to release His vengeance on those who harmed you; that's not your concern. But do expect God to deliver you. The righteous have many troubles and the Lord will bring them through each one (SEE PS. 34:19). Blame has no case against the power of Christ-hope in Him when your hope fails; He will sustain you and give you hope for the future!

HEB. 11:1, 12:2, 6:19; PS. 34:19; JOHN 11:15

June 28

"You go before me and follow me.
You place your hand of blessing on my head."
PS. 139:5 (NLT)

God is with you...right now. Know, think on and remind yourself of this truth constantly. You are never alone-God goes before you and follows behind you with His hand of blessing on you. Don't turn your back on the privilege of His Presence that lives in you or the supernatural power of speaking His Word.

God promises to bring you through every trial-seek Him and He will meet you where you are-His power is perfected in your weakness. If you're having trouble concentrating He gives you clarity, if you're grieving He comforts you, if you're anxious He gives your mind peace... there's no psychiatric or medical condition that can separate you from His provisions, no hurt that's too big for Him to heal or request that's too small for Him to listen to. His love heals you and His hope holds on for you. Remain in Him and He will remain in you-enabling His power to flow through you to overcome whatever you're facing! God's hands aren't tied because of a struggling economy, frozen job market or real estate downturn. He makes a way in the wilderness, flows rivers in the desert and makes dry, brittle bones come alive! He's mighty to save, gives hope to the hopeless and life to dead and broken relationships that are laid before Him!

God is with you...right now. Will you let His love comfort you...right now?

PS. 139:5; 2 COR. 12:9; HEB. 6:19; ZEPH. 3:17; JOHN 15:5; ISAIAH 43:19; 1; COR 4:20

June 29

"And ye shall know the truth, and the truth shall make you free."
JOHN 8:32 (KJV)

It takes guts to speak God's truths, but He makes a way...if we will get out of the way! Many reason they can't speak truth for fear that the people they love will get angry, leave or be in conflict with them. Jesus models how we're to handle difficult situations-confront sin in love so restoration can take place. No confrontation leads to...no restoration! Avoiding difficult subjects leads to shallow relationships, which are not rooted in truth. God's truth is the mortar that seals a relationship. It takes guts to have godly relationships and God will make a way for you...*if* you follow His truths. Don't let the enemy intimidate you...go on-you have the guts to speak God's truth...it's the foundation of every lasting relationship! For God has not given us a spirit of fear, but of power, of love and of a sound mind

JOHN 8:32

June 30

"Behold, I stand at the door and knock. If anyone hears my voice and opens the door, I will come in to him and eat with him, and he with me."
REV. 3:20 (ESV)

Until we know we're approved-we fear ridicule and rejection from others. Jesus boldly carried out the requests from His Father because He knew He was loved-trusting God to sustain and supply all His needs. God's love gives you the courage to follow Jesus; His love is your lifeline-continuing to increase your freedom as you move closer to Him.

Do you feel misunderstood or disconnected? Do you have secrets you will take to your grave for fear others would not accept you? Do you only show parts of you, fearing the other parts of you would be rejected? Go to Jesus, your only source for answers. He's waiting to show you love. His love gives you life, direction and purpose, forgetting the past and looking forward to what lies ahead. Embrace God's truth...you're His masterpiece-created to do the good things He planned long ago!

Have you completely surrendered to Jesus-making Him not only your Savior but also your Lord? If you're holding back from Him, you will also hold back from others. Your relationship with Jesus is reflected in your relationship with others. You will never experience the fullness and completeness Christ wants to offer you-until you completely surrender. Where the Spirit of the Lord is-there is freedom! Let God open up your mind to understand His Word. You were designed by Him to connect intimately, be vulnerable and walk with others to carry out His plans.

Get quiet and listen...the Advocate, Strengthener, Standby, Holy Spirit, Whom the Father sent to represent Jesus and act on His behalf, will teach you all things. He will remind you of and bring to memory everything you need to know. You are loved my friend-let God show you how you can love and connect with others the way He designed...be vulnerable and experience authenticity!

REV. 3:20; PHIL. 3:13; EPH. 3:20; LUKE 24:45; 2 COR. 3:17; JOHN 14:26

†

July 1

"And now these three remain: faith, hope and love.
But the greatest of these is love."
1 COR. 13:13

Jesus took it all-He is Risen! And we arose, too, when we received Him as our Lord and Savior, giving us faith, hope and love, and the greatest of these is love (SEE 1 COR. 13:13). God's love works all the time, with anyone and in every situation. Before we can *give* God's love-we have to *receive* His love. Many stumble trying to give love they haven't yet received.

We have a tradition in our family-a commitment to being cognizant of the power of love given to us at the cross...every day. This vulnerability keeps us real-we all have weaknesses. Acknowledging them and sharing allows us to accept where we are and focus on growth instead of perfection. When we can accept where we are...we can then accept where others are, genuinely allowing us to encourage others to become what God calls them to be, affirming that apart from Jesus' love we can do nothing! Celebrate the power of love given to you at the cross...every day. He is risen and so have you!

MATT. 22:37-40, 28:6; 1 COR. 13:13; JOHN 15:5; 2 COR. 12:9

July 2

"For we are God's masterpiece. He has created us anew in Christ Jesus, so we can do the good things he planned for us long ago."
GAL. 6:9 (NLT)

You are a work in progress...keep moving! Walk out your progress. Some days you will fall down a thousand times and you will get back up a thousand times...just keep moving forward-don't stop! Let us not become weary in doing good, for at the proper time we will reap a harvest if we do not give up! (SEE GAL. 6:9).

Get back up, friend; the work God's started in you...*He will bring to completion*! God will continue His perfection through you until the day Jesus Christ returns! You are His masterpiece... don't ever let anyone tell you differently! You are a work in progress-keep moving!

GAL. 6:9; PHIL. 1:6; EPH. 2:10

July 3

"Now if we have died with Christ,
we believe that we will also live with him."
ROM. 6:8 (ESV)

If you've received Jesus Christ as your Lord and Savior...your past is gone, dead at the cross! Yet many devalue their worth in God's eyes based on their past. The past is dead-they're saved, but their *mind* isn't. Their mind still lives in the past. I know this well because it's the number one issue I help Christians with in my counseling practice...but I also lived that way for a long time. For years I tried to gauge my worth based on my past. Finally I began to agree with God's truth, *even though I didn't feel it I accepted it as truth* and began to speak it aloud every day.

My agreement with God's truth opened the door for the Holy Spirit to give me revelation that I was free from my past...that's why where the Spirit of the Lord is, there is freedom (SEE 2 COR. 3:17). As I daily renewed my mind with His truth, I came to believe it, and the more I believed it the more I spoke it, the more

I spoke it, the more the truth cancelled out the lies I had believed for years...finally, I came to a balanced place and believed my Father's truth. I still renew my mind daily-it's not something that we can ever stop. God is love and His Word is our hope.

ROM. 6:8-9 (ESV); 2 COR. 3:17; 2 TIM. 2:11

July 4

"And I am sure of this, that he who began a good work in you will bring it to completion at the day of Jesus Christ."
PHIL. 1:6 (ESV)

Unresolved issues have never stopped God from working through people...but people have. God will bring to completion what He started in you-*if* you will let Him. Give yourself away...let God have all of you! If you're waiting for your issues to be resolved before you move forward and begin the season God's calling you to...you'll be waiting until the day you see Jesus face to face! Trust in God with all your heart, don't let reasoning steal what you know to be true-seek God in all you do and He will make your path straight!

God will correct your issues along the way-don't resist correction or feel like you're a bad child. God corrects those He loves-He corrects you to make you right, not wrong! Will you accept yourself as God accepts you? God's not shocked by what you can't do...so why are you? Will you let God's ability meet you at the end of your ability? If so, then rise up...He will fulfill His purpose through you!

PHIL. 1:6; 1 COR. 2:5; PROV. 3:5-6; 2 COR. 12:9

July 5

"Produce fruit in keeping with repentance."
LUKE 3:8

Many quickly apologize for their offense...but no behavior change follows. We should quickly apologize, then ask God to search our heart and give us wisdom into the behavior we're apologizing for. Many fights are the result of arguments that have had an apology tagged on the end of them..but there was never a resolution, so they resurface over and over, only for the last words to be, "I've told you 100 times I'm sorry!" The root of the reason that the apology is being requested must be understood before a genuine apology can resolve an ongoing argument...then genuine repentance is manifested in behavior changes! The apology is spoken, then action follows that seals the words spoken.

LUKE 3:8, 6:37; EPH. 4:38

July 6

"Oh, that we might know the LORD! Let us press on to know him.
He will respond to us as surely as the arrival of dawn or the coming of rains
in early spring."
HOSEA 6:3 (NLT)

See to it that no one takes you captive through hollow or deceptive philosophies, which depend on human tradition and the basic principles of this world. Don't be wise in your own eyes-seek God. He will bring health to your body and nourishment to your bones (SEE PROV. 3:7-8). Renew your mind with the Word to stay balanced in daily living.

You're flirting with disaster when you entertain teachings that credit humanity, the earth or nature. Many choose to believe some of God's truth, then mix it with other beliefs, but...Jesus is the only way, truth and life (SEE JOHN 14:6). No person is to add to God's truth or take away from it; if they do...they shut the door on His presence and the guaranteed protection of peace in their minds and hearts!

Don't drown in the grandeur of self-deception and forfeit the peace of God's presence that's available to you. Turn, repent and run to Him...He will refresh you like the spring rains that water the earth.

HOS. 6:3; COL. 2:8; PROV. 3:7-8; ROM. 12:2; JOHN 14:6; PHIL. 4:7

July 7

"So do not throw away your confidence; it will be richly rewarded."
HEB. 10:35

For years I hid behind my "Christian comfort zone." I honestly didn't know I was hiding, because when we're desperate to make something work we lose perspective, and I had lost mine. Deception had me believing that I'd finally gotten it all together, but most of my time was spent...trying to keep it all together. As long as I looked right, I thought I could feel right. Then Jesus introduced me to the "Big V"...vulnerability. I've been walking this journey of vulnerability; it's risky but well worth the prize...I will hold tight to the confidence promised in Jesus and His truth that sets me free!

HEB. 10:35; JOHN 8:32; EPH. 3:12

July 8

"Instead, let the Spirit renew your thoughts and attitudes."
EPH. 4:23 (NLT)

Getting saved gets you a new spirit...but *not* a new mind! You've got to renew your mind with God's Word every day of your life until you see Jesus face to face! "*The words I speak to you are Spirit and life.*" Your mind must be renewed with Jesus...the way, truth and life!

Time with Jesus is your lifeline-to not have time to renew your mind is like saying you don't have time to breathe! Apart from Him your mind withers and becomes exhausted and depleted because of its finite ability. God's Word gives your mind the ability to exceed its own finite abilities...the insight to discern what otherwise would confound you, and to believe and firmly stand on the promises of God-even when all looks lost!

Don't forfeit your lifeline; the Holy Spirit will give you a holy revelation of knowledge! Renew your mind daily...don't reject the way, the truth and the life offered to you!

EPH. 4:23 (NLT); ROM. 12:2; JOHN 6:63

July 9

"A new command I give you: Love one another. As I have loved you, so you must love one another."
JOHN 13:34

Love in the church...yes, no, maybe? Many have an unrealistic expectation that they will not be hurt in the church. Anywhere you find people, you will find hurt. People in the church will hurt you, but God gives us His Word to work through hurt. I'm thankful for the genuine love I receive from my church family-doing life together...it's real!

Nothing is perfect; the church consists of people, and offenses happen. I've offended others and others have offended me, but with God's love, I've been redeemed from the harm I've imposed on others, and I embrace the forgiveness God gives me to extend to others. Anywhere you find people-you will find hurt...but, dear God, don't let this keep us from loving one another in the church!

God's ways work when we work them His way. I'm thankful for God's love reaching through others to love me, and His love in me reaching to them. Yes...love is in the church!

1 JOHN 4:7; LEV. 19:18; JOHN 13:34

July 10

"I am the vine; you are the branches. If you remain in me and I in you, you will bear much fruit; apart from me you can do nothing."
JOHN 15:5

The issues you continue to reason away with theories or ignore altogether keep you from moving forward in the peace, confidence and destiny promised to you long ago. You are dissatisfied, borderline angry and not where you want to be; don't waste one more day with the protest that you've done all that God's asked of you. This isn't about what you're doing...it's about what you're believing!

Listen closely: God's not going to give up on you-don't give up on Him! Ask Him to search your heart and forgive hidden offenses; release your pride and let go of denial...the Holy Spirit will help you face the truth and expose the issues that are holding you back! You can't correct yourself-only the Holy Spirit can do it, but...he requires your cooperation. Denying His help keeps your mind in constant turmoil.

Expect to be uncomfortable-the truth hurts but it also sets you free! God gives wisdom generously without finding fault. Will you ditch your plans and listen to the wisdom God desires to give you?

JOHN 8:31-32, 15:5; JAMES 1:2-8; PS. 66:18-19

July 11

"...for it is pleasing when you keep them in your heart and have all of them ready on your lips."
PROV. 22:18

The greatest freedom in my walk with Christ has been in professing the Word aloud, writing it down, and putting my eyes on it regularly. During difficult seasons in my life when my heart was breaking, I would say Scripture aloud over and over and over; it was my lifeline to hold onto. But I remember to say Scripture the same way in good seasons as well, and it enables me to see the promises of God with clarity and gives me hope while I transition from one season to the next.

Write down the truth and speak it aloud throughout the day...God's peace guards my mind and my heart: "He has good plans for me; I can do all things through Christ Who strengthens me; I am complete in Christ; where the Spirit of the Lord is there is freedom." These aren't just words, they are God's Word, His promises that stand forever. They are full of power and will save, change and transform your life! Don't give up; renew your mind. God's got good plans for you!

PROV. 2:10, 22:18; JAMES 1:5

July 12

"I have said these things to you, that in me you may have peace.
In the world you will have tribulation. But take heart;
I have overcome the world."
JOHN 16:33 (ESV)

Feeling fear and being fearful are different. It's normal to feel fear in this world-God told us we would. Jesus said, *"do not be afraid, I've overcome this world!"* (SEE JOHN 16:33). Being fearful arises out of a spirit of fear that steals the peace promised by God.

Feeling fear engages the internal security system God designed in every person; it sets off an alarm to signal danger in the mind, like smoke sets off a fire alarm to signal a fire. It's God's design to alert us to danger so we will run to Him. We seek His safety and believe He will protect us although we may be engulfed in danger. His protection keeps us from being devoured by the world!

Being fearful results when a person struggles to believe God's promise of protection. They think God may or may not protect them. Their decisions are based on what they're *feeling*...they prefer their feelings over God's truth, which results in instability. Feelings change based on circumstances but God's truth remains constant *despite* changing circumstances.

Will you seek God when you're feeling fear to guard against being fearful?

2 TIM. 1:7; MATT. 8:26; JOHN 16:33 (ESV)

July 13

"We can rejoice, too, when we run into problems and trials, for we know that
they help us develop endurance."
ROM. 5:3-5 (NLT)

Pain is an inevitable part of life. God promises to hold our hand and walk us through it, but we have to be willing to *face* it and trust Him to do what He promises. If we deny the pain or resist His help, we turn from the door of hope that's at the end of every pain. That door of hope is God's hope and God's hope never disappoints! Will you let God walk you through your pain, which leads to His door of hope?

ROM. 5:3-5 (NLT); HAB. 3:33; LUKE 21:19

July 14

"...yet for us there is but one God, the Father,
from whom all things came and for whom we live."
1 COR. 8:6

Nothing, nothing, nothing...is too big for our God! One touch of His hand...and your world can change in a nanosecond. You have to trust Him, friend...if you want to watch Him transform your nothing into something. Trusting Him is required to walk where it appears you can't...and to believe when it looks like there is nothing to believe in, and to keep on moving forward when you don't think you can.

He will supply all your needs while you are believing Him and following Him. Remember, through Him all things were made; without Him nothing was made that has been made. Let Him make something...from your nothing. He's for you, so there's nothing, nothing, nothing...that can be against you.

PHIL. 4:19; JOHN 1:3; ROM. 8:31; 1 COR. 8:6

July 15

"Who shall separate us from the love of Christ? Shall trouble or hardship or
persecution or famine or nakedness or danger or sword?"
ROM. 8:35

Lean into God and His Word when life presses on you-it's your confidence. When you're overwhelmed and feel you're out of resources with no plans-that's when you're pressed to know the power that's at work within you. If you stick with God, you'll find out He's faithful. These seasons increase your faith, heighten your sensitivity to the Holy Spirit, and enable you to know and walk in the truth that sets you free!

Do not be mistaken: God will challenge your beliefs, flush out your insecurities and purge your pride. You're vulnerable and raw but also certain of God's love for you-knowing your value is in Who you belong to-not in what you do. You trade your false confidence for His unwavering boldness, and your need to prove for His approval. As you renew your mind with His truth you learn to walk by faith and not by sight. Daily you push back and take another step into the unknown-there are times when weariness depletes every cell in your body and you consider quitting, but then God sends His undeniable encouragement that reenergizes your entire being and you know you can do it because His Spirit fuels you. You come to know without a doubt where you stand with God, that His love sustains, comforts and protects you. Every one of His promises is true. He supplies all your needs!

Apart from Him you can do nothing-but with His strength, you can do all things! All your hope is in Him because of Who He is-not what He does. The greatest part of these seasons being over isn't so much that they're over, but it's what you know when they are...that you're loved by your Father, that He will never leave you, and that He has good plans for you! Will you trust God to do a work in you so you can know the power that's...at work within you?

Eph. 3:19-20; John 8:32, 15:5; Phil. 2:13, 4:13

July 16

"In him was life, and that life was the light of all mankind."
John 1:4

Jesus will help you...but you have to let Him. He won't force Himself on you-He's gentle, kind and caring. He wants you to invite Him. You choose if you're comfortable with Him being close to you. He's waiting; He's your bridge to the Father. Go on, ask Him...He's waiting for you. What is it you need help with: self-esteem, a relationship, finances, heartache, job search, being real, forgiveness, time management, jealousy, school choice, anger, a disease, assertiveness, direction, friendship, grief and loss, parenting, hearing God?

Whatever you need help with...Jesus will help you, but you must let go. What you keep from Him is for you to handle-what you release to Him...He will handle. Jesus never messes up, His plan is perfect, He fixes what was broken, restores the lost, makes your path straight, makes the blind see and the deaf hear, He makes something from nothing, heals the hurting, binds up the wounds of the brokenhearted, gives hope to the hopeless. He shows up when others don't, holds you when others won't, reveals what others can't; He has no barriers, He's unstoppable, He's the name above all names...Jesus! His love completes us-He is the way, truth and life.

Jesus will help you...but you must let go. He's your bridge to the Father. Go on, ask Him...He's waiting for you.

COL. 2:10; JOHN 1:4, 14:6; ISAIAH 61:1

July 17

"The LORD is close to the brokenhearted
and saves those who are crushed in spirit."
PS. 34:18.

What we hand to God...He takes-what we don't hand to Him, we keep. Listen closely, there's nothing holy about not taking your hurts to the Lord. Regardless of how small they are-they eventually pile up. When was the last time you honestly looked at your pile? The size of your pile doesn't matter...whatever its size it stands between God and you and those you love, and it keeps you from completely moving forward!

Ask Jesus to look at this pile with you. He will show you the hurts you minimized or dismissed. He will give you the courage to face things you never thought you could face. You've got to remember Jesus came to heal our broken hearts and bind up our wounds. Maybe your pile has hurt in it from a person who's passed away...they may be gone, but they didn't take your pain with them. Look in your pile...that's where it is. Today, will you let Jesus begin to bind up every one of your hurts?

What a relief to know we're not tethered to the wounds we have received from or imposed onto others! Our Father God is our Healer and Comforter. He will restore us completely with His love! Today, will you receive the healing you need to get past the pile of hurt you've been avoiding?

PS. 147:3; 1 PETER 2:24; ISAIAH 43:18; 2 COR. 3:17; ROM. 8:28

July 18

"Let us then approach God's throne of grace with confidence, so that we may receive mercy and find grace to help us in our time of need."
HEB. 4:16

Jesus will escort you into the throne room of our Father any-time day or night-you don't need an appointment or ever have to wait. Prayer doesn't have to be long or loud, rehearsed or repeated; prayer pours out words from your heart...at times inaudible groanings you don't even understand. You can pray anytime, anywhere and anyplace. Prayer is an open door to our Father-it's a privilege...don't turn your back on it.

Prayer is where you receive our Father's love. He tells you that you matter, you're chosen and that He has good plans for you! It's where He heals the broken parts of your heart-He whispers that His love heals all your hurts and gives hope for the future. He promises to restore more than was ever taken from you if you will put your trust in Him. Prayer is a time to grieve and let go-verbalizing fears of the unknown...it's a time to weep, grieve and lay down your plans for the those of the Father.

Prayer is a time our Father assures you that you've got what it takes because He's put everything you need in you-it's where you're certain He hears, understands and cares; where He nur-tures, encourages and validates you. Prayer is your safe retreat, where your Father comforts and guides you, reminding you that you're never alone, because He's with you always! Prayer is a privilege-will you let Jesus escort you to the throne room of our Father?

JOHN 14:6; JER. 29:11; ISAIAH 61:1-3; HEB. 4:16; EPH. 3:12

July 19

"Seek the LORD and his strength; seek his presence continually!"
PS. 105:4 (ESV)

God promises that as long as we seek Him, He will bring us through each trial. I believe God. I'm sure you do, too, but I still get overwhelmed and tired, and have meltdowns at times. I move through them, not because I'm a spiritual giant...but because Jesus Christ lives in me! And thank you, Jesus, I'm stronger after each trial, which increases my hope and trust in Him! Every time we reach an end, the Holy Spirit is waiting to supply us with the same power that raised the beaten and dead body of Jesus from the grave! His power is perfected in our weaknesses.

I have to be purposed in keeping my eyes on Christ; if not, the impossibles overtake me. I move forward in deliberate steps with the bold confidence of Christ's strength in me-knowing He will make a way. I don't entertain how He will make a way... I've already decided He will because He can't lie. Still, doubt pounds on the door of my mind-screaming all my insecurities, failures and insufficiencies, and each one of them is true. But I know...Christ's power is perfected in my weaknesses! Apart from Him I can do nothing, but with Him I can do all things... thank you, Jesus, and Amen! Will you let Jesus Christ do the same for you?

I TIM 6:12; JOHN 15:5, 16:33; PS. 34:19, 105:4 (ESV); ROM. 8:11; 2 COR. 12:9

July 20

"For the LORD your God is living among you. He is a mighty savior. He will take delight in you with gladness. With his love, he will calm all your fears. He will rejoice over you with joyful songs."
ZEPH. 3:17 (NLT)

You've been violated and experienced many let downs in life. You were robbed, but are you going to allow the past to also rob you of your present and future?

God didn't rob you...others did; don't hold a grudge against God. Your emotions are distorting and separating you from His truth and love. God will set you free from the bondage of past pain-He will restore what was stolen, given away or never received-giving it all back and more, but you'll never know this truth...unless you trust Him!

Following God doesn't exempt you from pain...but it does promise He will bring you through the pain! You will have more heartbreak and hurt in the future, but God will soothe you through each one. God's in control over what you see and don't see-He holds creation together in His hands. Faith isn't based on what you see God do...it's based on Who you believe He is! Will you trust Him? He's mighty to save?

PROV. 14:12; ZEPH. 3:17 (NLT); COL. 1:16-17

July 21

"So do not fear, for I am with you; do not be dismayed, for I am your God. I will strengthen you and help you; I will uphold you with my righteous right hand."
ISAIAH 41:10

Limiting God with your limits...opens a door for doubt to distort what God can do. Questioning and doubting what God can do in your situation limits His ability to help...you. Do you believe He will do for another, but not you? Ask the Holy Spirit for revelation; you're believing a lie. You're not exempt from God's possibles. Doubting also places a heaviness of hopelessness deep in your spirit, further distorting your spiritual vision. Renew your mind with God's promises and read Scripture to be encouraged.

Look at LUKE 1:27-38: a virgin willing to be ridiculed by society, possibly stoned to death, much less what Joseph, her fiancé, would think of her, and a million other "what-ifs." She didn't know how things would unfold, being pregnant but never having been with a man...who's going to believe her? But she didn't look at her impossible situation, instead she trusted God saying, "let it be done to me according to what you have said."

Move forward in this season of your life...knowing what you face is impossible for you...but with God nothing is ever impossible. Continue to thank God for making a way. You are bringing the glory of Heaven before you when you thank Him for what He has not yet brought to fruition. Think about the times when your child or someone has thanked you for what you had not yet done for them. I know as a parent and grandparent, I can hardly wait to bless my kids when they have confidence in me delivering what I promised them. The same holds true for God; when we thank Him in the middle of our trials, knowing with confidence He will provide for us, we are showing Him we believe. It's a ROMANS 4:17 promise: calling those things that be not as though they are. Continue to thank God for turning your impossible into His possible. Don't allow doubt to distort what God can do.

LUKE 1:27-38; ROM. 4:17, 12:2 ; ISAIAH 41:10

July 22

"For God is working in you, giving you the desire and the power to do what pleases him."
PHIL. 2:13 (NLT)

Jesus died to give you an abundant life...to have a peace that surpasses human understanding *in spite of trials*. Seek the Holy Spirit and ask for wisdom to walk in the promises of God. When you get real with Jesus...He will get real with you. You may feel you've messed up too much, wasted time or are just not valued enough to be used by God. These are your feelings and they are real...but they are *not* God's truth!

God chose you-He loved you first, He purposed long ago every good work you would do. Ask Jesus to help you not doubt Him...He gives wisdom and sufficiency to all who call on Him. God wants you to succeed in what He purposed you to do-He's for you not against you! You have what it takes, everything you need to do what He's asked of you. Jesus lives in you, the Holy Spirit guides you and God has planned every second of your life. The only way you won't fulfill what your purposed to do is if you opt out and do life your way! God even gives you the desire and power to obey Him *if you ask.*

One more thing: you're exhausted because you're trying to re-solve impossible situations with human wisdom. Put your faith in God's power, not your wisdom. Don't seek from man what only God can do! If you're still breathing...God's still at work. Keep moving, breathe in, breathe out, get some rest, think on what's pure, lovely and right, and spend time with those who will encourage you but also speak God's truth. God won't give up on you, don't give up on Him. He will stay with you during hard times...He wants to know if you will stay with Him?

ISAIAH 41:10; 2 COR. 5:7, 12:9; PHIL. 1:6, 2:13 (NLT); EPH. 2:10; ROM 8:31

July 23

*"Now faith is being sure of what we hope for
and certain of what we do not see."*
HEB. 11:1

Be informed, prudent and purposed in decisions and consider worldly information, but your hope must be in God and His power...not man's wisdom! God's ability to provide isn't de-pendent upon current interest rates, government leaders or school officials, financial forecasts or career projections, in-duced psychosis or genetic predisposition, personality traits or resiliency skills, bank approval, knowing the right people, maybe, sometimes, or "if we're lucky".

These are all real issues, of course, but your help comes from the Lord. Will you hope in Him instead of mans's wisdom?

HEB. 11:1; 1 COR. 2:5; PS. 121:2

July 24

*"And being fully persuaded that, what he had promised,
he was able also to perform."*
ROM. 4:21 (KJV)

Are you facing an impossible situation? The first thing you need to do is immediately submit your mind to the Holy Spirit and ask for help, then acknowledge the reality of the situation and profess aloud that you are giving it to the Lord! If you allow your thoughts to linger and look at the impossible, your mind will sink in despair because you don't have the ability to figure it out! God, of course, can, but until He lets you know, you will need to rest in Him while you go about your daily business. You do that by focusing on His Word and professing it over and over. I've listed some Scriptures as examples. You might prefer others, but, wither way, have them within reach so you're ready to profess them. Finally, remember: the Holy Spirit lives in you. He is your Helper and Advocate to get you on the other side of this.

God is able to do exceedingly abundantly above all you think or ask, make all grace abound to you and give you sufficiency in all things, give you a peace that surpasses all understanding, supply all your needs, do whatever He promises, keep you from stumbling and present you blameless before God, and bring to completion the good work He started in you. And, God is able to make donkeys talk, open up and roll back massive bodies of water, convert one meal to feed 5000, and do anything He pleases. If you're wondering...God *is* able. The question is: will you trust Him to be *your* able?

ROM. 4:21 (KJV); EPH. 3:20; 2 COR. 9:8; PHIL. 1:6, 4:7; JUDE 1:24; NUM. 22:28; EX. 14:21; JOSHUA 3:16; JOHN 6:5-13

July 25

"Do not [earnestly] remember the former things;
neither consider the things of old."
ISAIAH 43:18 (MSG)

Letting go of what was...the former familiar. You're in a new season-to say you feel vulnerable, insecure and awkward is an understatement. The past is gone; there's nothing there-let it go...reach forward to what lies in front of you. God wants to show you something new, but you won't see it ahead...if you're still looking back. Life is a perpetual motion forward-it will continue whether you choose to move with it or not. Say "yes" to the life God wants to show you-He's made a way...will you follow Him there?

ISAIAH 43:18-19 (MSG); ISAIAH 65:17; 2 COR. 5:17

July 26

"...to bestow on them a crown of beauty instead of ashes, the oil of joy instead of mourning, and a garment of praise instead of a spirit of despair."
ISAIAH 61:3

Blame wants you take matters into your own hands and undo the wrongs done to you, but you can't...only the love of Jesus can undo what happened to you. Your feelings are valid and blame's recall is accurate, but neither have a case against the power of Christ that lives in you!

The love of Jesus heals broken hearts and saves those crushed in spirit; He restores and redeems what was lost, stolen, given away or never received! Jesus will undo every wrong done to you, but you have to let go of blame in exchange for the love He wants to give you...don't take matters into your own hands. Will you receive the freedom He's offering you today?

ISAIAH 61:1-3; PS. 34:18-19

July 27

"Here on earth you will have many trials and sorrows. But take heart, because I have overcome the world."
JOHN 16:33 (NLT)

Bad things happen to good people and there will be things you won't understand for the life of you until you get to Heaven! What a relief to know God's love is bigger than anything this world can throw at us! His Spirit lives in us-testifying with our spirit! Only with His love can we move through the inevitable pain and uncertainties this life brings. His love gives us His perfect peace, but we must be purposed in receiving it by spending time with Him, renewing our minds with the Word and being sensitive to the prompting of the Holy Spirit. Jesus said we'd experience distress, trials and frustrations, but to have courage, be confident, certain and undaunted, because He's overcome the world!

God's promises stand...you have to be purposed in taking them every hour of the day-choosing to believe when you see no indicators. Agree with God's Word-it will strengthen you and increase your stamina while knocking down discouragement.

Jesus has overcome this world...this is the truth; He can't lie! Ask the Holy Spirit to help you every time doubt knocks on the door of your mind, otherwise anxiety will rush you and lead you into despair. Don't allow doubt to linger. Immediately call on the name of Jesus!

Stick with God. He's your hope! His love sustains you and His hope holds on for you-making a way when you can't see the way. This is your promise, but a promise is only as powerful as it is believed...do you believe?

JOHN 16:33; HEB. 6:19; MARK 9:24; EPH. 3:20; 1 COR. 13:8

July 28

*"My soul faints with longing for your salvation,
but I have put my hope in your word."*
PS. 119:81

God does His best work in us when we've left our familiar but not yet arrived in our new season. We're uncertain, unfamiliar, unsettled...pride purged, false confidence knocked out, beliefs challenged. This is the middle part; where God's love approves us not for what we do or don't do, but for who we are in Him. When we know God's love... we know we've got what it takes-because He says so!

PS. 119:81; 1 COR. 2:10; MATT. 5:45

July 29

*"By God's grace and mighty power, I have been given the privilege of serving
him by spreading this Good News."*
EPH. 3:7 (NLT)

As Christians, we're always to be in forward motion and making a difference for God's glory. Intensity can change according to the season of life, but the perpetual forward motion never stops. We're saved to fulfill the plan and purpose to which God has called us.

Seeing our lives from God's perspective enables us to know we're equipped, not because of what we're able to do, but because of what the Holy Spirit will do through us!

1 Cor. 10:31; 1 Ptr. 4:11; Eph. 3:7 (NLT)

July 30

"Early will I seek you"
Ps.63:1

It's inconceivable for you to think you don't have time for God because of the things you need to do or have to take care of...because the things you do and have to take care of are under God's authority and everything belongs to Him. You want to be efficient, maximize your time and not allow stress to eat you alive every day...then go to God first every morning and spend time with Him.

God is over everything and holds everything together with His hands; what you have belongs to Him and He will guide you to steward it with success. God is available to you all day and all night...He will listen to your heart all day and He will stay up with you all night and comfort you. You can talk to Him about anything and everything-He loves you and wants an intimate relationship with you. Will you let Him love you today?

Matt. 6:33; Col. 1:17; Prov. 3:5-6; Luke 12:31 (NLT); Ps. 63:1

July 31

"Therefore we are buried with him by baptism into death: that like as Christ was raised up from the dead by the glory of the Father, even so we also should walk in newness of life."
Rom. 6:4 (KJV)

Many hold on to relationships that no longer exist...they are dead. Even though the relationship is over-the person hasn't gotten over it. They still cling to the past, trying to revive what's no longer there, still trying to find meaning in something that's passed-an identity that no longer exist.

Two points that are critical 1) your identity is only found in Jesus; and 2) if you make your identity in someone or something then, when it no longer exists...neither do you. If you hold on to the past that's where you will live, which doesn't allow you to be in the present...so you're the walking dead. As long as you you're looking back...you can't exist in the present, or move forward.

Today, will you ask God to forgive you if you've put your hope in anything other than Him? And then will you let Him show you how to put your hope in Him? I pray the God of Hope will overflow you with His hope right now in the mighty name of Jesus-Amen!

Rom. 6:4, 7:6; Heb. 12:1

✝

August 1

"The LORD is my strength and my shield; my heart trusts in him, and he helps me."
Ps. 28:7

If you are breathing you have issues; no person is exempt. When you get to Heaven *then* you won't have any. Until then, receive the revelation the Holy Spirit will make known to you: where the Spirit of the Lord is, there is freedom. This truth sets you free, enabling you to receive His love and approval, allowing His light to shine through you. God won't abandon the plan He started in you. Don't allow what you are not to get in the way of who God says you are. What you lack or what you're up against doesn't stop God's plans-He will give you every provision you need to to walk out what He asks of you. Take comfort in the truth that your hope is in His power, and not in the mercy of man's wisdom. That should make you shout!

You can trade in your frustrations, weaknesses, every wrong in the world, sleepless nights, grinding your teeth, IBS, headaches, regrets, hurt, anxiety, irritability, fear of being passed over, back up plans, reasoning of potential outcomes, betrayal of friends and loved ones, opposition and those who undermine you because...Jesus has overcome *every* person, situation or outcome that would interfere with His plans! Nothing, no one, nada can undo God's promises; this generation will not pass away until all things take place (SEE LUKE 21:32). Cooperate with God, let the Holy Spirit give you revelation and comfort you-then you can lay down who you think you should be and become the person God made you to be...His masterpiece planned long ago to do the good works He purposed for you!

So relax and know that if you're breathing...you have issues-we all do. When you get to Heaven you won't have any because God's work will be complete *in* you. Until then, will you trust God to fulfill His call *through* you?

1COR. 2:5, 12:9; EPH. 2:10; 2 COR. 3:17; JOHN 8:32; COL. 2:10; MATT. 5:16

August 2

*"I love those who love me, and those who seek me
early and diligently shall find me."*
PROV. 8:17 (AMP)

Who told you those lies? Have your children ever come home from school upset and crying because another child made a hurtful comment to them or said mean and untrue things about them to others? The first thing we do as a loving parent is ask, "who told you those lies?" Then we hug them and look them directly in the eyes and tell them to not believe the lies they were told. We remind them of Who they belong to and their identity in Christ, that they are fearfully and wonderfully made-God's masterpiece, and another person can't determine their worth or value. *We replace the deception with God's truth!*

Are you believing any of the lies the world is telling you...that you missed your chance, you're too old, it's too late for you to fulfill your dreams, you don't matter, you have nothing to offer, you will never overcome your past? Go to your Father with these lies and He will ask you, "who told you those lies?" Then He will tell you to not let any person take you captive through hollow and deceptive philosophy that depends on human traditions and basic principles of this world rather than Christ!

God will replace the deception you're believing with His truth... which trumps all the fleeting opinions of the world! Your part is to continually (all the time throughout the day) renew your mind with His truth so that your mind is transformed. Seek His will for you so you don't conform to who the world says you are!

ROM. 12:2, COL. 2:8, JOHN 8:31-32; PROV. 8:17 (AMP)

August 3

"We love him, because he first loved us."
1 JOHN 4:19 (KJV)

Do you have a grudge against God? If you do, be honest with Him because He's the only One Who can get you on the other side of it. You can fight against God your entire life...you will have as much success beating your fists against a brick wall! Holding onto this grudge gives you a false sense of control, but you're the only one who's suffering. God didn't make bad things happen to you and holding onto a grudge against Him won't make what happened to you go away. See, your grudge against God doesn't put you in a position of power...it places you in a position of loss. As long as you're mad at God, you're cutting off your help from Him and you're holding hurt in your heart. When you lay down the grudge against God, you open the door to His help. You give Him the hurt you've been carrying-this is called *forgiving*. He takes all this hurt and re-places it with His love...this is called *restoration*!

His love will heal every broken part of your heart. Forgiving isn't dismissing the wrong you experience or the hurt you felt...it's *choosing* to no longer carry it in your heart. You can't deal with this burden through your strength and you don't have to, but until you release it...you will continue to. You can be real with God and He will be real with you. He will answer you, but you have to decide if you will listen. *"I sought the Lord and He answered me; He delivered me from all my fears. Those who look to Him are radiant, their faces are never covered with shame."*

PS. 34:4-5; JOHN 10:10; PHIL. 1:6; MATT. 6:33; 1 JOHN 4:19 (KJV)

August 4

"I tell you the truth, if you have faith and don't doubt, you can do things like this and much more. You can even say to this mountain, 'May you be lifted up and thrown into the sea,' and it will happen."
MATT. 21:21 (NLT)

Don't resent where you are right now...God's conditioning and preparing you for the next season. He's pushing you to your edge-it's making you stronger. Every season has trials, so don't be surprised by them; they're part of life. Without God, trials would do you in-but because of God you're guaranteed to move through them. God's getting you in shape spiritually, emotionally and physically, running you through drills of patience, endurance and focus-the requirements to sustain and maintain you during each season. To be successful you must rely on God completely and have faith in Him constantly. Don't resent where you are right now...God's conditioning and preparing you for the next season!

PHIL. 4:13; MARK 11:22; PS. 34:19

August 5

"Even to your old age and gray hairs I am he, I am he who will sustain you.
I have made you and I will carry you;
I will sustain you and I will rescue you"
ISAIAH 46:4

God tells us to cast our cares on Him and to not have anxiety about anything. The response I hear to this when I'm counseling someone is, "I know but how am I supposed to not have anxiety when____?" People fill in the blank differently, but their thought patterns are the same...they're trying to fix an impossible situation with a human solution! The human mind is isn't designed to fix impossible situations apart from God's help. Attempts to do so default into anxiety mode...because human solutions can't fix impossible situations! Deception has them believing that their *problem* is the impossible situation, but the problem is the way they're *thinking about* the impossible situation.

You will be faced with impossible situations until the day you see Jesus face-to-face; until then you can rest in the promise God makes to you..."*Even to your old age and gray hairs I am he, I am he who will sustain you. I have made you and I will carry you; I will sustain you and I will rescue you.*" You rest in this promise by desiring to believe it, and God will help you believe. Then daily you profess this truth, ask the Holy Spirit for revelation of it, write it down were you can see it throughout the day, and then stand on it, even when it looks impossible! You don't have to know *how* God will deliver His promise to believe that He *will*. Will you cast your cares on Him today?

ISAIAH 46:4; PS. 55:22; MARK 9:24

August 6

"But now, Lord, what do I look for? My hope is in you."
PS. 39:7

Have you been praying over a situation for a long time? God honors our steadfast hearts in prayer, but be careful to not get caught in a subtle snare...putting your hope in what you're praying for instead of hoping in Who God is. This will lead to grief because your hope is contingent upon prayers being answered, versus God's hope that sustains you.

God's hope promises to satisfy us and He does answer prayers, but not always like we want them to be answered, because His ways are higher than ours. He's God and we're not. God's hope gives a peace that surpasses human understanding, holds on when we can't and gives a confident expectation for what is to come. His hope never disappoints!

Will you make a decision to trust God regardless of the outcome of a situation? Will you hold tight to God's hope...right now?

HEB. 6:19, 11:1; ROM. 5:3-5; PS. 39:7

August 7

"My grace is sufficient for you, for my power is made perfect in weakness."
2 COR. 12:9

Don't settle...nothing compares to knowing the love God has for you and being known by Him; it's where your security and identity come together to form the foundation for the authentic person He designed you to be! You were uniquely created and purposed to do good works and to make a difference in this world for God's glory! His love enables you to rest in His sufficiency...you're approved so you no longer feel compelled to prove. You're valuable because you belong to Him-not because of what you do for Him! Embrace this truth-renew your mind with it; it will change your life! But you won't know it until you "walk out" what you profess to believe about Him! I pray you will accept all the love God has for you and live out the authentic life He planned for you long ago!

LUKE 18:27; 1 COR. 1:27; ACTS 4:31; 2 COR. 12:9; EPH. 2:10; PS. 127:1-2

August 8

"You will guard me and keep me in perfect and constant peace as my mind [both its inclination and its character] is stayed on You..."
ISAIAH 26:3 (AMP)

God's Word and doubt will always wage war inside of your head; your spirit says believe but your mind says you missed it! These battles don't stop until you see Jesus face-to-face. Don't let this reality get you down; you have the full-time help of the Holy Spirit to overcome and be victorious in every battle! He never leaves you and gives you His grace, a supernatural help...to be spiritually tenacious! Set your mind to this truth every day, then move forward with the help of the Holy Spirit!

PHIL. 4:7; ISAIAH 26:3 (AMP); JOHN 14:27

August 9

"But you are not like that, for the Holy One has given you his Spirit,
and all of you know the truth."
I JOHN 2:20

Having an understanding of the enemy's motives along with knowing how God uses trials in your favor enables you to be hopeful, confident and expectant despite the hardship you're experiencing. When you submit the hardship to God and expect Him to bring you through, you give Him the opportunity to use it for His glory while the Holy Spirit teaches you to endure and pace yourself during the difficult season.

In the natural what God asks is impossible...that's why He has to carry it out through us. In my own personal experience and over the years of professionally working with clients, I have seen that most every prompt from God requires walking in the unknown. I've experienced Him lead me through places were I didn't have a clue as to what He was doing until after I went through, but this I know with all my heart: *God keeps walking with us and He never leaves us!* This is how each of us experience our personal relationship...in our personal experience with Him!

He's taught me to be comfortable with not knowing, which is counterintuitive to what the world teaches. But when we take this risk, it's the craziest, safest, most exciting and fulfilling place to ever be! Will you get comfortable in letting God show you how to face trials and increase your trust in Him, so you can walk out what He asks of you?

JAMES 1:2-4; I COR. 2:13; 2 COR. 2:13-15; I JOHN 2:20

August 10

"In my desperation I prayed, and the LORD listened;
he saved me from all my troubles."
PS. 34:6 (NLT)

Don't carry around your pain one more day and accept it as your identity. Your identity is in Christ - *not* in what you did or what was done to you! I'm not trying to be insensitive, but I want you to know the truth: God loves you dearly. He will take each ugly and mean lie and give you His life-changing truth, trade out the heaviness of depravity for the lightness of His confident dignity, replace the years of rejection with His complete acceptance, and take the hopelessness you see and give you His hope that never disappoints!

Your part is to unconditionally accept God's love for you, renew your mind and believe when it seems crazy to do so! Your identity isn't what you've been through-your identity is in what was done *for you* on the cross! Jesus took on hell and won. The Son has set you free and the Holy Spirit is your Helper to bring to fruition the plans God made for you long ago! You are free indeed!

Will you release your pain into the hands of God so He can use it for His glory?

PROV. 3:5; PS. 34:19; PS. 34:6 (NLT); ISAIAH 61:1-7; GEN. 50:20

August 11

"My people are being destroyed because they don't know me."
HOSEA 4:6 (NLT)

Need direction in life? Go to Jesus; no one is denied. Be transformed in your heart, mind and body in the gospels of MATTHEW, MARK, LUKE and JOHN-read the words of Jesus and take comfort: *Ask and it will be given, seek and you will find, knock and the door will be opened to you. Daughter, your faith has healed you-go in peace and be freed from your suffering. Whoever can be trusted with very little can also be trusted with very much. Peace I leave with you; my peace I give you. I do not give to you as the world gives. Don't let your hearts be troubled and don't be afraid.*

Speak God's Word; embrace the love of Jesus and live the life He gave you; allow the Holy Spirit to guide you so that you do not conform to the world, but are transformed and renewed in your mind to do the pleasing will of God! Many perish for lack of knowledge. God's Word is life-He and His Word can't be separated, and His Words are full of supernatural power.

God gives us the privilege of His Word; if we read it and renew our mind with it we will be transformed and walk in the confidence, peace and victory He promises! Will you renew your mind with the Word and be transformed?

MATT. 7:7; MARK 5:34; LUKE 16:10; JOHN 14:27; ROM. 12:2; HOSEA 4:6

August 12

"But he gives us more grace."
JAMES 4:6

Nothing in life compares or will ever give you more... than Jesus, the "More Than Enough" Who already lives in you. He will supply all your needs and give you more than you dare ask or imagine, so that in all things and at all times you have more than you need, which provides you with a peace that transcends all understanding, offers His hope that holds on when you can't, fills you with joy and peace, and overflows you with hope as you trust Him, making His power perfect in your weakness!

Jesus is more than enough...offering you everything that you need. He lives in you. Will you let Him be your "more than enough" today?

PHIL. 4;19; EPH. 3:20; 2 COR. 9:8; PHIL. 4:7; HEB. 6:19; ROM. 15:13; JAMES 4:6

August 13

"...it is to one's glory to overlook an offense."
PROV. 19:11

Are you holding onto unforgiveness, swearing you will never forget the wrong done to you? Listen closely: unforgiveness keeps the harm done to you alive in your heart-keeping you chained to the person and the offense. Forgiveness doesn't *excuse* the wrong done to you. What happened to you was wrong, but releasing it transfers the burden off of your heart and into the hands of Jesus. He's your Vindicator and Redeemer-the only Bar of Justice! You can try all your life to overcome what was done to you, only to end up mad, sad and empty hand-ed...but Jesus can give back what was stolen or never received!

Forgiveness is one of the hardest things God asks of us; it doesn't just happen "naturally". It's a mental exercise along with a heart's desire. Don't be alarmed when, after you make the decision to forgive, you still are experiencing hurt and anger. Just keep asking the Holy Spirit for strength. Consistency and desire, along with the Holy Spirit's help, promise to bring you through this! Forgiveness is a gift. Will you hand the harms you've carried in your heart to Jesus today?

PROV. 19:11; EPH. 4:32; MATT. 5:44, 6:14-15

August 14

*"Praise the LORD. Give thanks to the LORD,
for he is good; his love endures forever."*
PS. 106:1

You are privileged...God gives you His time and His Word be-cause He loves you. Don't turn your back on this privilege. Read, speak and memorize His comforting words, not because you should...but because you can. Spend time with Him daily; fill up with His love for you. Give thanks and praise Him. Let God go before you each day....He says you are His and He has redeemed and summoned you by name. That's right; He knows your name, friend...deep waters and rivers will not sweep over you, and you will not be burned when you walk through fires.

God is with you and will never leave you. Uncertain about about your career? Commit to the Lord whatever you do, and your plans will succeed. Are you being taken to court and falsely accused? The Lord won't let you be condemned when brought to trial. Do you need to confront a difficult situation? Read JOSHUA 1:9, *"do not be terrified; do not be discouraged, for the Lord your God will be with you wherever you go."* Feeling like you can't take one more day of a certain situation? ISAIAH 41:10 says, *"Fear not [there is nothing to fear], for I am with you; do not look around you in terror and be dismayed, for I am you God. I will strengthen and harden you to difficulties, yes, I will help you; Yes, I will hold you up and retain you with My [victorious] right hand of rightness and justice."*

Wherever you are, you are never alone, because your Father is with you...don't turn your back on your privilege. Begin to speak the words of your Father and be encouraged...He has a good plan for you. Peace be with you, friend.

PS. 37:33, 106:1; ISAIAH 43:1-2; HEB.13:5; PROV. 16:3; JER. 29:11; JOHN 14:27

August 15

"I would like to learn just one thing from you: Did you receive the Spirit by the works of the law, or by believing what you heard?"
GAL. 3:2

If you believe your value in life is dependent on what you can or cannot accomplish for God, then you will feel accepted when you succeed and rejected when you fail. This belief leads to misery and places you in a perpetual agitated state because you're not defined by what you do or do not do...you're defined by "Who" lives in you and "what" He did for you!

You can't save or change yourself...if you could you wouldn't need a Savior! *"Are you so foolish and so senseless and silly? Having begun [your new life spiritually] with the [Holy] Spirit, are you now reaching perfection [by dependence] on the flesh"* (SEE GAL. 3:3 AMP). We received the Holy Spirit the day we believed and accepted Jesus as our Savior. The Holy Spirit is at work in us and is our source for deepening our walk with Jesus...*not* our ability to keep rules.

God isn't impressed with how many rules we can keep, but He *is* pleased when we walk in the unknown and follow Him with confidence! And this is also how we increase our faith in Him, because we see that He provides along the way! Will you step out in faith today?

ROM. 10:17; GAL. 3:2-3, 5; 1 THESS. 2:13

August 16

"If you abide in my word, you are truly my disciples,"
JOHN 8:31 (ESV)

Whatever you need help with...Jesus will help you. He wants to set you free, but you must let go of your grip so He can. Release your mind from the constant circling of potential outcomes and scenarios. This is fear disguised as concern, and it is trying to paralyze your mind.

Your efforts can't fix this problem...but Jesus can and will...*if* you will let go of your grip! What you keep from Him is for you to handle-what you release to Him...He will handle. Jesus never messes up, friend. If you hold to His teachings, you will know the truth and His truth will set you free!

2 COR 3:17, JOHN 8:31-32, 15:7-8 (ESV)

August 17

"But the Advocate, the Holy Spirit, whom the Father will send in my name, will teach you all things and will remind you of everything I have said to you."
JOHN 14:26

Jesus modeled vulnerability. He remained authentic-true to being the person God called Him to be. He could do this because He knew Who He belonged to. His Father was "well pleased" with Him; He was approved. Until a person knows she is approved she fears ridicule and rejection from others. Jesus boldly carried out requests from God because He knew He was loved-trusting God to sustain and supply all His needs.

God's love gives you the courage to follow Jesus. His love is your lifeline-continuing to increase your freedom as you move closer to Him. Do you feel misunderstood or disconnected? Do you have secrets you will take to your grave for fear others would not accept you? Do you only show parts of you-fearing the other parts of you would be rejected? Go to Jesus, your only source for answers. He's waiting to show you love. His love gives you life, direction and purpose. Forgetting the past and looking forward to what lies ahead, embrace God's truth...you're His masterpiece-created to do the good things He planned long ago! Have you completely surrendered to Jesus-making His Will...your will?

If you're holding back from Jesus, you will hold back from others; your relationship with Jesus is reflected in your relationship with others. You will never experience the fullness and completeness Christ wants to offer you-until you completely surrender. Let God open up your mind to understand His Word. You were designed by Him to connect intimately, be vulnerable and walk with others to carry out His plans.

Get quiet and listen...the Advocate, Strengthener, Standby, Holy Spirit, Whom the Father will send in My name-in my place, to represent Me and act on My behalf, will teach you all things. He will remind you of and bring to your remembrance everything I have told you. You are loved, my friend. Let God show you how you can love and connect with others the way He designed... be vulnerable and experience authenticity!

REV. 3:20; PHIL. 3:13; EPH. 2:10; 2 COR. 3:17; LUKE 24:45; JOHN 14:26

August 18

"A person's wisdom yields patience;
it is to one's glory to overlook an offense."
PROV. 19:11

Most agree they're offended in some way each day; some big and others small, but it's the offenses from other Christians that can knock us out of the race that God's put us in...if we let them. Being offended by another Christian hurts, but mostly surprising because we're on the same team and we don't expect injury from them. We expect help from them. As hurtful as this is-it's real. But, you can learn how to overcome as God instructs.

Here's what you can do to ensure you stay in the race your Father's called you to. 1) Acknowledge your injury; your hurt is real and your feelings are valid. To dismiss what you went through only puts a "Christian-ese" Band-Aid on and results in permanent injury. Proper treatment requires you to release your injury to God-then He can heal you. You can then get back in the race; 2) Know these truths: another person can't diminish your purpose, devalue your worth or destroy your destiny, because....you're God's masterpiece. He's approved you and He has good plans for your life! These are God's truths for you, but they won't make a difference in your life...unless you choose to believe them for you; and 3) Be prudent and ask God for wisdom-He gives it generously.

God requires you to *forgive* everyone, He doesn't require you to *believe* everyone. A person can say they're sorry each time they cause an offense, but if they're not making changes, they're looking the part but not changing their heart. Unless notice-able changes are evident-there's no heart change and you'd be foolish to expose yourself to the same situation and expect a different response.

Apply these steps each time you're injured. It's hard to believe our Christian teammates would cause harm, but it's real. Don't lose heart-God oversees this race and He sees everything that goes on. Keep your eyes on the prize, be patient, endure, re-main steadfast...so you may receive, carry away and enjoy to the full what God has promised!

EPH. 2:10; COL. 2:10; JER. 29:11; PROV. 14:25; GAL. 6:9; HEB. 10:36

August 19

"But thanks be to God, who always leads us as captives in Christ's triumphal procession and uses us to spread the aroma of the knowledge of him everywhere."
2 COR. 2:14

Most delays and detours on the journey God calls us to are due to the self-imposed roadblocks of unbelief! We know we heard the Spirit give us direction, but we reasoned the impossibility in our mind, with thoughts like "what if I don't have enough; it's not possible, no way can that happen; I might miss God people will think I'm crazy," and so on.

God has never once expected us to come up with the answers or asked us to figure out a way to overcome the impossibles we see...but He *does* expect us to rely on Him for the provisions needed. Then, as we're moving forward in faith He provides us with what we need while He directs our next step. And this is how we learn to walk by faith not by sight, moving forward in God's confidence and His strength to take down one roadblock of unbelief at a time! So move forward in His confidence, get comfortable in trusting and believing He will provide all you need during the journey while on the way to your destination.

PROV. 3:5-6; 2 COR. 5:7

August 20

"As each has received a gift, use it to serve one another,
as good stewards of God's varied grace:"
I PETER 4:10 (ESV)

You don't choose a passion...God chooses you for a passion! When you know Him and are known by Him-your passion rises up! It has to; it's God's design. His love gives you the fuel to drive it! A passion doesn't rely on popular opinion or wait for approval; you have to carry it out whether you're paid for it or not! You naturally flow in it, not because of *your ability*, but because of *God's ability in you.*

But here's the tricky part: only through *opposition* can a passion be refined to sustain the course of time. And this is where many people drop out. They become offended, take their passion and go home! And it's exactly what the enemy wants...to debilitate and send them home! This is where a choice has to be made: obey God and fulfill the passion, or sit around and talk about your injury!

Remember that God puts a passion in us-we have the privilege of carrying it out. When we're offended we must seek God for healing and direction; He gives us the stamina and endurance to be refined, and His love and comfort enable us to sustain the course! Many want to argue the unfairness of it. God never said things would be fair, but He *did* say He'd bring to completion what He started in us! Ask Jesus about things being unfair...then remember how God brought to completion what He started in Him! So, how are you coming along on carrying out your passion?

PS. 37:5-6; PROV. 3:5-6; JOHN 19:17-27; 1 PETER 4:10 (ESV)

August 21

"But when you ask, you must believe and not doubt, because the one who doubts is like a wave of the sea, blown and tossed by the wind."
JAMES 1:6

God knows how hectic your schedule is. He knows more about it than you do. None of us are exempt from life's hectic schedules, but if we're believers, we have a Helper Who promises to guide us in managing them and gives us the wisdom and stamina to maintain them also...*if we ask*.

God is clear. He wants us to ask Him for wisdom and He promises to give it generously without finding fault-*but* when we ask we're to believe He will provide and not doubt. The person who doubts is like a wave of the sea blown and tossed about; he believes his livelihood is subjected to the hectic schedules life imposes. This is a fixed false belief that has to replaced with God's truth, then this truth has to be *maintained* by renewing your mind every day with God's promises.

Every one of God's promises is true and full of power, but *a promise not believed has no power*...no matter how true it is. God's truth is your lifeline to overcoming the reality of hectic schedules. Replace fixed false beliefs with God's Word, seek the Holy Spirt, sit with and talk to Him. Do this day in and day out to execute the truth and power that God promises!

JAMES 1:2-8; MATT. 21:21; EPH. 4:14

August 22

"Be kind to one another, tenderhearted, forgiving one another, as God in Christ forgave you."
EPH. 4:32 (ESV)

Holding onto blame holds you back from living the life God has planned...He's factored in everything to include all the wrongs you've done and all the wrongs done to you. Choosing to forgive yourself and others allows God to take care of what

matters. He's capable and will exceed your greatest expectations - but you have to let go of blame...will you?

PHIL. 4:19; ISAIAH 61:1-3; 1 COR. 2:5; EPH. 4:32 (ESV)

August 23

"May you be strengthened with all power, according to his glorious might,
for all endurance and patience with joy."
COL. 1:11 (ESV)

Your best is not enough...that's a hard statement to read-but it's
true. God will meet you at the end of your best-every time, if
you rely on Him to give you strength. Where your strength
ends-God's grace begins. His ability connects to the end of your
ability. His grace is sufficient for you-His power is made
perfect...in your weakness. (SEE 2 COR. 12:9)

What's overwhelming you...a job, financial concerns, parenting, marriage, career path, friendships, your future, uncertainty
regarding the course of your life, a child with special needs,
betrayal, a doubting mind, grief so heavy it weighs you down
daily, figuring out how you will get through school and manage
your family, how will you ever get out of debt, and on and on?
God sees what you're going through, so release it to Him.

God will give you the strength to do the things He's called you
to do, but you must rely on Him. Where your strength ends-His
begins. Do your best-give what you have and then God will give
you the endurance and patience you need to keep moving forward. Will you accept His grace and let His power be made
perfect...in your weakness?

PHIL. 4:13; 2 COR. 12:9; COL. 1:11 (ESV)

August 24

"...so that your faith might not rest on human wisdom, but on God's power."
1 COR. 2:5

Oh, the freedom that's felt when we can rest in the truth that God is our source for anything we need or desire in this life...where the Spirit of the Lord is, there is freedom. What a relief to know that our future isn't determined by the wisdom of men but rests in God's power. Until you can rest in God and believe His promises, you'll be at the mercy of others-looking to them to deliver what you need or desire. God is your only source but you give people this authority when you put them on the throne instead of God. I did this for years. I said I believed God's promises, but I put my hope in man's wisdom, not God's power, to deliver my destiny. My prayers focused on complaints, frustration and fear instead of thanksgiving, hope and love. I would faithfully seek Christ, only to consistently rely on people to deliver what I asked for in prayer.

God works through people-we're His vessels, but if there's an unwilling vessel He will use another one. This doesn't exempt us from unfair things happening while God situates things for us, but we can be confident He's with us...a righteous man will have many troubles and God will deliver him from each one. Everyday trouble will send you a personal invitation to join the doubt and discouragement club. Decline the invite! There will always be a teachers who treat your child wrong, financial concerns, crazy bosses, job cuts, Christians who do bad things, unfit coaches, people who let you down, poor financial forecasts, board members who lie, untrustworthy neighbors, tough times in the economy, dishonest congressmen and so on...and *not one of them determine your destiny*-only God does.

Trust Him-believe His promises...and He will make the your righteousness shine like the dawn and the justice of your cause like the noonday sun. Will you accept the freedom God offers you and rest in Him?

PS. 34:19, 37:6; 1 COR. 2:5; 2 COR. 3:17

August 25

*"And give thanks for everything to God the Father
in the name of our Lord Jesus Christ."*
EPH. 5:20 (NLT)

Every day I speak God's truth and choose to agree with it, even though I may feel nothing like what He says I am. I still say: I'm His masterpiece (EPH. 2:10), fearfully and wonderfully made (PS 139:14), unblemished and holy (EPH. 5:27), more than a conqueror (ROM. 8:37), He has good plans for me (JER. 29:11), He will exceedingly abundantly more than I ever dare ask or imagine (EPH. 3:20), I'm favored-God is pleased and delighted with me (PS. 90:17, 41:11, 147:11), and many more, but thats the general idea.

Your past died at the cross with Jesus, it's done. You must decide if you believe it's true, not because you *feel* it, but because Jesus *said* it. But if you think on your past, you will keep it alive in your mind. Speak God's truth so you will know His truth and be free (JOHN 8:32). Give all of yourself (mind, body and spirit) to Christ-replace your deception with His truth and be transformed into seeing as He sees (ROM. 12:1-2). Be deliberate in thinking on God's truth-if not, you're thinking on what opposes His truth...*there's no in-between.* Be purposed in receiving His promises-they're yours but you must *claim* them. Your past is dead at the cross...will you let it die in your mind too?

EPH. 2:10, 5:27; PS. 41:11, 90:17, 139:14, 147:11; JER. 29:11; ROM. 8:37; JOHN 8:32

August 26

*"There is therefore now no condemnation to them which are in Christ Jesus,
who walk not after the flesh, but after the Spirit."*
ROM. 8:1 (KJV)

Make a decision to not go on any more lunch dates with condemnation! Jesus sees past...your past. He sees you as God's unique creation with a good future. If you're experiencing any condemnation, it's not from Jesus, so strike it down with the Word. You are fearfully and wonderfully made, more than a conqueror, soaring high like an eagle, there are good plans to prosper you-giving you hope and a future, if God's for you who can be against you.

Agree with what Jesus sees, not what condemnation is asking you to see! No more lunch dates with condemnation-he's not your friend; he wants to steal the promises of God from you. Tell him it's time to go...that you've got a future full of good plans from God to fulfill.

ROM. 8:1-2(KJV); PS. 31:7 (NLT), 62:1-2

August 27

"The integrity of the upright guides them,
but the unfaithful are destroyed by their duplicity."
PROV. 11:3

Every day integrity...don't compromise the seemingly small things and miss out on the big things God wants to entrust to you! Life will give you plenty of opportunities to be tempted and tested-you choose whether you will pass or fail. God is always giving you opportunities to pass, while the enemy is forever trying to get you to fail. How many times have you been given extra change or not been charged for an item, etc? When these things happen do not claim them as God's favor-*God's not blessing you...He's testing you*!

Temptations you face are no different from what others experience-God is faithful and He won't allow the temptation you're facing to be more than you can handle. God wants you to pass-He will show you a way out...you decide if you will trust Him when He does.

Whoever can be trusted with very little can also be trusted with much, and whoever is dishonest with very little will also be dishonest with much.

"The integrity of the upright guides them, but the unfaithful are destroyed by their duplicity." (SEE PROV. 11:3). Everyday integrity...don't compromise yours.

I COR. 10:13; LUKE 16:10; PROV. 11:3

August 28

"If we are thrown into the blazing furnace, the God we serve is able to deliver us from it, and he will deliver us from Your Majesty's hand."
DAN. 3:17

Throughout scripture, the people who believed God in the impossible situations they faced where the same ones who witnessed His miraculous provisions. Don't you know Shadrach, Meshach and Abednego were ready to meet the Lord when they were thrown into the fiery furnace. Still, they stood firm, believing God. They didn't know *how* God would provide for them, but they held onto His truth...that He *would provide* for them!

When you set your mind in advance to believe God will provide everything you need in every situation...you've made a bridge that will walk you through every burden you will ever face. That bridge is Jesus! With Jesus you can do all things He strengthens you to do. This mindset keeps you focused on Jesus as your bridge and keeps desperation from flooding your mind! The burden remains, but you're not responsible to resolve it-it's not on you...it's in Jesus' hands. You move ahead in what you know to do, which will seem crazy in the natural. This may lead you right into the fiery furnace; if so, know Jesus is with you and He will never leave you.

Most burdens require us to walk into the fire to stand on what we say we believe. This is how we build our faith. Nobody wants to walk in the fire, but after we walk out we know that no devil in hell can ever take what we believe! And each fire brings a greater revelation of our powerful, mighty and sweet Jesus! The more we know Him, the more we know that nothing can ever separate us from His love! Will you put your hope is in Him all day long and His let His joy complete you?

JOHN 15:11, 16:33; PHIL. 3:10, 4:13; HEB. 6:19; PHIL. 4:7; DAN. 3:17; MATT. 5:16, 19:26; JER. 29:11; PS. 25:5

August 29

"If it is possible, as far as it depends on you, live at peace with everyone."
ROM. 12:18

Conflict leads to increase connectedness if viewed and resolved from a godly perspective. Jesus modeled dealing with conflict in the gospels-He was unwilling to settle for anything less than the truth and freedom God promised.

Many avoid conflict because it takes time, effort, work, honesty, and vulnerability, bringing flaws into the light and taking re-sponsibility, preferring the other person's feelings and making apologies. *The process is tiring...but the investment is priceless!* Every conflict process is an opportunity to increase truth in the relationship. Truth is the cornerstone for freedom to be exercised-walking out the purpose God planned for your life.

Those willing to address conflicts invest their time, mind and hearts, and it pays off-returning high yields of peace and en-joyment throughout the course of the relationship. Those un-willing to address conflict settle for strain and strife, a baseline of dissatisfaction robbing them of the freedom that truth promises. Are you willing to address conflict so you can live in the truth and freedom God offers?

EPH. 4:24-28; JOHN 8:32; PHIL. 2:14; PROV. 8;7; 2 COR. 3:17; ROM. 12:18

August 30

"Do not be conformed to this world, but be transformed by the renewal of your mind, that by testing you may discern what is the will of God, what is good and acceptable and perfect."
ROM. 12:2 (ESV)

Dare to believe...God gives each of us an imagination to see what He sees-to give us hope for our future. Within seconds our imagination can elicit all five senses and recall an event from yesterday, or go back 30 years and remember a specific event. Your imagination is designed to see the promises of God. See yourself as an overcomer, loved and valued. See relation-ships being restored, burdens lifted, new career, a ministry, family members being saved.

Use the power of your imagination the way God intended: for His glory and honor...believing His promises. Do not allow Satan to use your imagination for harm, to create despair, or to be overwhelmed with potential bleak outcomes. You must immediately come against the strongholds he tries to set up in your mind...he is a liar! Ask Jesus for help...He's knocking on the door of your heart-let Him in to help you with doubt, fears and old hurts that continue to haunt you and whisper lies of despair. See what God sees for your life...He has good plans! Dare to believe!

ROM. 12:2; REV. 3:20; JER. 29:11

August 31

"And God is able to make all grace abound to you, so that having all suffi-ciency in all things at all times, you may abound in every good work."
2 COR. 9:8 (ESV)

God never trades even...give Him what you've got and He will give you what He has! It's an uneven trade every time, with you always giving far less than what God gives back to you! God will generously provide all you need, with plenty left over to share with others! Your mind will never comprehend how God's ways work. Doing the math won't get you the answer...but having faith will!

Don't allow reasoning to rob you of the promises God has made to you. Today will you take the risk and give God your first and best-trust Him with every concern in your life and not hold anything back? God never trades even!

2 COR. 9:8 (ESV); MARK 11:22; PROV. 3:9-10

†

September 1

"But we do not belong to those who shrink back and are destroyed,
but to those who have faith and are saved."
HEB. 10:39

Most delays and detours on the journey are due to our own self-imposed road blocks in our mind! We know we heard God in our spirit give us direction in an area of our life, but we reasoned in our mind how impossible it would be to carry out by saying things like..."what if I don't have enough, it's not possible, no way can that happen, I might miss God, people will think I'm crazy," and so on.

God doesn't expect us to have the answers for what He asks of us...He wants us to rely on Him for the provisions needed to move forward on the course He's called us to! Then, while we're moving forward He provides what we need and directs our next step. This is how we walk by faith, not sight! And, with each step we gain in God's confidence we take down another road block in His strength! Keep moving friend...you're making progress!

PROV. 3:5-6; 2 COR. 5:7; HEB. 10:39

September 2

"My comfort in my suffering is this: Your promise preserves my life."
PS. 119:50

Hope gone; a mist fading...then no more. You poured your life into what's now gone. What do you do now; how do you go on? You can't; you've already tried. You're out of resources with no plan. But, dear God, whatever you do, don't try to handle this alone any longer. Your strength is gone and your mind isn't clear, so... call on the name of Jesus! His hope anchors your soul, and keeps you holding on when you can't. He knows pain and grief-He took on hell when He gave His life for you. And because He did-the tomb's empty...God's hope makes the dead rise up and live-forever! Don't try to figure this out. Follow Jesus and He will lead you directly into God's Hope.

PS. 39:7, HEB. 6:19, 10:36; PS. 119:50, 105

September 3

"But we have this treasure in jars of clay to show that this all-surpassing power is from God and not from us."
2 COR. 4:7

God will do exceedingly, abundantly, more than you could ever imagine, beyond your ability...according to the power that's at work within you. The degree you believe in the power that's alive and at work within you will determine the level of manifestation released through you! God has equipped you with everything you need to fulfill every plan He's made for you. Your part is to believe in Him, seek Him first in all you do and then give all you have on the altar for His glory!

Daily, be purposed in reading the Word and spending time with God, placing His written Word on your phone and around your home, hanging out with friends who will hold you accountable, and speak truth to you, and most of all have faith constantly! If you focus on the facts - your actual inabilities - you will become overwhelmed and hand over the triumph that God's truth promises you. Don't be shocked when trials come to remind you of your weaknesses-they will. During each trial allow God's power to be perfected in your weakness! God goes before you and follows behind you. He never leaves you to your own ability. Put your faith in God's power...not the wisdom of man, and you will see Him do exceedingly, abundantly more than you could ever imagine!

2 COR. 4:7, 12:9; JOHN 6:29; PHIL. 2:13; EPH. 3:20; PS. 139:5; 1 COR. 2:5

September 4

"..that according to the riches of his glory he may grant you to be strengthened with power through his Spirit in your inner being."
EPH. 3:16 (ESV)

Being rooted in God's love allows a person to release the persons who offended them and the wounds received, or to release themselves from the offense and the wounds they imposed. Where the Spirit of the Lord is, there is freedom! God's love heals and binds up wounds, restoring what was lost, stolen, taken or imposed. Human love makes sincere attempts, but ultimately reaches an end. God's love has no end! I see this often in working with people...they too quickly respond with the "right" Christian behavior, which is to forgive or apologize, but there's no revelation behind their decision...so there's no resolution. Any issue that is resolved and leads to revelation is done via Holy Spirit intervention; our human love is unable to have revelation apart from Him.

Change happens on the inside and then works its way to the outside and it's the heart where change begins! Many attempt to address the hurt with their human love, but don't process the pain with the Holy Spirit, Who turns information into revelation. Without revelation, a person may believe in their mind they have insight, but a mind's reasoning apart from the Holy Spirit leads to dead ends! And this death is moving forward without God's love! You don't have to. God is with you! Will you let Him help you?

Prov. 16:25; Eph. 3:16-17; 1 Cor. 16:13

September 5

"Instead of shame and dishonor, you will enjoy a double share of honor."
Isaiah 61:7 (NLT)

Don't carry your pain another day or let it be your identity. Your identity is in Christ, *not* in what you did or what happened to you. No pain is in vain in the hands of God. He doesn't waste pain, but you have to release it so God can use it!

Instead of shame and dishonor, you will enjoy a double share of honor, possess a double portion of prosperity in your land and everlasting joy will be yours! Will you release your pain into the hands of God today?

Prov. 3:5; Ps. 34:19; Isaiah 61:7 (NLT)

September 6

"When we tell you these things, we do not use words that come from human wisdom. Instead, we speak words given to us by the Spirit, using the Spirit's words to explain spiritual truths."
1 COR. 2:13 (NLT)

The enemy's a master at mind games and he will trip you up by questioning your motives from a human perspective, but not a Spirit led revelation. The mind can't comprehend what the Spirit reveals-it has to accept it through faith, which is revelation from the Holy Spirit. When you begin to reason what the Holy Spirit prompts you to do, your mind rejects how ridiculous the request is. This is where the enemy gets you off course. So, you have to renew your mind with God's truth, *"humanly speaking it is impossible, but not with God"* (SEE MARK 10:27). Put your faith in God's power, not man's wisdom. Moving ahead in faith is how you strengthen your "trust muscles" by having God lead you, and believing the anointing He put in you to hear Him guide you.

1 JOHN 2:27; 1 COR. 2:5, 13 (NLT); MARK 10:27

September 7

"We were buried therefore with him by baptism into death, in order that, just as Christ was raised from the dead by the glory of the Father, we too might walk in newness of life."
ROM. 6:4 (ESV)

You don't have to prove your worth. Jesus did that for you on the cross. Your part is to walk in the power that raised Him from the dead! That power is His Spirit, the Holy Spirit, Who is alive in you to glorify God by carrying out the plans He made for you long ago! Don't try to reason this truth in your mind...you will talk yourself out of believing God's truth.

But you can renew the spirit of your mind, which is submitting your mind to the Holy Spirit's lead and He will give you the desire and power to walk in God's truth! No person can walk in God's truth apart from the Holy Spirit; what God asks of us is impossible, but He never expected us to do anything independent of Him. So seek God in all you do, every hour of the day, in both big and small things because your Father God loves you and is interested in every big and small thing you do!

ROM. 6:3-6 (ESV), 12:2; EPH. 4:23

September 8

"Jesus replied, 'What is impossible with man is possible with God.'"
LUKE 18:27

Don't settle...nothing compares to knowing the love God has for you and being known by Him. It's where your security and identity come together to form the foundation for the authentic person He designed you to be, and to carry out the good plans in this world for His glory. His love enables you to rest in His sufficiency...you're approved so you no longer feel compelled to prove! You're valuable because you belong to Him-not because of what you do for Him, but you won't know this until you walk out what you profess to believe about Him! I pray you will accept all the love God has for you and walk out the authentic life He planned for you long ago...don't settle!

LUKE 18:27; 1 COR. 1:27; ACTS 4:31; 2 COR. 12:9; EPH. 2:10; PS. 127:1-2

September 9

"Be careful what you are hearing. The measure [of thought and study] you give [to the truth you hear] will be the measure [of virtue and knowledge] that comes back to you—and more [besides] will be given to you who hear."
MARK 4:24 (AMP)

This is such an encouraging scripture. God is truth and He clearly tells us that if we seek Him we will find Him! And the more we seek Him the more revelation of truth we will have about Him. This revelation of truth is what sets us free to know our identity is found exclusively in Him!

Knowing our identity is in God enables us to move through difficult seasons of isolation, stand up against opposition and most of all know His love and be known by His love! His love is the sustenance of our being; it's why we exist, can love others, and do the good works He planned long ago! Will you be purposed in putting thought and study into God's truth so you can know Him and be known by Him?

MARK 4:24 (AMP); LUKE 6:38, 11:8-10; MATT. 13:12; 1 COR. 8:3; LUKE 11:8-10

September 10

"These things I have spoken to you, so that in Me you may have peace. In the world you have tribulation, but take courage; I have overcome the world."
JOHN 16:33 (ESV)

Despite the grace and truth God offers us to turn mistakes around, many of us get caught in yet another mind game of the enemy; he comes at us with "how many times are you going to let God down?" Don't take the bait of Satan. It's true, we mess up a bunch, but God's grace and truth are bigger than any mess we can make! Grace accepts us where we are and God's truth shows us where we are! The two work in tandem to help us overcome any mess!

God wants you to succeed-He made you because He first loved you, but He also purposed you to do the works that He planned long ago. Focusing on areas where you've messed up keeps you from experiencing God's love. If you're not experiencing His love, you won't be able to receive His grace and truth. Without grace and truth you're not able to carry out what He's called you to do...you see the vicious cycle, right? Will you agree with God's truth, even when you don't feel it? How you feel doesn't change God's truth...but God's truth will change how you feel! God's not going to give up on you...so don't give up on Him!

JOHN 8:32, 15:5, 16:33 (ESV), 14:26-27

September 11

"You have granted me life and favor, and Your providence has preserved my spirit."
JOB 10:12 (AMP)

Doubt is powerful because it's based on facts. When it knocks on the door of your mind and screams: "you don't have the ability to do what God calls you to do." It's correct - *you* don't.

This is a fact. For you to do what God calls you to do, you have to completely rely on the Holy Spirit's power that lives in you...*this is the truth*! What a relief to know God's truth trumps facts; although you're limited in ability and strength, when tethered to God's strength you can do all things because God's strength flows through you!

So face it! Doubt's accusations are based on facts, but big whoop...your strength is totally dependent on the power that raised Jesus' dead body! It's not about what you can do, it's about what the power of the Holy Spirit does through you! And this is the truth that trumps facts! So think on this truth and ask God to help you when doubt knocks on the door of your mind. God will give you the desire and power to follow Him with the help of the Holy Spirit at work within you. Will you let Him?

Job 10:12 (AMP); 1 Cor. 15:57 (ESV); 1 John 5:4

September 12

"Every word of God proves true;
he is a shield to those who take refuge in him."
Prov. 30:5 (ESV)

Don't let this wilderness season discourage you...it seems like you're going nowhere, but God is developing you-He never wastes pain! We never like these seasons, but it's the only way God can build our endurance, perseverance and confident expectation.

How can we endure unless there's something we need to push through? Is there any other way to persevere other than press back when we're pressed on? And, finally, how can we have a confident expectation in God unless we're placed in a season where we know He's undeniably our only Source?

Don't be discouraged; remember this...every end leads to a new beginning, a closed door leads to an open door, and an old season must end for a new one to begin! *"For I am about to do something new. See, I have already begun! Do you not see it? I will make a pathway through the wilderness. I will create rivers in the dry wasteland.*" (SEE ISAIAH 43:19). Lift your head, continue to move forward-God has a good plan! Will you see with your eyes of faith?

ISAIAH 43:19; PS. 3:3, 5:12; PROV. 30:5 (ESV)

September 13

"In him and through faith in him we may approach God with freedom and confidence."
EPH. 3:12

Set your mind free...submit it to God's truth and seek the Holy Spirit for direction. He has all the answers! The mind apart from the Holy Spirit's direction will manifest agitation, fear and an overall uneasiness. When facing trials, we have a tendency to only take the big ones to God and handle the smaller one ourselves-this is called denial. Apart from God we don't handle anything, but pride will convince us we don't need to bother God with the little things...oh, the deceptive things we entertain to massage our ego! Will you submit your mind to God's truth today in all you do?

EPH. 3:12; HEB. 4:16; ISAIAH 26:3 (AMP)

September 14

"I will not be seized with alarm and struck with fear, for it is my Father's good pleasure to give me the kingdom."
LUKE 12:32 (AMP)

God promises victory to every Christian; no person is exempt and there's no unique situation that His love can't overcome! God only asks one thing of us, and that is to believe in His Son, Jesus Christ. And it's this one truth where the mind sets up roadblocks-we just can't wrap our mind around this truth. And the reason we can't is...*we* can't! Only the Holy Spirit can translate this information of truth into revelation of truth, then our mind can choose to believe it. Jesus did all the work for us-we can't add any works to it. This places us in a vulnerable and humble position.

There's nothing we can do to earn or pay back what Jesus did for us other than to humbly receive it with unqualified assurance...this removes us from the equation of salvation and completely gives full credit to Jesus Christ our Savior and Lord! We can't earn the love Christ freely gives, nor can we achieve or take credit for His death on the cross or the power that raised Him from the dead; He freely gave us everything that was His the day we gave our life to Him!

So all this leads to the reality that you can't save or change yourself...if you could you wouldn't need a Savior! God doesn't invite you to give up your life for His then figure out how to follow Him. He lovingly calls you to Him, to rest in, depend on and seek Him for everything you need and desire. God will never give up on you...don't ever give up on Him. Keep the Word in your mind, put your eyes on it, speak and profess it-believe it with all your heart, mind and soul constantly...and you will be prosperous in all you do! *"Are you so foolish, senseless and silly? Having begun [your new life spiritually] with the Holy Spirit...are you now reaching perfection by depending on your ability?"* (SEE GAL. 3:3 AMP)

GAL. 3:3 (AMP); LUKE 12:32 (AMP); I CHRON. 16:34

September 15

"Casting down imaginations, and every high thing that exalteth itself against the knowledge of God, and bringing into captivity every thought to the obedience of Christ."
2 COR. 10:5 (KJV)

What is the wall that's keeping you from fulfilling the dreams and desires God put in your heart long ago? Do you believe the situation you're facing is too messed up, broken, hopeless or lost? Can you even remember why you stopped dreaming or shut off your desires? Are you just going through the motions to put another day behind you? Are anger, irritability, and anxiety more familiar to you than faith, hope and love?

There is no wall big enough to keep you from fulfilling what God's planned for you, other than the wall of your thoughts opposing God's truth. God is waiting for you to invite Him to tear down the wall in your mind. He will meet you there at the wall of thoughts that are opposing His truth and He will begin to demolish the strongholds in your mind! Will you invite Him today? God's Word is like a hammer that breaks rock into pieces...there's no wall of strongholds that it can't take down! Will you invite God today to help you knock down the walls that are keeping you from fulfilling the dreams and desires He put in your heart long ago?

PROV. 3:5-6; MARK 4:19; EPH. 4:23-24; 2 COR. 10:5 (KJV)

September 16

"Do not be conformed to this world,
but be transformed by the renewal of your mind."
ROM. 12:2 (ESV)

Your spirit was saved at salvation, but your mind wasn't! Your mind has to be "saved" every day for the rest of your life, until you meet Jesus face-to-face! To live the saved life and walk in the victory God has promised, you have to renew your mind with His word.

Many days negative thoughts, potential disasters and threats of not having what you need are waiting to take you under with the intent to steal the life Jesus promises. To counter and over-come these thoughts, you have to renew your mind with God's truth: meditate on the Word, hold tight to it and put our eyes on it. But, be careful, don't confuse your feelings with God's truth. Some days I don't feel like a conqueror; I feel afraid, awkward and anxious, *but God says* I am more than a conqueror...so I agree with Him even though I don't feel like it.

I profess the Word over and over, write in on index cards, post it on my phone, highlight it in my Bible, keep it tucked in my heart, and close to my reach so my eyes can see and read it. Eventually, breakthrough comes...not because I am strong, but because God's Spirit is strong in me and His strength is made perfect in my weakness!

ROM. 6:4, 8:37, 12:2 (ESV); EPH. 4:23

September 17

*"We can rejoice, too, when we run into problems and trials,
for we know that they help us develop endurance."*
ROM. 5:3 (NLT)

What you profess to believe about God and you is revealed when you face adversity in life. Adversity knocks down props, messes up routines and removes façades presented to others...making a way for the authentic person God designed you to be and for you to be comfortable with you!!!

Embrace adversity; it grows your faith, develops your character, and sets you free...you don't have to make a way for yourself-God has already done that. But you *do* have to agree with His truth and be willing to take risks, especially leaving your comfort zones and being ready for opposition. When you accept the revelation that God's planned every second of your life, you will begin to let go of anxiety about being overlooked, not being good enough or not having what it takes.

Each time you face adversity, you have an opportunity to lay down who you think you are and become more of who God says you are-His masterpiece...created to do the good works He planned long ago. Are you ready to ditch your plans for His?

JAMES 1:2-8; JOHN 8:32; EPH. 2:10; ROM. 5:3 (NLT)

September 18

*"For freedom Christ has set us free; stand firm therefore,
and do not submit again to a yoke of slavery."*
GAL. 5:1 (ESV)

You are free, but you won't live like it until you accept that truth first in your mind. This requires you to be engaged in a constant active mental process of renewing your mind with God's Word and continually seeking the guidance of the Holy Spirit to execute and walk in the Word. This is a full time job, but so is anything you think in your mind!

Rise up and receive the freedom Jesus gave you the day He saved you; His death took the power of sin off of you so you would have the freedom to walk out the good plans God made for you long ago! You were created specifically to make a difference in this world; to let God's light shine through you! You are free indeed...will you rise up and live like it?

John 8:36; 1 Cor. 7:22; Gal. 5:1 (ESV)

September 19

"Let us examine our ways and test them, and let us return to the LORD."
Lam. 3:40

We justify being mostly faithful to God...reasoning that at least we are more faithful than most. But *mostly* isn't *completely*, and less-than-completely isn't acceptable to God. "Mostly" leaves room in our heart for someone or something else. It interferes and weakens our direct relationship with God. In counseling, this is called triangulation: a third party is involved in a two person communication. This weakens and breaks down communication between the two. Anything we allow to be placed between us and God weakens our relationship with Him. The first commandment says to have no other gods, so if we're being mostly faithful, we've allowed another god in our heart. Justification focuses on being mostly faithful to the first commandment to reasoning..."I'm walking out numbers 2-10." This is a huge problem because if the first isn't kept...the others don't matter!!!

Think about it this way: a spouse justifying he or she is mostly faithful because of providing financially, caring for the children, verbalizing love, etc. If they're not completely faithful-the covenant is violated; the other things don't matter! Accepting mostly faithful would adulterate the exclusiveness of the marriage covenant with the other spouse. And neither can God allow us to adulterate our exclusive covenant with Him. The good news is He meets us in our understanding and will show us what's in our heart that's interfering in our relationship with Him. Will you ask Him to search your heart?

Ex. 20:1-17; Ps. 139:23-24; James 1:5; Lam. 3:40; Mark 12:30

September 20

"He will be the sure foundation for your times, a rich store of salvation and wisdom and knowledge; the fear of the LORD is the key to this treasure."
ISAIAH 33:6

Are you uncertain about some things, not sure how to proceed...setting goals, need advice in your marriage, family or profession, carrying a dream in your heart that's so impossible you don't even speak it, overwhelmed with finances, having boundary issues? Then spend time with Jesus-He knows what you need to succeed! You have many plans, but only His prevail! Don't be deceived, apart from Him you can do nothing, but with Him you can accomplish what He calls you to! Seek Him first...until you do nothing else matters!

JOHN 15:5; MATT 6:33; ISAIAH 33:6

September 21

"Set your mind on the things above, not on earthly things."
COL. 3:2

Spend time with Jesus daily studying scripture. How can you know what His promises are unless you read them? Many say they don't have time, but...how can you not have time to invest in your future! Expect opposition daily- these trials strengthen you; every time you're pushed on...press in and back and you will become stronger, like a muscle being developed to peak performance! Embrace trials, they mature you! God's always ready to give wisdom...*if you ask*. Are you going to respond to God's call? Don't forgo the future He planned for you...you will miss absolutely loving the rest of your life! *"Yet, I am with you always!"* (SEE MATT. 28:20)

JER. 29:11; PS. 73:26, 139:16; PHIL. 3:10, 4:13; ROM. 8:31; JAMES 1:2-5

September 22

"Truly I tell you, if anyone says to this mountain, 'Go, throw yourself into the sea,' and does not doubt in their heart but believes that what they say will happen, it will be done for them."
MARK 11:23

Don't be shocked when doubt side-swipes you while you're following God and being faithful. First, following God doesn't exempt us from hardships, but following *does* promise He will bring us through them. Second, the enemy wants you to think that if you're going through a difficult season, you're somehow messing up or missing God, so he questions you from an appearing prudent perspective with questions like...are you being selfish, maybe God doesn't trust you, are you sure you heard God correctly? All of these are valid questions and they might be true, but they don't eliminate you! When we're following God, His love is sufficient in filling in the gap for all the areas we are insufficient. He doesn't expect us to have it all together...He expects us to rely on Him to keep it all together!

Remember: the enemy gets you off course when he challenges your thoughts from a human perspective, which are logical. That's why it's critical you renew your mind with the Word daily then ask the Holy Spirit for revelation of what you're reading in the Word. This enables you to move forward in Spirit-led revelation and not be bound to the logic of human wisdom! This process enables God to add His super to your natural, and you will move forward despite the side-swipes of the enemy! Are you ready?

MARK 11:23; MATT. 17:20; JAMES 1:6

September 23

"I called out to the Lord & He answered me; He delivered me from all my fears-those who look to Him are radiant... their faces are never covered with shame."
PS. 34:4-5

If you've been hurt by someone who was supposed to love you...you will have a hard time believing that God chose to love you first. Only the love of God can begin to reverse your fragmented view of you and stop your mind from replaying the harsh words spoken over you, and heal the hurting parts of your heart. The wrong done to you bruised your memory and wounded your heart, but it didn't determine your value...Jesus did that when He died on the cross for you!!! Replace the wrong that was imposed on you with the truth of who God says you are...His chosen one-a masterpiece purposed to do the good works He planned long ago! If someone didn't love you like they were supposed to that doesn't make something wrong with you.

Will you make a decision to agree with who God says you are, then agree with it in your mind over and over and over...until the voice of condemnation is replaced with the love of Jesus Christ?

EPH. 1:11; PS. 25:5, 34:4-5; ISAIAH 61:1-3

September 24

"But thanks be to God!
He gives us the victory through our Lord Jesus Christ."
1 COR. 15:57

Listen to how you talk to yourself...it matters a bunch; so much that it determines the course of your life! You will not rise above your view of yourself or live the life God planned unless you're talking to yourself with His truth. You're His master-piece, more than a conqueror, and He supplied all your needs despite the dead dreams staring back at you...renew your mind with His truth even when you don't see or feel it! What you see and feel change-God's truth never changes...it's your anchor of hope when life looks and feels hopeless! How you talk to your-self matters a bunch, so much that it determines the course of your life!

HEB. 6:19; ROM. 8:37, 12:2; 1 COR. 15:57

September 25

"...yet I will rejoice in the LORD!
I will be joyful in the God of my salvation!"
HAB. 3:18 (NLT)

Dear child, come sit with Me; you're anxious and troubled about many things...I want you to know about My hope. My hope isn't like the hope in the world, where hope is based on a "maybe it will happen" hope or and "if you're lucky" hope. My hope is rooted in My truth and I can't lie! My hope goes ahead of you and follows behind you. It holds you together when life is falling apart. My hope promises clarity to the racing thoughts in your mind, comfort to the unknown groans from your soul, and flushes out the deep-rooted shame in your heart. My hope takes your depravity and gives you My dignity, exposes lies of rejection, and replaces each one with My loving truth!

My hope tells you that you matter to Me and you belong to Me. You are My child and I love you dearly! My hope rises up from within you to fight an army, scale a wall or stand alone if you need to! My hope enables you to believe when it looks crazy to do so, gives you the stamina to endure otherwise unbearable circumstances while continuing to believe I will come through for you, and lets you rest in Me.

My hope is your lifeline-available any time of the day or night, your shelter and comfort...it's always your home to run to! Most of all, child, I want you to know My hope is always for you and never against you- know My hope and be known by it; it will satisfy you all the days of your life and never disappoint you! Dear child, will you please put your hope in Me and let Me care for you?

ROM. 5:3-5, 8:31; PS. 139:5; HAB. 3:18 (NLT)

September 26

"The teaching of your word gives light, so even the simple can understand."
PSALM 119:130 (NLT)

Be purposed in embracing humility daily, and recognize that you can't successfully manage day to day living apart from the guidance of the Holy Spirit. Seek His truth for guidance in every area of our life-all big and small situations and everything in between. He will help you balance family, work, relationships, understand the desires of your heart, develop healthy friendships, choose an outfit for a party, have the right words to make a sincere apology, know which over the counter medicine to pick for a sick child, call a friend just when they needed encouragement, coordinate childcare, give you hope in a hopeless situation, etc. Don't ever minimize the gift of the Holy Spirit...He is your lifeline for stable living!

Be purposed in training your mind to ask the Holy Spirit throughout the day what He would say to you regarding the issue you're thinking about. This mental process keeps your mind submitted to His leading and prompting while keeping you tethered to His grace, which gives you the ability to exceed your own ability in executing tasks of daily living. Praise God you are never alone and thank Jesus He went away so we would always have a Comforter, Counselor and Advocate!

PSALM 119:130 (NLT); 2 COR. 6:6; ROM. 15:13; JOHN. 14:26, 16:13, 17:17

September 27

"...for though the righteous fall seven times, they rise again,"
PROV. 24:16

Trials, heartaches and disasters in life...hardships none of us escape. The best plans don't prevent them, nor does a strong walk with Christ spare us! God never promised believing Him would exempt us from hardship, but He did promise He would bring us through each one!

Do you completely trust God to bring you through hard seasons? If you mostly trust Him, you're not completely trusting Him and this leads to anxiety. Anxiety develops in the mind when an outcome is uncertain; it's our internal alarm to signal danger. The alarm goes off when we feel unsafe. If our alarm is working correctly we run to God when facing a hardship with certainty He will provide. We cause a malfunction when the alarm goes off and we try to take on the burden independent of Him or partially trust Him. To correct the error, we have to renew our mind with His truth: He is with us, will provide what we need and will bring us through it!

Your outcome is certain as a follower of Christ. God says to not fear or be dismayed. He will strengthen and uphold you. Believing God doesn't require you to know how He will deliver, but it does require you to believe He will, otherwise you forfeit the comfort He gives. If you struggle believing, ask the Holy Spirit to help you. He's your Helper and Comforter, and He will give you revelation! Only by faith can you believe God's promises, and only the Holy Spirit can give you the faith needed to believe!

And that brings this reality of truth full circle...we're not exempt from hardships, but we are promised that God will bring us through each one. Will you believe God to bring you through?

PS. 34:19; ISAIAH 41:10; HEB. 11:1; PHIL. 2:13, 4:19; ROM. 12:2; PROV. 24:16

September 28

"Fight the good fight of the faith."
1 TIM. 6:12

The long and hard seasons send us to the battlefield. It's where we come to know without a doubt...God loves us and He is for us! The decision to stay and fight when we feel like going home makes the enemy so stinking mad that he can't see straight and he will try everything he knows to take us down!

The enemy was sure you were going to give up by now, but he underestimated your revelation of knowing where your strength comes from! You have set your face like flint, refusing to back down; this revelation has ignited every neuron in your body...you know God's for you and the power that raised Jesus from the dead is alive and active in you! The harder the enemy pushes on you, the more you lean into the Holy Spirit's power at work in you! And this fierce fight of faith partners with God to bring His good plans to fruition through you!

I know one thing for sure...all of Heaven is cheering for you! Keep shining your light, baby. You're making a difference for Christ and He's pleased with you!

Rom. 8:31; Ps. 121:1-2; Mk. 10:32; Isaiah. 50:7; Eph. 6:13; 1 Tim. 6:12

September 29

"Let all that I am wait quietly before God, for my hope is in him."
Ps. 62:5 (NLT)

Despite the despair that's inevitable in life we're promised a hope that soothes our soul, joy that overflows and peace that surpasses human understanding. These are God's promises. Many ponder, debate and speculate meaning, validity and reliability, but at the end of the day it doesn't make them any less true! Jesus tells us in John 16:33, "I *have told you these things, so that in Me you may have peace-in this world you will have trouble, but take heart...I have overcome this world!"* Will you receive the hope, joy and peace that Jesus offers you each day?

Heb. 6:19; John 15:11; Phil. 4:7; Ps. 62.5 (NLT)

September 30

*"You go before me and follow me.
You place your hand of blessing on my head."*
Ps. 139:5 (NLT)

If you're feeling discouraged or overwhelmed let this truth give you hope...hardships and heartaches are inevitable in life-no person is exempt, but every person is promised a way out! The Lord's angels encamp around His loyal followers and delivers them; He pays attention and hears their cry for help. He saves them from all their troubles! He's near to the brokenhearted and delivers those who are discouraged!

Save yourself much grief; accept that you will not know the "why" to many situations but you can be comforted knowing God is with you. Put your hope in His power not your wisdom. The Lord promises to comfort you during hardships and heartaches...will you let Him?

PS. 34:7, 15-19, 139:5 (NLT); I COR. 2:5, 4:7

✝

October 1

"Remember not the former things, nor consider the things of old."
ISAIAH 43:18 (ESV)

Release your grief...rise up...lift your head...don't spend one more second on "if". We are to grieve losses...for a period of time, but then we're to go on. God wants to take you into a new season...He's waiting on you. Release your grief to Him, so you can move into your new season. You're trying to live in two places and it's impossible. If you're living in the past...you can't live in the present. Come now, it's time, friend, let Jesus have all your hurts.

PS. 73:26, 142:5; ECC. 3:1-8, 11; ISAIAH 43:18 (ESV)

October 2

"Come quickly to help me, my Lord and my Savior."
PS. 38:22

When life devastates you...God is with you. His love holds you tight and will never let go-He's your Refuge, Shield, Fortress, Strong Tower and Deliverer...your hiding place to rest your heart, mind and soul! God pours His hope through you to lift you above the reality of the devastation...look to Him for relief. He turns your darkness into light while He whispers that He will make a way for you.

The enemy waits for vulnerable times like these to break down the door of your mind so he can spew his lies of despair every-where. He will try to convince you that you will never overcome. To counter his attacks on your mind it's crucial that you keep your eyes on God's Word. It is your confidence for maneuvering through life and especially during trials like these! Daily profess the Word, memorize and post it in every room of your home so that you see it coming and going, put it in your car, on your phone and on your desk at work-keep within arm's length at all times! When life devastates you...count on the Lord to be with you. He is mighty to save!

PS. 27:1, 38:22; EX. 15:2; ISAIAH 12:2

October 3

"You have searched me, LORD, and you know me."
PS. 139:1

Don't forfeit God's plans for you because you just can't imagine how He can use you. No worries! He's planned every second until the end of the ages! He knows what you're going to do before you do because He's already there! Makes your head spin, doesn't it?

Every desire, mistake, motive, regret, intention, choice, sorrow, idea and dream you've ever had is a culmination of seconds called...your life! And God's got all your life planned out, but He needs you to partner with Him by focusing on His Word-it's your map for the course He's planned for you. Will you commit your life to Him and let Him make your righteousness shine like the dawn and the justice of your cause like the noonday sun? God is ready to help you in all you need to do today...are you ready to let Him help you?

PS. 37:5-6; MATT. 6:33; PSALM 139:1-4

October 4

"You were running the race so well.
Who has held you back from following the truth?"
GAL. 5:7 (NLT)

Stay in the race...you will be pushed and knocked out of your lane many times. Expect opposition from others-questioning your motives, seeing if you've got what it takes. Don't allow what they say to distract you; just because they say so...does not make it so! Persevere, look ahead-this race isn't about what you can do...it's about what your Father God is doing through you!

You're running this race because you're called to it. God has purposed you. Many will want you to prove your ability to run; don't engage in this kind of conversation with others or inside of your own head! Your proof is in Who chose you for this race...enough said. Keep your eyes straight ahead and keep running! Toss off what others say or it will weigh you down and keep you from finishing the race. Fix your eyes on the prize, keep your pace and endure, so you may fully accomplish the will of God-receiving, carrying away and enjoying what is promised. Do it...God made you for hard!

GAL. 5:7 (NLT); PHIL. 3:9-12; HEB. 10:35; ISAIAH 41:10

October 5

"Heaven and earth will pass away, but my words will never pass away."
MATT. 24:35

What's your view...are you in or out? Do you consider leaving when things get hard and tell God that He needs to show you something or..or what? What are you going to do; where would you go? Pick a team-you can't play both sides or you'll be ripped apart; it's double-minded thinking! You know what the Word says, but if you continue to look to the world to meet your needs...you will lose your mind-really you will!

News flash: the worldly view self-serves and will serve itself before it serves you, and then it will tell you, "hasta la vista, baby!" Take a stand-submit your mind to God's truth, not to what you feel. Your feelings are unstable and unreliable...God is stable and reliable-He is your source...not the world!

ISAIAH 55:11; I PET. 1:23; HEB. 4:12; 2 COR. 2:14; JAMES 1:8; MATT. 24:35

October 6

"Direct your children onto the right path, and when they are older,
they will not leave it."
PROV. 22:6 (NLT)

You're not alone in parenting...you've got God; He's got everything covered. You can't control how life happens to your children...but you *can* prepare them for life. Teach them how to call on the name of Jesus...how to pray and spend time with Him. Walk out what you believe. Explain that Jesus has overcome and conquered anything they will ever face. Let them know you've been given the privilege and responsibility to parent them, but they belong to God, and that makes you feel safe...because He's the greatest Superhero of all time! Be honest when they ask questions; things happen we can't control, but we're never alone-God never lets go of our hand. God doesn't promise we will not face danger, but He does promise that He will be with us when we face danger. God commands His angels to watch over children (SEE PS. 91:11-12) and He's before all things. He holds everything together (SEE COL. 1:17). You're not alone in parenting...you've got God, and He's got everything covered!

JOHN 16:33; DAN. 3:27; ISAIAH 43:1-2; PS. 9:11-12; COL. 1:17; PROV. 22:6 (NLT)

October 7

"Whoever does God's will is my brother and sister and mother."
MARK 3:35

You can't control how your family treats you-their acceptance is desired but not always possible. Trying to make them accept you shackles you in chains to their view of you. How they treat you has nothing to do with your value...it's a reflection of their unresolved issues overflowing on to you!

Families of origin don't always connect as planned. God knows this and it's why He gives us a spiritual family to love and support us. Acknowledge the pain in your family of origin then seek God to help you grieve and accept it-He will give you everything you need!

God is faithful. His love accepts and completes every person who calls out to Him...He promises to stay with us to the very end and will walk us across the finish line! Will you let Him?

MARK 3:35; MATT. 6:25-34; EPH. 1:5

October 8

"For we are God's masterpiece. He has created us anew in Christ Jesus, so we can do the good things he planned for us long ago."
EPH. 2:10 (NLT)

You're toiling in your effort and exerting strength to achieve what you believe will satisfy you while you plead with God to just give you these few things you're asking for. You say you don't understand why God is withholding your modest request when He could so easily provide for you. I'll tell you why...for starters, God doesn't enable us to live in the spiritual poverty that many are willing to settle for. If a child of His insists on it, He will continue to allow him to encounter circumstances that will return their heart to Him. Next, He wants you to live the abundant life Jesus died to give you-far beyond what your mind can imagine, but it requires you to let your plans die. Dying to self allows the power of God to pour through you-it's called His grace: where you end...He begins! Finally, you just don't know what you don't know.

God purposed you to do good works long ago, but you have to put your hope in Him, not people, situations and circumstances! You're living like a junkie desperately looking for a fix and willing to do about anything for relief because you can't see beyond the desperation of the moment! God knows this and He's not giving up on you, so don't give up on Him! He will see you through this...if you will let Him.

Listen closely: nothing gives us relief like the love of God. All else pales in comparison. When you renew your mind with God's truth and embrace His grace, you will know He's for you, not against you, and His truth will set you free to be the authentic person He designed! Will you put your hope in God? Until you do, you will seek from the hand of man what only the hand of God can deliver!

John 8:31-32; Eph. 2:10 (NLT); 1 Cor. 2:5; Rom. 8:31; Phil. 1:6, 2:13, 4:7

October 9

"A friend is always loyal, and a brother is born to help in time of need."
Prov. 17:17 (NLT)

Getting real with ourselves is the catalyst to working through our issues. Ask God to search your heart and give you revelation so you don't allow the same issues to repeat over and over in your life, and rob you of being the authentic person He designed you to be! After the Lord shows you the issues that are hindering you, ask Him to bring people into your life to help you work through them. Sharing with trusted godly people who can accept you where you are, while holding you accountable to what you need to do to move through where you are, is the practical application of grace and truth in your life.

If a person believes they're lovable only when they have it together, then they will hold back the parts of themselves that are weak, bad and imperfect. This of course prevents them from being real. Authentic relationships are founded on being real. Transparency and vulnerability are required to connect! You are vulnerable when exposing your heart, but there's power when you experience another person accepting all of you. You discover that it is possible to be loved and valued...even with imperfections! Knowing you don't have to be perfect to be loved is critical to move through life and stay on the course God calls you to. Will you get real and let God's perfect love uproot the behaviors that are hindering you from experiencing the connectedness in relationships He designed for you?

Ps. 139:23-24; Prov. 17:17 (NLT); 1John 4:12, 18-19

October 10

*"Be strong, and let your heart take courage,
all you who wait for the LORD!"*
PS. 31:24 (ESV)

You're strong because the Spirit of God lives in you! Don't be shocked by constant opposition and trials-God said to expect these schemes from the devil. You're promised victory through the blood of Jesus Christ. The Holy Spirit lives in you and will work through you to glorify God...if you let Him!

You must engage in the battles to experience the victory! Not fighting keeps you in bondage to what torments you. Put on the full armor of God: the belt of truth, breastplate of righteousness, shoes fitted with the gospel, shield of faith, helmet of salvation, and the sword of the Spirit-praying on all occasions! Life is hard, but God has equipped us with His full armor to move us through hard times, and to come out on the other side of each...victoriously!

EPH. 6:10-20; PS. 27:14, 31:24 (ESV); 1 COR. 16:13

October 11

*"...to make her holy, cleansing her by the washing with water
through the word"*
EPH 5:26

To change how you *feel*-you have to change how you *think*. Many people believe they are wrong because wrong was done to them. Until they change how they think...they will continue to feel wrong. These wrongs manifest into unresolved hurt, which is like a toxic leak in the body. Every time a person thinks on and/or revisits the hurt, toxins seep into every cell, causing damage to the heart, mind and soul. No person can manage this damage, but the Holy Spirit can!

Only the Holy Spirit can purge your hurt. He releases His truth over and through you. His truth washes away every mean and nasty word spoken to you, cleans your wounds that developed from the wrong imposed on your body, and He places His overflowing hope in your soul! God's Word is truth; it is a healing balm to the heart, mind and spirit-His Word restores, redeems and renews...it makes old into new, lost into found, hopeless into hopeful, and breathes life back into what was considered done and dead!

God's Word washes, cleanses and heals us-it's the antidote for all hurt. Will you consistently think on His truth? It will change how you think, which changes how you feel!

Titus 3:5; Acts 10:38; Luke 6:19; Matt. 14:36; 1 John 1:9; Ps. 51:2

October 12

"You will keep in perfect peace those whose minds are steadfast,
because they trust in you."
Isaiah 26:3

Your identity is found in your relationship with Jesus Christ-nothing else. The One Who gave you life...gives meaning to your life! Embracing the revelation that your identity is in Christ enables you to *believe* God is for you. Knowing His love is for you is the foundation needed for you to develop into who He says you are. This knowing who you are in Christ then enables you to walk out what He asks of you!

Don't be naive...walking out the life Christ calls us to allows us to experience a peace that surpasses all understanding and a joy that overflows, as well as...seasons of suffering. These seasons are the only way to develop our overall character of perseverance, patience and endurance...the keys needed for an unshakeable faith in Christ! This unshakeable faith in Him is our ongoing development of our identity in Him...knowing Him and being known by Him. Seek to know Christ and be known by Him...it's the greatest thing you will ever do in life!

Phil. 4:6-7; Isaiah 26:3; Ps. 34:8

October 13

"My sheep listen to my voice; I know them, and they follow me."
JOHN 10:27

The day you were saved, God gave you His Holy Spirit so that you would have 24/7 guidance. Be careful to remain in close fellowship with Him. Speak the Word aloud throughout the day and immediately toss out thoughts that oppose His truth. He will prompt your direction throughout the day. Ask for clarification if you don't understand. Don't become anxious if you don't think you're hearing Him, because He wants you to so you can understand His Word.

He wants you to feel confident in His ability to guide you and for you to trust Him. You will become more comfortable as you renew your mind and consistently overcome worldly reasoning. Renew your mind at least every hour-this keeps you sensitive to His still, small voice. Be purposed in hearing the Holy Spirit and you will know Him intimately. Like anything else, the more you do it, the more comfortable you are!

JOHN 10:4, 10:27; PHIL. 4:6-8

October 14

"...and if you embrace this kingdom life and don't doubt God, you'll not only do minor feats like I did to the fig tree, but also triumph over huge obstacles."
MATT. 21:21 (MSG)

Indecisiveness opens the door to mental torment, but...*a decision opens the door to freedom*! God will flow His ability through you if you remain in Him and keep Him in you. Being indecisive in trusting God is being double minded - one day you trust God...the next day you're not sure. This thinking leads to mental torment!

Making a decision to trust God enables you to mentally transfer the burden of the reality you're facing into His hands. This truth gives you relief. The reality you're facing hasn't changed, but your *perspective* has. You no longer feel responsible to re-solve the burden because it's no longer in your hands; it's now in the hands of God! Your decision to trust God enables you to move forward in His confidence, which enables you to walk in freedom and not be a slave to the burden you're facing...despite the reality of it! Be decisive and believe God...your mind will appreciate your decision!

MATT. 21:21 (MSG); JAMES 1:6; MARK 11:23; EZ. 17:22-24

October 15

*"For the LORD grants wisdom! From his mouth come knowledge
and understanding."*
PROV. 2:6 (NLT)

Know your triggers-the things that emotionally charge you, then make a decision, *with God's direction*, on how you will respond. This enables you to set your mind in advance on how you will respond, versus trying to maintain control after you're already in an emotionally charged situation (which rarely works)!

Such a decision enables you to direct your emotions instead of them directing you. Not making your mind up in advance to a familiar trigger is you knowingly lending your mind to craziness...because you know what is ahead for you! We may not have the power to change a situation, but we do have the power to determine in advance how we will respond! Crazy is responding to the same situation the same way....over and over and over! Don't go crazy. Ask God for direction prior to facing a situation that triggers your emotions and He will give you wisdom generously without finding fault!

JAMES 1:5, 15:7; PROV. 2:6 (NLT); MATT. 7:7

October 16

*"...and to know the love of Christ that surpasses knowledge,
that you may be filled with all the fullness of God."*
EPH. 3:19

Spending time in prayer is vital for your identity in Christ to be developed. Your stability thrives on the intimacy you have with Him. Spending time in prayer isn't something you have to do...it's something you *get to do*-it's a privilege. You need this time with Jesus to rise up and be Who He says you are. It's your time to praise, honor and thank Him, loving Him for Who He is. Praising Him...strengthens you. Your Father God is the...I AM, the Alpha & Omega, El Shaddai, Jehovah Jireh, Savior, Comforter, Protector, Provider and Creator of the universe! He loves you-He lives in you, and He knitted you together with His very own hands.

Your Father always has time for you....He approves of all of you, flooding you with His confidence, directing and correcting you-whispering dreams and ideas into your heart, comforting and assuring you He's got everything covered, and that you don't need to be anxious or afraid. Time spent with your Father is safe, intimate and validating. It's during this time together that He shows you your value and worth; your authentic identity is found and continually developed in Him.

When you go into the world- you know who you are, not because of who *you* are...but because of *Who you belong to*; you are His! His confidence in you directs your steps. Time with your Father: guard it, don't allow anything or anyone to take you away from being with Him. Seek God, love Him with all your heart, receive His love...let Him be your Father-His love completes you! He will give you more than you could ever ask for or could even dream about; spend time with Him-it's your privilege!

COL. 1:17, 2:10; PS. 139:13; MATT. 6:33; EPH. 3:19-20

October 17

"Fearing people is a dangerous trap, but trusting the LORD means safety."
PROV. 29:25 (NLT)

Vulnerability is an unedited snapshot of our complete self; it exposes the parts of us that we hide for fear of rejection by others. Being vulnerable is a risk that opens us up to be judged by some, but it's the glue required to connect and experience authentic relationships with others in the body of Christ as God designed!

Feelings of rejection are insidious; they convince us to hide parts of us that would be potentially rejected, and present the parts that would be potentially accepted, but we never feel completely accepted because we don't allow anyone to really know us! But, when we embrace the acceptance the Lord gives us we're released from the bondage rejection imposes on us! Humbly accepting God's love enables us to know our value *isn't tethered to what we do, but it's rooted in Who we belong to* and what He's done for us! Accepting this truth allows God's love to break off the chains of rejection that stunted our development, and we begin to grow into the person God designed us to be, doing the good works He planned long ago!

Don't be naive; vulnerability is a risk to be accepted and some *will* reject you, but remember this: their rejection doesn't mean something is wrong with you...it means something is wrong with them! The experience of being accepted and being yourself as God intended far outweighs rejection by a few. God's perfect love casts out all fear...will you let His love cast out yours?

Prov. 29:25 (NLT); Phil. 3:3; Isaiah 12:2; Ex. 15:2

October 18

"I love those who love me, and those who seek me diligently find me."
Prov. 8:17 (ESV)

God does not force His truth...nor can we. The burden of proof...is not on us. We present the truth and God's Word is the evidence. Each person has the freedom to choose what he or she will believe. Our hearts are sincere in wanting them to know the truth-it's easy to get caught in a battle of "wanting" to make them see and hear, but we can't. God can, but He won't force them-the Holy Spirit is on standby to give revelation to any person who's ready to receive it.

God gives us free will to believe. He will never force His truth; He wants us to want Him because we desire His love and presence, not because we are pressured or guilt-induced. God is love, and He loves us very much. His love is full of power-a force to be reckoned with, but He will never force us into loving

Him back nor should we believe we can force another to receive His truth. Our best gift to those we want to "see and hear the truth" is to walk out what we believe, holding unswervingly to His truth, and standing firm during good times and bad ones - not allowing circumstances or another person to compromise our walk. Where the Spirit of the Lord is, there is freedom.

2 COR. 3:17; ISAIAH 61:1; PROV. 8:17 (ESV)

October 19

"Then I will give you rain in due season,
and the land shall yield her increase..."
LEV. 26:4 (KJV)

I am speaking to some who might be reasoning themselves out of God's plans. There's nothing holy about staying in a season that God says is over. His anointing provides for each season He calls us to. If we stay beyond the call...it ain't pretty! The mind seeks order and resolution-it's God design. We don't like to leave a season before we've finished our job; we cling to GALATIANS 6:9,"*don't grow weary, for in due season you will reap a harvest.*"

Listen closely: "due season" is the operative phrase-you will see a harvest in the "due season" God's called you *to*...not the one He's called you *from*. Staying makes you disobedient, and you will labor in vain unless the Lord is with you (Ps127:1-2). If you believe the Holy Spirit whispered that it's time for you to leave a season-then you need to get moving!

GAL. 6:9; PS. 127:1-2; LEV. 26:4 (KJV)

October 20

"For the LORD is good and his love endures forever..."
PS. 100:5

I pray today you will stop the charade of trying not to look hurt. Instead give your hurt to Jesus...He heals hurt. He's waiting to exchange with you...your sorrow for His everlasting love. He will soothe the ache inside of your soul and fill the empty, lonely places in your heart with His love. I can't convince you of this truth; you have to take the risk, but I can promise you...His love works with *anyone, anytime and any place.* Will you let Jesus take your hurt and heal you with His love?

JER. 29:11; JOHN 14:6, 15:4-5; PS. 100:5

October 21

"Do not be anxious about anything..."
PHIL. 4:6

To come against racing thoughts in your mind...seek God first. He promises to supply all our needs. God is clear. He's got the situation covered; He's an anxiety crusher! We're not to worry-*ever*! When we believe this, He goes to work...by the way, all those questions that anxiety wants you to panic about? God's got each one covered. Have faith in His ability to handle your inability. When you do...God will give you words to speak, the courage and stamina you don't have, lead you to people who can help you, give you fresh ideas, work through devastating grief, restore dead relationships, forgive the unforgivable, connect you to the job matched to your skills, lead you to a friend who will understand and walk with you, find the school with the teacher who knows how to work with your child, see the doctor who has a cure for your disease, connect you with the loan officer who considers you instead of your FICO score, gives you the opportunity you've needed to market your concept. But, most of all...God's there for you-He loves you and He will handle anything you're up against...if you will put your faith in Him!

God's love soothes your mind, heart and soul, letting you rest in Him no matter what you're facing. Will you let His love bring your mind into a balanced focus of His truth?

PHIL. 4:6; MATT. 6:33; MARK 11:22; EPH. 3:20

October 22

*"But thanks be to God! He gives us the victory
through our Lord Jesus Christ."*
1 COR. 15:57

Your willpower doesn't work, but grace does. You can't deliver yourself...but Jesus can! His grace adds power to your will, which exceeds your own ability. Your willpower motivates you to begin, but it's Jesus' power that sustains you to continue on to completion! *If you depend on human willpower then you deny the power of the cross!*

Daily, seek the Lord instead of seeking to overcome; your intentions are sincere and seem right, but put the focus on your external performance instead of the internal power of the Holy Spirit. It's the power that happens on the inside of you that changes your life! You can do all things God calls you to do... and nothing apart from Him! If we could save ourselves-we wouldn't need a Savior! Will you seek the power of Jesus Christ today and let Him add power to your will...it will change your life!

1 COR. 15:57; ROM. 8:37; 2 COR. 2:14

October 23

"Let all that I am wait quietly before God, for my hope is in him."
PS. 62:5 (NLT)

Setbacks in life...you're back in a place you swore you'd never be again. Disappointment slaps you- failure overwhelms you. You worked hard to leave a place you despised, but here you are...*again*. You've climbed out of this same pit many times, but this time...you're done. You're embarrassed, hopeless and don't understand what's wrong with you. Shame and condemnation begin to flood you.

You must know three truths about where you are right now: first, your willpower doesn't work, but *grace* does. You can't deliver yourself from this...only Jesus can. Willpower motivates you to start the race, but it's Jesus' power that sustains you, allowing you to complete the race. Each morning seek Jesus instead of seeking to overcome. *Nothing* is overcome unless it's done via Jesus. Thank Jesus in the morning and throughout the day for the strength He will provide to you. Don't entertain thoughts that if you try harder, you can sustain...*it's a setup for a setback*. It's in your weakness that God's power is made perfect. Next, renew your mind. Profess and believe that you're delivered, even when you see no indication of deliverance. God calls things that be not-as though they are. Agree with God, who He says you are...*not* what you feel you are. God never condemns you. He doesn't want you to condemn yourself, either; condemnation guarantees failure. Finally, consistently seek Christ and have faith constantly. God's truth must be applied to every area of your life-completely surrender all of your life to Him...holding nothing back. Ask Jesus to examine, correct and enable you, because you can't...*but He can and will.*

God will meet you where you are...love Him with all your heart, all your soul and all your mind. Do these three things daily and look forward to the peace God will provide to you. Seek the Lord and He will answer you; those who look to Him are radiant, their faces are never covered with shame. He has good plans for you. Will you let Him be your anchor of hope?

JER. 29:11; HEB. 6:19; PS. 34:4-5, 62:5 (NLT)

October 24

"...for it is God who works in you to will and to act in order to fulfill his good purpose."
PHIL 2:13

You are saved to make a difference for God's glory...not to just participate in your personal interests or hang out until you go to Heaven! God uniquely designed you to carry out the works He planned for you long ago. Your trust in Him empowers you to carry them out. You've reasoned and justified various excuses from the trials and troubles you've encountered, but none of them are acceptable; they all come back to your ability. It's not *your ability* that enables you to do what God calls you to do...it's *your willingness* to let *His ability* work through you. God's got ability.

He needs availability. Are you available?

I PETER 4:11; PHIL. 2:13; EPH. 2:8-10, 3:20

October 25

*"I have swept away your sins like a cloud.
I have scattered your offenses like the morning mist."*
ISAIAH 44:22 (NLT)

None of us are exempt from our emotions taking the lead in our thoughts. We've all experienced moodiness, ungrateful-ness, selfish, lustful, prideful, greedy, superior, inferior, and legalistic attitudes that lead us into sin. But as soon you realize your sin, turn to God and repent; He blots out the sin and His Presence refreshes you to experience "godly sorrow", which is God-focused sorrow, not worldly, self-focused sorrow. God-focused sorrow gives you mental clarity, through which you're able to gain insight into how your thought patterns led you into sin and how your sin affected others. You're able to apologize with a sincere heart and ask for forgiveness from those your sin affected.

Sadly, many turn away from God out of guilt. This is worldly sorrow...they're sorry they got caught, they feel bad for messing up and they don't want to face God. They think He's mad at them. God is not mad *at* them...God's mad at what sin *does to* them! Jesus took on hell and won so sin would have no power over us, but when we turn away from God, when we reject His forgiveness and His freedom, we opt to stay in bondage to the sin Jesus died to free us from!

And this is exactly what the enemy wants you to do...if he can deceive you into thinking God is mad at you, then you will turn away from Him and not receive His gift of forgiveness, which would set you free from carrying the burden of sin. Meanwhile, the enemy is waging war on your emotions and having you to focus on what you feel. You will feel bad because you're rejecting the refreshing God's forgiveness would give you! Don't entertain the enemy's stinking lies one more sec-ond...if you're in sin run to God as fast as you can! He's waiting for you to repent, so He can blot out your sin and refresh you!

ACTS 3:19; ISAIAH 44:22 (NLT); ROM. 6:10-14; 1 COR. 15:55-57

October 26

"...but the righteous person will live by his faithfulness..."
HAB. 2:4

Will you lay down the frustration you've been carrying around and pick up the faith God offers you? How much longer are you going to try and control something you never had control of to begin with? Your emotions and feelings are overtaking you because you're trying to manage your situation apart from God's help. Pride is going to take you down...but you're too deceived to know it!!! Faith is evidence of what you do not see, and the evidence of those things you hope for. (SEE HEBREWS 11:1).

Faith in the love of Jesus will move you through impossible circumstance that otherwise would suck the life out of you. Faith is believing in what God *will do, and can do,* and is nothing about what *you* can do. When you face frustration, take your position of faith, stand firm, and say "Father, you see what I'm up against, I can't handle this, but You can. Help me to believe in Your ability...although I see an impossible situation before me, that You can make a way, because You love me and will always be with me. Don't let me doubt your Mighty Hand in this-I want to believe You and trust."

HEB. 11:1; HAB. 2:4; 2 COR. 4:18, 5:7; ROM. 1:17; GAL. 3:11

October 27

"So I say, walk by the Spirit,
and you will not gratify the desires of the flesh."
GAL 5:16

To experience the peace that transcends human understanding, walk out the abundant life promised and know the truth that sets you free...you have to believe in and follow the Word of God-be Spirit-led. God's Word will never fail us; it's alive and active, it judges the thoughts and attitudes of the heart. Many peddle the Word for their glory instead of God's-they're false teachers! Be rooted in the Word and continually built up by it, aligning all your thoughts to it. Don't be deceived by the philosophy of man, intellectualism, following human tradition..."*just crude notions following the rudimentary and elemental teachings of the universe and disregarding [the teachings of] of Christ (the Messiah).*" (SEE COL 2:8 AMP)

As Christians, we live in and work with the world in doing good, but we're not to acquire the worldly ways that are in opposition to God's truth. Every person has the prerogative to believe as he or she chooses. We're to live in harmony with others but we're to never endorse beliefs opposed to God's truth...by adding or taking away from it. God's truth never changes-it's not subject to understanding of era, seasons, or the understanding or endorsement of the human mind! Be Spirit-led in all you do!

ROM. 8:14; GAL. 5:16; 2 COR. 2:17; HEB. 4:12; I COR. 1:20, 26-29, 2:14

October 28

*"And again He says, My trust and assured reliance
and confident hope shall be fixed in Him."*
HEB. 2:13 (AMP)

Don't confuse your part with God's part. When Jesus asked Phillip to feed the 5000 people He didn't expect Him to feed them...it was a test to strengthen His faith! Phillip became agitated at the request because his resources weren't enough-he viewed his situation from a human perspective instead of an opportunity for God's intervention and provision. The little boy's lunch wasn't enough either, but when placed in the hands of God...was more than enough!

Don't limit what God can do through you because you don't see a human solution. God doesn't need human solutions...*He needs willing hearts who believe* He can take their not enough and turn it into more than enough! Will you offer God what you have of your treasure, time and talent?

JOHN 6:1-15; HEB. 2:13 (AMP); 2 TIM. 1:7 (AMP)

October 29

"When he spoke to me, I was strengthened and said, "Speak, my lord, since you have given me strength."
DAN. 10:19

Every time we find ourselves pushed up against a wall and feel we've reached our limits...we are correct, we have. But, our end allows God's beginning. He shows His mighty hand and takes us to the next level of perseverance, pouring the power of His Spirit through us! We have limits-*God has none*...He's before all things we see and don't see, and holds all things together. When we abide in Him, we stay connected to Him and bear much fruit, enabling us to be more than conquerors! His strength is our authentic confidence to have the mind of Christ! Will you let Christ flow through you to do the things He designed you to do? Take the focus off of what you can or can't do and put your focus on Christ...His Spirit lives in you!

PHIL. 4:13; 2 COR. 12:9 (NLT); DAN. 10:19; JOSHUA 1:7; DEUT. 5:32

October 30

"God's way is perfect. All the LORD's promises prove true. He is a shield for all who look to him for protection."
2 SAM. 22:31 (NLT)

When truth transforms to trust...when someone we love is hurting, we hurt too, and want to help them overcome their situation. Often, our sincere motive to help actually hinders them. *We confuse loving them with rescuing them.* Loving them is being available emotionally and physically, reminding them of God's truth, giving them the freedom to seek Christ and to trust Him to provide a way.

Rescuing them puts you...between them and God. This makes you their problem-solver and cheats them out of a personal experience of seeking Christ with confidence when they're faced with adversity. You must remove yourself as the go-to person so your loved one will seek Christ *first*...instead of you. If you continue to rescue, you are interfering with Holy business. Release those you love to God; trust Him to provide what they need. Remember...He loved them first.

One of the most powerful ways we can help those we love is to model our trust in Jesus, believing He will make a way, even when we do not see a way. We model standing firm on what we know...versus how we feel, believing He will provide all our needs. A person can be told the truth that God will provide a way, but the *truth transforms to trust*...when they do not see a way and then God makes a way. You will never know if God will handle your situation until you give Him a chance to handle it...will you let Him?

2 SAM. 22:31 (NLT); DEUT. 32:4; PS. 12:6

October 31

"I pray that out of his glorious riches he may strengthen you with power through his Spirit in your inner being."
EPH. 3:16

Pride lies. It wants you to believe you're above being offended-especially if it's a small offense that you should easily dismiss because you know the Word and you've got a strong walk.

Listen closely: a strong walk is only as strong *as it is dependent on God!* The only way to remain strong in your walk is to depend on God for *everything*...to include working through small offenses! Apart from God you can do nothing, but with Him you can do all things He strengthens you to do. Bottom line: what you release to God is dealt with in His strength, and what you keep from Him is dealt with in your strength. Who's strength will you depend on?

JOHN 15:5; PHIL. 4:13; EPH. 3:16; 2 COR. 12:9

✝

November 1

"Teach me your way, LORD, that I may rely on your faithfulness;
give me an undivided heart, that I may fear your name."
Ps. 86:11

The common denominator...surrendering to God's love and a willingness to be used by Him! God can't accept egos and pride-they compete with His glory, but surrender and willingness weave perfectly into His plans. We complicate and delay being used by God when we begin a reasoning monologue of debate in our mind with Him like: can we trust Him with our situation, if our past is too much for Him to handle, and/or if we're qualified for what He's called us to do...seriously? Say these questions out loud and listen to how ridiculous they sound when talking about the Creator of the Universe and what He's capable of doing!

God challenged me one day when I was struggling to believe if I was hearing Him correctly, so I questioned aloud His power and plan, and...I burst out laughing! Then the Lord led me to read Scripture and look at the people He uses: Moses killed a guy, had to overcome major self-esteem issues, and he had no specific training in crossing the Red Sea; David didn't go to giant-killing school, he had major sin, but God called him a man after His own heart; Peter's fishing trade didn't qualify him to preach, but his love for Jesus did, even though he denied Jesus three times. The common denominator...they surrendered to God's love and had a willingness to be used by Him! So what about you: are you in or out? I pray you won't miss how God's planned to work through you!

Ps. 86:11; Jer. 42:3; Prov. 3:6, 16:18; 1 Cor. 1:26-27; Eph. 3:14-21; Matt. 16:24

November 2

"And so we know and rely on the love God has for us. God is love.
Whoever lives in love lives in God, and God in them."
1 John 4:16

Grace, truth and love...the requirements to walk in the victory God promises! God will bring to completion what He started in you, until the day you meet Jesus Christ face-to-face. Your part

208

is to agree with His plan so that you can! First, embrace God's *grace*. It accepts where you are. Next, know His *truth*. It tells you what you need to do about where you are. Finally, receive God's *love*. It empowers you to follow through on what you need to do!

Look closely at the pattern in God's plan. He accepts, tells and empowers you...your part is to embrace, know and receive what He provides. God is the giver and you are the receiver...that's a secure no-fail plan! That's how much God loves you. He's covered all the bases, so that you can succeed and walk in the victory He promises! God will never quit on you...will you commit to not quit on Him?

ROM. 3:24 (AMP); EPH. 1:7; 1 JOHN 4:16; 2 PETER 1:12

November 3

> *"For the LORD takes delight in his people;*
> *he crowns the humble with victory..."*
> PS. 149:4

Don't deny the reality of what you're going through...but don't deny God's help either! Jesus said, *"humanly speaking it's impossible, but not with God... everything is possible with God!"* Will you give God the impossibles you're facing today-the ones from yesterday and the ones you will face tomorrow? Will you let Him comfort you when...your bank account doesn't have enough to pay bills, you're dealing with a harsh supervisor, your gas tank is empty and you need to get to work, family demands are draining you, you struggle with letting go of betrayal, a loved one is self destructing, your heart aches with grief, your marriage is falling apart, depraved thoughts engulf you, fear presses you against the wall, or a medical diagnosis changes your lifestyle?

Will you let God make a way for you when you can't see a way? The issues you face are impossible-this is reality, but not for God...*this is truth*! Commit all of your thoughts to God, do not try to think this through, you will be sucked in an abyss of hopelessness! Instead, put your hope in God alone.

He holds on when you can't, His peace will flood your mind and He will direct your steps in how to get through this impossible! Will you trust Him to?

PS. 16:11, 149:4; JOB 36:11

November 4

"This is my command--be strong and courageous! Do not be afraid or discouraged. For the LORD your God is with you wherever you go."
JOSHUA 1:9 (NLT)

Define yourself...give every part of yourself to the Lord. Don't dismiss anything! He's the Master of making nothing into something. He will do greater than you dare ask or imagine...ginormous dreams! Your mind can't wrap around what Jesus is able to do in you-He's ready and waiting. Your part is to embrace the power that's at work within you, which is believing the power of the Holy Spirit's work in and through you. This requires you to give all of yourself to the Holy Spirit; yielding to His power at work in you-don't hold anything back. *What you keep from Him confines you; what you give to Him...defines you!* Be defined, shine your light, let the Holy Spirit make a difference through you. Do it!

JOHN 1:3; EPH. 3:20; MATT 5:16; JOSHUA 1:9 (NLT); 2 TIM. 2:15

November 5

"Now faith is confidence in what we hope for and assurance about what we do not see."
HEB. 11:1

Adversity...going through it and knowing Jesus! Going through it takes you to an uncertain, uncomfortable and unfamiliar place, where your pride is purged, false confidence eradicated and beliefs challenged-a time of Holy revelation of Jesus' love. His love is for you and His Spirit lives in you-unwavering, unmovable and unstoppable, and you *know* deep in your spirit you belong to Him. It's a beautiful, risky and confident place to be...trusting He will walk you through places where you can't see, give you the strength to press on when you have none, and give hope and life to a situation that's considered dead. Know that He will provide all you need, not to just get by, but more than you could dare ever ask for. Jesus loves you...will you let Him show you?

2 COR. 5:7; ISAIAH 40:29; ROM. 4:17; PHIL. 4:19; EPH. 3:17-19

November 6

"So we fix our eyes not on what is seen, but on what is unseen, since what is seen is temporary, but what is unseen is eternal."
2 COR. 4:18

Don't ponder, debate, and speculate God's truth...you will lose ground and become confused! Blessed are those who hear the Word of God and obey it! Believing God is a *choice, not a feeling.* We choose to believe, then walk out what we profess, walking by by faith, not sight. This is how we spiritually strengthen our believing muscles. Jesus said He's deprived this world of the power to harm you. He's conquered it for you! Let this give you courage during trials, knowing you don't have to figure out how you will overcome them.

Focusing on this truth releases you from the desperation that can consume your thoughts! Believe and let Jesus Christ flow His power through you to accomplish the good plans God called you to long ago. Agree with Christ and give Him an opportunity to finish the good work He started in you, bringing it to completion. He's the way, the truth and the life...know His truth and you will move forward in the freedom He promises you! Christ knows what you're facing this very second...will you choose to believe He's got you covered...this very second?

2 COR. 4:18, 5:7; EPH. 2:10; PHIL. 1:6; JOHN 14:6; JOHN 8:32

November 7

"The Spirit of God, who raised Jesus from the dead, lives in you."
ROM. 8:11 (NLT)

Your status is not your identity...be careful, the world wants to label you with statuses to qualify your value then call them your identity. Don't confuse a status with your identity; statuses change throughout life but your identity remains the same in Christ; you are His child, there's only one you and He loves you!

God uniquely made you with individual fingerprint and DNA that no other person has ever had or will ever have. You're a masterpiece fearfully and wonderfully made with a purpose to do good works God planned for you long ago. Embrace this truth. It's crucial for your emotional and spiritual development, and to sustain the journey the Lord has called you to. The world will make numerous attempts to steal your identity and tell you who you are and what you can plan to accomplish in life. Your status is a label given by the world like single, married, divorced, renter, home owner, professional, unemployed, tax bracket, home address, etc. They are labels *not* value indicators, and they don't define you...you define them!

You belong to Christ. His love defines, authenticates and completes you! Purpose to know Him and you will be known by Him. His love for you is your identity! Statuses change... God's love and your identity do not!

Rom. 6:4, 8:11 (NLT); I Pet. 2:10; Ps. 139:13-16; Eph. 2:10

November 8

"This is what the LORD says: "Don't let the wise boast in their wisdom, or the powerful boast in their power, or the rich boast in their riches."
Jer. 9:23 (NLT)

God is your source...not the world. Many profess God's truth with their mouths while they follow worldly views in their minds and hearts. We live in this world. We're to be informed of, but not conformed to. Our mind is to be submitted to God's truth to walk in the victory He promises; our security is in God alone! His Word is our confidence and the answer to anything we need-He's over all we see and all we don't see.

When facing an impossible situation acknowledge the reality of it then immediately *praise and thank* the Lord for His provisions!

Do not lean on your own understanding...but in *all* your ways acknowledge the Lord and He will make a way for you!

PROV. 3:5-6; JER. 9:23 (NLT); ECC. 9:11

November 9

"For the LORD your God is living among you. He is a mighty savior. He will take delight in you with gladness. With his love, he will calm all your fears. He will rejoice over you with joyful songs."
ZEPH. 3:17 (NLT)

Expectations are determined on the inside of you, not in outward circumstances. Life can be cruel and unfair at times, but you can have a confident expectation that Jesus has overcome. Despite what your eyes see, expect change. The joy of the Lord is your strength! The end you see is impossible for you...but not for God! Your expectations aren't in what you can do or see; your expectations are in God. He will work out the impossibles you're facing, *if* you keep your eyes on Him. Keep a confident expectation in Him!

HEB .11:1; ZEPH. 3:17 (NLT); COL. 1:17; 2 COR. 5:17; JOHN 16:33; NEH. 8:10

November 10

"Humble yourselves before the Lord, and he will lift you up."
JAMES 4:10

Acknowledge the impossible situation you're up against because it is real, then humble yourself before the Lord and trust Him to empower you with the grace to overcome it! Many are sincere, but refuse to acknowledge what they're up against for fear it will give the enemy a foothold or somehow reflect a lack of faith. But the impossible they're facing is still a reality whether they acknowledge it or not!

Admitting what you're up against is necessary in order to align your thoughts with God's Word and to confidently position yourself in His truth. This mental process is grace at work in your mind...enabling you to move forward in the reality of the situation, while enabling you to rely on the power of the Spirit

Who lives in you! God will do more than you dare imagine, *if* you will take the risk to trust Him! Don't deny, minimize or try to handle the impossible situation you're facing. Immediately turn to God's truth...it trumps the reality of the impossible you're facing!

JAMES 4:10; EPH. 3:16-20; 2 CHRON. 7:14

November 11

"Faith is the confidence that what we hope for will actually happen;
it gives us assurance about things we cannot see."
HEB. 11:1 (NLT)

Get your game face on...this is a tough season of spiritual conditioning; you will get through it. My Spirit lives in you! I give you what you need along the way. I go ahead of you and My hand of blessing is on you. Many things I ask seem absolutely absurd to you...*it's because they are!* Do you think that Mary's mind could wrap around carrying the Messiah in her womb and giving birth to Him, or can you imagine what was going through Moses's mind when he was backed up against the Red Sea with Pharaoh's army about to kill him? These situations were humanly impossible. Both Mary and Moses moved forward not knowing how I would provide, but that's what faith is all about...believing in Me!

Listen closely: when I ask you to do something I *never* expect you to accomplish it apart from *completely* relying on Me. As you move forward in faith believing in Me, I will give you what you need along the way. Many decline the good plans I made for them long ago. They want *details* and *resources* before they will move forward. Will you believe in Me and decide to walk by faith, not sight, so you can live out the good plans I made for you long ago? If so, then get your game face on and let's go!

HEB. 11:1 (NLT); EX. 14:21; 2 COR. 5:7

November 12

"I will give them hearts that recognize me as the LORD. They will be my people, and I will be their God, for they will return to me wholeheartedly."
JER. 24:7 (NLT)

Do not believe the lie that your genetic predisposition, family of origin, personality traits, ethnic background, social experiences, educational disadvantage or poor choices will keep you from living God's best for you! Nothing has the power to stop God's best...*other than your excuses.*

The excuses you make are rooted in thought patterns developed over the years and that have culminated in you believing you don't have anything God needs. What makes your thoughts convincing is that they are partially true: you don't have what God needs, but you do have what He desires, and that is your *heart!*

Giving God your heart allows Him access to empower you with His love. Until you embrace the revelation that God's love is the source of *all* your needs, you will believe the lie that you're exempt from God's best! Today, will you make the decision to receive God's love and let His Word wash your mind with truth? Will you be purposed in doing this every day and allow His love to empower you to walk in His best for you?

JER. 24:7 (NLT); EZEK. 11:19, 36:26-27; DEUT. 4:29

November 13

"Whoever trusts in his own mind is a fool,
but he who walks in wisdom will be delivered."
PROV. 28:26 (ESV)

Life is hectic...it's a host of complex realities! We're not exempt from experiencing these realities, but we can be confident God's grace and truth will move us through each one! God's grace accepts us where we are in our understanding, and His truth is honest in how we are to proceed. Making a decision to stand on God's Word *before* we experience the complex realities of life is the key to maintaining stability during them. But not making a decision in advance defaults our thoughts into indecisiveness, which inevitably leads to misery every time!

God's truth and grace equip us and enable us to deal with every aspect of life. Nothing escapes the scope of wisdom God gives us! Still, many labor in vain by trying to manage their life with none or some of God's grace and truth, but anything less than all of it cheats them out of having God's hand on them in everything they do. God's hand is our protection and provision, but He won't force Himself on us.

God's grace and truth give us the ability to unravel the complexities of the realities we face every day. Will you seek God's help for your hectic life before you resort to your reasoning?

PROV. 3:5-6, 16:3, 28:26 (ESV); JAMES 1:5; JER. 9:23

November 14

"So we fix our eyes not on what is seen, but on what is unseen, since what is seen is temporary, but what is unseen is eternal."
2 COR. 4:18

Don't allow your emotions to overtake you. Faith is evidence of what's not seen and the evidence of those things we hope for (SEE HEB. 11:1). When you face a frustrating situation, take your position of faith, stand firm and say, "*Father, you see what I'm up against, I can't handle this, but You can-we do not know what to do but our eyes are upon you.*" (SEE 2 CHRON. 20:12).

Most days I come across impossible situations and I've learned through enough mistakes and trials to submit to God and profess that if He doesn't handle things, they won't get done, because I can't unless He equips me. My daily prayer is "I choose to believe You can make a way, because You love me and will always be with me. Don't let me doubt You. I want to believe and trust You. Thank you for taking care of me and those I love and things I value."

The more I stand on His provisions in my life-the more faith I have in Him to handle what will frustrate me if I try to take it on. God's ways work all the time in every situation and with everyone. What will you choose...faith or frustration?

PHIL. 4:13; MARK 9:24; HEB. 11:1; 1 JOHN 4:8; 2 CHRON. 20:12, 15, 17

November 15

"...who saved us and called us to a holy calling, not because of our works but because of his own purpose and grace, which he gave us in Christ Jesus before the ages began..."
2 TIM. 1:9 (ESV)

Don't grieve what's gone...or dread what's ahead, clinging to what becomes dust in your hands, blowing away into nothingness. As Christians, we're to keep moving forward, doing what God calls us to do, even when we're weary. God's promised a harvest, and it will come. Stay focused on what's unshakeable: God's love.

Each year that passes is a year closer to the future of forever, our eternal home. But for this day and this time, you have a call, a job; you're to be a steward of God's love that's alive in you and you're to make a difference in this world! Don't delay or be distracted by what doesn't matter one more day. You're saved...rise up; you've got work to do!

Stay focused, keep moving, don't give up and God will make your righteousness shine like the dawn and the justice of your cause like the noonday sun! Now that should get you excited, so act like it ...because we'll be talking about this forever!

GAL. 6:9; EPH. 2:10; 2 TIM. 1:9 (ESV); PS. 37:6

November 16

"You will not have to fight this battle. Take up your positions; stand firm and see the deliverance the LORD will give you..."
2 CHRON. 20:17

"I'll have faith or go crazy...and I'm not going crazy." Years ago I coined this term. I was in a desperate situation and I made up my mind to choose to believe God's Word. I was discouraged and deceived; I'd come to the end of myself trying to figure life out. I thought I was being responsible, doing my part as I waited on God to do His part. But I wasn't *waiting* on God...I was managing my life independent of God, then praying for

Him to bless my efforts! I didn't realize I was being self-sufficient; to me it was being responsible, but I was denying the power of God's love to flow into and work through me. I didn't deliberately reject His love...I just didn't know how to rely on the sufficiency of His love.

I came to the end of my efforts and myself; I had to choose to have faith or go crazy. Like the woman with the issue of blood, I reached out to Jesus in desperation to save me...one touch-He completely transformed my heart to believe and follow Him! I surrendered all of me that day and began walking by the faith that I professed with my mouth-relying on His sufficiency for *everything* I needed. That was years ago, and these days when I face an impossible, which is nearly each day, I *press in and stand firm* on His sufficiency.

I still allow deception to trip me at times, but immediately I rise up and speak God's Word against the lies the enemy speaks in my mind. Each trial is an opportunity for me to strengthen my faith in God, mature spiritually and gain wisdom. Impossibles are part of life; we can't handle them, but God will, if we invite Him. So, what will you choose...faith or crazy?

JAMES 1:2-8; 2 CHRON. 20:17; 2 COR. 5:7, 12:9

November 17

"Be sober-minded; be watchful. Your adversary the devil prowls around like a roaring lion, seeking someone to devour."
1 PETER 5:8 (ESV)

God writes our stories...we choose to walk them out. It hurts when our loved ones aren't walking out the story God's written for them. But, remember: the final chapter is yet to come! You can't convince someone to stop their destructive patterns of behavior or accept help. Only the Holy Spirit can convict (convince) a person to change, and then empower them to do so. Don't try to guilt or coerce a person into changing or take their behavior personally, although you may be personally experiencing it! It's painful to watch a person self destruct, especially when it's a loved one.

It's such a helpless feeling to watch loved ones as they're determined to do life their way and refuse the help that would put them on the right path! Be careful. You know the enemy is trying to devour them, but he's also after you! He will wake you in the night with anxious thoughts, have you rearrange plans because you feel responsible for their choices, replay guilt tapes of all of the "should-haves" you should have done, and on and on.

Just remember this truth: God is the perfect Father and *His* child Adam rebelled against Him, but He didn't take responsibility for Adam's choice to rebel. However, He did continue to speak the truth to Him and give Him opportunities to take responsibility for his behavior. You can't change this situation. You don't have the power, no matter what you do; your hands are tied...but your prayers aren't! Your prayers have access to the throne of Heaven...so pray, baby, pray!!! And know that in this the perfect parent, your Father God, is with you and will be your sufficiency...and your loved one's sufficiency. After all, God writes our stories...and the final chapter is yet to come!

JOHN 10:10; 1 PETER 5:8 (ESV); PHIL. 4:6-7; EPH. 4:15; 2 COR. 3:5, 9:8

November 18

"Through these he has given us his very great and precious promises."
2 PETER 1:4

Your past died at the cross with Jesus, it's done. You must decide if you believe it's true, not because you feel it, but because Jesus said so. But if you think on your past, you will keep it alive in your mind. Speak God's truth so you will know His truth and be free. Give all of yourself (mind, body and spirit) to Christ. Replace your deception with His truth and be transformed into seeing as He sees. Be deliberate in thinking on God's truth. If not you're thinking on what opposes His truth...*there's no in between.*

Be purposed in receiving His promises; they're yours, but you must claim them.

JOHN 8:32; ROM .12:1-2; PHIL 4:8; 2 PET. 1:4

November 19

"Come to me, all of you who are weary and carry heavy burdens,
and I will give you rest."
MATT 11:28

You're exhausted and fatigued...and Jesus is waiting for you. His yoke is light, His love gives relief, He will refresh you and you can rest in Him. Many are sincere in their attitude, desiring to do what's right and being committed to taking care of day-to -day responsibilities, being emotionally and physically available to family, giving their time to a ministry, helping out a sick friend, etc. But sometimes life begins to spin out of control and you become exhausted and fatigued in carrying out the desires of your heart! This is where the fine line is: whatever has to be done, God will help us do it, but we have to rely on His strength in order to carry it out...not call on Him when we think we need His help!

We all get out of balance at times, but when we seek Him first, then we can keep balance because He will give us the power, insight and strength to serve Him! Will you commit all you do to the Lord and rely on Him to lead you in all He has you to do?

MATT. 11:28; JER. 31:25; JOHN 4:14

November 20

"Commit everything you do to the LORD.
Trust him, and he will help you."
PS. 37:5

When people desire to trust God, He meets them at their trust level. He gives them the power and desire to to rely on and trust in Him. They rely on God's sufficiency instead of self-sufficiency. This truth is put into practical application when a person renews his mind with God's Word, and is then able to move through otherwise impossible seasons of life! Each step he takes in God's truth strengthens his "believing muscle," which gives power to take another step. God equips those who trust with a spiritual tenacity to keep pressing with His confidence to overcome!

Many reject God's offer because they prefer to cater to their emotions instead of preferring God's truth; they want "proof" before they trust Him. When they don't get the "proof" they're looking for from God, they map out their own plans to prevent and/or overcome the inevitable bad, wrong and unfair things of life and to achieve their personal desires. They're convinced they are right. They've put their faith in human wisdom instead of God's spiritual discernment; the thing about deception is...it deceives the one who entertains it! Their ways give them a false sense of being in control, and they forfeit God's good plans for their life.

Will you trust in the Lord with all your heart and not lean on your own understanding, preferring His truth to your emotions? If so, you will live a life beyond your wildest dreams because there's never a dull moment when you're doing what God designed you to do!

PROV. 3:5-6; PS. 37:3-5, 55:2; 1 JOHN 5:4 (ESV)

November 21

"This is an easy thing in the eyes of the LORD..."
2 KINGS 3:18

God's presence goes where you go...He will stay up all night with you because you're afraid, or to just talk about life, He laughs and cries with you, enjoys your company, corrects you to make you right, holds you up when your knees buckle, speaks boldness through you to deliver His truth, and reveals knowledge necessary to complete His plans! He flows His confidence and stamina through you to accomplish what's humanly impossible, goes before you, follows behind you, and keeps His hand of blessing on you! His Word is a lamp to your feet and a light to your path. He breaks down gates of bronze and rips apart iron, makes an ax head float, moves mountains, rolls back waters, makes a donkey talk, and extends daylight for 24 hours; you can count on God's presence making a way for you!

God's presence will satisfy and comfort you all the days of your life-He's always loved you and is committed to completing the good work He started in you long ago! He will never leave you and will provide everything you need and more...*unless* you shut the door on Him! Think on His Word day and night to keep the door to His presence open. He promises to protect your heart and mind, and He will turn around every evil intended to harm you if you let Him. Allowing your mind to reason in ways that add to or oppose His Word shuts the door to His presence, leaving you to defend yourself against the world! Will you keep the door open to Him?

2 Kings 3:18; Mark 10:27; Joshua 10:12; Num. 22:28; Isaiah 58:11

November 22

"And I am sure of this, that he who began a good work in you will bring it to completion at the day of Jesus Christ."
Phil. 1:6 (ESV)

God partners with our pain for His glory. He doesn't waste any of it, but you won't know this until you release it to Him! You have to *choose* if what you profess with your mouth is also what you believe in your heart-*completely*. Believing God's Word, even when it doesn't make any sense, enables the Holy Spirit to guide you through what seems like a hopeless abyss. The pain still hurts but you're able to bear it with the comfort the Holy Spirit will flow through you! His love enables you to endure and stay focused, knowing the pain has an end, *and will be used for God's glory*. Along the way, the Holy Spirit will give you revelation. He will continue to open your mind to understanding and tell you things you didn't know!

Finally, be confident in this: God will continue the good work He started in you long ago, until He brings it to completion on the day Jesus Christ returns!

Will you hand your pain to God and let Him transform it into a purpose for His glory that will not only benefit you, but others too?

JER .29:11; LUKE 24:8; JOHN 8:29; PHIL. 1:6 (ESV), 2:13; PS. 119:18

November 23

"God is faithful, who has called you into fellowship with his Son,
Jesus Christ our Lord"
I COR. 1:9

Don't allow false accusations to take your eyes off of the destiny God's planned for you. Handing offenses to Jesus doesn't dismiss the harm done to you, but it does keep you from carrying the harm in your heart. God vindicates; *your* job is to trust Him and move forward. How you respond to false accusations determines how long you stay under them. What a relief to know the burden to correct wrongs done to us...isn't left up to us!

Jesus models this in the Gospels. He constantly dealt with accusations from His family, hometown and religious leaders during His ministry, and He consistently sought His Father for direction and comfort. Jesus didn't take matters into His hands, He consistently stood on the Word, stated the truth of Who He was and Who He belonged to, and trusted His Father to vindicate Him. Jesus prayed for direction and compassion then moved forward with His Father's agenda. That frees us to get on with life and do the work God's called us to...are you ready?

HEB. 10:23; PROV. 29:25; EPH. 2:10; I COR. 1:9

November 24

"Come to Me, all you who labor and are heavy-laden and overburdened, and
I will cause you to rest. [I will ease and relieve and refresh your souls.]"
MATT. 11:28 (AMP)

Gate of Grace...the place we come when we've tried everything we know, we're used up, weary, depleted and at the end of ourselves. It's where we surrender to the sweet love of Jesus! The Gate of Grace is where the Good Shepherd resides; His yoke is light; He's gentle, kind, and will guide us in wisdom. Enter into His rest. His grace accepts you as you are, while His truth guides you to where you need to be. His love comforts, encourages and supplies all your needs along the way!

The reasons are numerous as to how we come to this point: sometimes it's from trying to do life our way, other times it's hardships imposed on us, and yet some are due to being naïve toward the course of life. No matter how we come to this point, the answer is always the same for overcoming...His name is Jesus, the Good Shepherd-He stands at the Gate of Grace ready to love us and put us back together again. Will you let the Good Shepherd help you?

MATT. 11:28 (AMP); JER. 31:25; JOHN 4:14; ISAIAH 40:29

November 25

"You intended to harm me, but God intended it all for good."
GEN. 50:20 (NLT)

Problems are part of life. They never go away; some you bring on and others are imposed on you. God promises to make a way regardless of how the problem comes to you, *if* you rely on Him. Accepting responsibility for how the problem is impacting your life enables you to move past it; rejecting responsibility keeps you stuck in it. The response I've heard over the years is, "but it's not fair!" And it's true; most problems *aren't* fair, but God never promised us fair...He promised us power! Every person has to decide if they will accept God's power or default to the reasoning of their mind.

God is clear throughout scripture that we live in an unfair world, but a relationship with Him enables us to overcome the unfair that we encounter. He uses what was intended for harm and turns it around for His glory, for those who love Him (SEE GEN. 50:20).

God promises that if we will seek Him we'll be...more than a conqueror, have all our needs supplied, do all things with His strength, have a peace that surpasses all understanding, walk by faith not sight, know Him and be known by Him! Problems come and go, but the love of God is constant; a force to be reckoned with for anyone or anything that comes against a child of God! And, *you* are a child of God...will you let His love give you what you need today in order to move you past this problem?

PS. 21:11; ROM. 8:28; GEN. 50:20 (NLT); PHIL. 4:7; 2 COR. 5:7; 1 COR. 8:3

November 26

"May the God of hope fill you with all joy and peace in believing, so that by the power of the Holy Spirit you may abound in hope."
ROM. 15:13 (ESV)

I'm thankful for God's hope...it gives me clarity when life overwhelms me, picks me up when grief knocks me down and soothes the ache in my soul for those I care for who won't care for themselves! When discouragement and doubt beat on the door of my mind and challenge what I believe, I defer to the Spirit of God Who lives in me. His hope floods my mind with certainty despite the uncertainty that stares back at me. His hope rises up from within me to believe what my mind doesn't see! I prefer God's hope to what I feel...I would lose my everloving mind if I didn't! God's hope gives me the guts to rise up, sit down or stand alone if I need to!

When I'm depleted, His hope fills me up, puts my feet on solid ground and gives me the strength to advance against an army and leap over a wall! God's hope enables me sound sleep and stamina to move through trials, while giving me a peace that surpasses human understanding. God's hope is my source and purpose...I can do what He calls me to do because His hope gives me reason to! My hope is in Him all day long! He supplies all my needs! Who do you put *your* hope in?

PS. 18:28-29, 25:5, 40:2; HEB. 6:19; PHIL. 4:19; ROM. 15:13 (ESV)

November 27

"Finally, be strong in the Lord and in his mighty power."
EPH. 6:10

Are you already feeling overwhelmed and agitated today with the things you need to do? If so, you're looking at your day through your strength, which lets the spirit of dread beat you up! Right now remind yourself of this truth in JOHN 14:27... *"Peace I leave with you; My [own] peace I now give and bequeath to you. Not as the world gives do I give to you. Do not let your hearts be troubled or afraid."* Stop allowing yourselves to be agitated and disturbed, and don't permit yourselves to be fearful, intimidated, cowardly and unsettled. Now, pull down that spirit of dread and then get prepared to move on with the day. Keep saying this truth as you move through it!

JOHN 14:27; EPH. 6:10; 1 COR. 16:13

November 28

"fear not, for I am with you..."
ISAIAH 41:10 (ESV)

If you become overwhelmed and begin to doubt how the impossible situation you're facing could ever be turned around, or how Jesus could ever restore your heart after the hurt you've gone through. Remember that the power that brought Jesus back to life is alive *in you*...the tomb is empty! What looked like a tragic end was a beautiful beginning...full of hope; God's promise to us. Jesus spent 40 days after His resurrection telling those He loved, "don't be afraid, it's Me." Hear that in your spirit today...don't be afraid. Your traveling companion is Jesus. His Spirit goes where you go. You're never alone...*ever!*

During each hurt, disappointment, rejection and broken dream He is with you. Expect to be restored beyond what you can imagine. Renew your mind daily with God's Word, say what He says about you, and don't be anxious or afraid. He's with you always. Nothing is impossible for our God! Do not fear or be dismayed about anything. He will strengthen you. His love is perfect and casts out *all* fear. He knows what you're facing this very second, and He's your traveling companion always. Jesus *will* help you...the tomb is empty!

LUKE 18:27, 24:3; JOEL 2:25; ISAIAH 41:10 (ESV); I JOHN 4:18; EPH. 3:20

November 29

"Take heart; it is I. Do not be afraid."
MATT. 14:27 (ESV)

There is no physical distance that can separate you from what you have not dealt with in your heart and mind. Many are deceived in believing that if they physically put distance between themselves and the situation that caused them pain, they can move on from it. *But we can't physically move on from what we haven't emotionally dealt with!* Until we face what we're running from...it will chase us down and ultimately debilitate us!

The only way we can separate and move on from the things that have caused us pain is to take Jesus with us back to where we experienced the pain. When we do, His love empowers us to stand up to what hurt us...not to prove who we are, but to assert Who we belong to! When we're known by Him, we have the courage and strength to stand up to the situations that *tried* to determine our identity. Facing the situation gives us the clarity that it wasn't the situation that had us chained to the past, it was the *emotions* that we experienced in the situation. This insight enables us to lay down the pain that tried to define us and accept the love of Jesus, where our authentic identity is found!

The love of Jesus breaks chains. Jesus doesn't make the past go away, but when we make Him our Lord and Savior, His love has the power to break off the emotions that chained us to the past. Our identity is not bound to the wounds imposed by others because Jesus has deprived this world of the power to harm us! Will you let Jesus break your chains?

JOHN 10:10; PROV. 19:20; MATT. 14:27 (ESV); JOHN 8:31-32, 16:33

November 30

"I correct and discipline everyone I love.
So be diligent and turn from your indifference."
REV. 3:19 (NLT)

Correction is to make you right...not wrong. You're made right in Christ's righteousness, but to walk it out requires a daily transformation for every Christian. Will you let Jesus bind up and heal the old wounds you still carry where someone harshly corrected you or had unrealistic expectations of you?

Until you let the love of Jesus heal you, you will be defensive and reject correction. You want to be approved and valued, especially by those you love, but your defensiveness keeps a wall up between you and everyone and everything you care about. With loved ones, it's an ongoing fight. They're trying to connect, telling you how they feel, but all you hear is criticism and hurt in your heart...that you are wrong! Your behavior may be wrong, but you're not wrong. You won't accept this until you allow Jesus to heal the wrong done to you. Those who love you want to address the wrong behavior in the relationship that keeps you and them from connecting, but you push them away. And then they walk away feeling defeated and even more distant from you; exactly what you don't want...their rejection of you. Will you let Jesus correct you to make you right...not wrong?

ROM. 8:1 (ESV); HEB. 12:8; REV. 3:19 (NLT); PROV. 3:12

†

December 1

"Take hold of my instructions; don't let them go.
Guard them, for they are the key to life."
PR. 4:13

God's Word is the key to having stability in an unstable world and moving forward with a confident expectation. God's Word works all the time, in every generation, in any kind of situation and with every person! It's your armor in daily battles, food for your soul and water for life...it's living and active and tells you things you did not know! It's a lamp to your feet and light to your path. It will heal every part of your broken heart and hold on for you when life depletes you. It gives you hope when there's no hope in sight, enable you to rise up with boldness and have an unshakeable confidence despite the inevitable adversity in life!

Don't turn your back on the privilege of knowing God's Word. It's your answer to any and every situation in life. Renew your mind with it every day and ask the Holy Spirit to give you the grace to walk it out...it's your key to stability in an unstable world!

PROV. 4:13; EPH. 4:23; ROM. 12:2

December 2

"For the LORD God is our sun and our shield. He gives us grace and glory. The LORD will withhold no good thing from those who do what is right."
PS. 84:11 (NLT)

Are you living in the freedom Jesus gives you daily? If you're not, what's getting in the way? Jesus' hope anchors you when this world overwhelms you. His peace surpasses all under-standing and His joy completes you. No devil in hell can steal, kill or destroy what Jesus died to give you...unless you release it to him. God has given us authority over the enemy; *this is a truth, not a feeling.*

To overcome the evil in this world, we must appropriate the truth we know...not what we feel. God's Word is the truth that never changes though our feelings change constantly. Know the truth and the truth will set you free, because where the Spirit of the Lord is, there is freedom. Live in the freedom Jesus offers you each day!

HEB. 6:19; PHIL. 4:7; JOHN 8:29, 10:10, 15:11; LUKE 9:1; 2 COR. 3:17; PS. 84:11

December 3

"Jesus came and told his disciples,
'I have been given all authority in heaven and on earth".
MATT. 28:18 (NLT)

The joy of the Lord is your strength...He can handle anything you release to Him! All authority in heaven and on earth have been given to Jesus. The burdens you face are subjected to His authority! When you release to Jesus the impossible you're facing, you move the burden off of you & into His hands. This allows you to experience the peace He promises because you are no longer trying to manage an impossible situation; your hope is no longer tethered to the burden which caused hopelessness, but now you're tethered to Jesus...Who never fails you! After releasing the burden to Jesus, you make room to receive His peace. His peace gives your mind the clarity needed to recognize the burden hasn't changed, but your perspective has. The burden is still there, but you're confident Jesus will handle it. You don't have to know how He will handle it to choose to believe He will! The joy of the Lord is your strength for every impossible situation you face in life. He will handle it...if you release it to Him. Will you let Jesus have it?

MARK 10:27; HEB. 6:19; PHIL. 4:7; MATT 28:18 (NLT)

December 4

"You did not choose me, but I chose you and appointed you so that you might go and bear fruit--fruit that will last--and so that whatever you ask in my name the Father will give you."
JOHN 15:16

Do not feel sorry for yourself...there's nothing sorry about you! Don't settle for this defeated mindset. How could anything be sorry about you...don't you know the Spirit of God lives in and completes you! The Holy Spirit stands ready to help you discern the balance between your emotions and life experiences. He also helps you understand how past emotions and experiences factor into your current thinking, thought patterns and decisions. Be deliberate in seeking Him daily, purposed to know what His Word says and He will give you wisdom. Be careful that your prayer time doesn't become a complaining time. God wants you to express your heart, purge yourself of everything before Him and He will fill you up with His Truth. But if you're mostly complaining and not being a "doer" of the Word, you will forfeit His comfort, guidance and love, and settle for staying stuck in a defeated mindset!

Retrain your thought patterns and be purposed in thanking God for His provisions in all you do today. Each time the defeated mindset pushes on you...push back on it with God's truth! This strengthens your "truth muscles" that keep you on the course God's calling you to!

JOHN 15:6, 16:24; ROM. 8:28, 37; 1 COR. 15:57; 1 JOHN 5:4

December 5

"A wise man will hear, and will increase learning;
and a man of understanding shall attain unto wise counsels..."
PROV. 1:5 (KJV)

Don't dread your job another day. Ask for wisdom. People seek to be defined *by* a job...but God seeks to define people *for* a job. *"For we are God's [own] handiwork (His workmanship)...[taking paths which He prepared ahead of time] that we should walk in them."* He has good plans. Many Christians miss their calling to be defined because they're busy doing good things for God...but not being still enough to hear Him give direction. We're not called to respond to every request. If you're caught in this trap you will often respond to valid needs, but it doesn't mean God has called you to those things.

Get with God; He wants you to know the paths He's prepared for you. Ask God to search your heart for direction and He will answer you. Talk this over with wise, godly counsel. We miss it at times, but we can confidently expect our Father to reveal His plan and redirect us. Be still and let God define you.

EPH.2:10 (AMP); JER.29:11; PS. 46:10, 139:23-24; PROV. 1:5 (KJV)

December 6

"The tongue has the power of life and death,
and those who love it will eat its fruit."
Prov. 18:21

Spoken words are powerful. They encourage and give life or discourage and give death. God gives us His Word to speak life-comfort, joy, peace, faith, hope, and most of all...love! When you're overwhelmed, immediately speak God's Word and agree with it; it will minister to your mind and heart. Keep the name of Jesus on your lips, ready to call out to Him during danger or despair! Give thanks to God throughout the day. His Word is your sword to protect you and give you confidence!

This world imposes a lot of hurt and pain, but in the midst of it we can speak life with God's Word-replacing hopelessness with hope, anxiety with peace, sorrow with joy, lies with truth, and call those things that be not as though they are! God's Word is full of power. Speaking it is a privilege. Don't turn your back on it; use it as God instructs you to! You have the power of life and death in your tongue...choose words of life!

Prov. 18:21; Matt. 12:36-37; Ps. 19:14

December 7

"And God raised us up with Christ and seated us
with him in the heavenly realms in Christ Jesus."
Eph. 2:6

When life is crumbling around you...do not fear! God is building up your faith in Him while He tears down the false securities in and around you, which obscure your view of the new things He wants to show you! Do not fear as you watch more crumble. He goes before you and follows behind you with His hand of blessing on you. Your hope is in Him-*not in what you see*! He will supply all your needs and give you more than you dare imagine...according to the power that's at work within you.

The same power that brought Jesus back to life and ascended Him into Heaven is at work within you! Your mind can't comprehend this truth unless you ask the Holy Spirit to give you revelation....and He will if you ask. Your decision to believe this truth by faith releases Christ's power through you. Do not fear; God will give you the desire and power to obey what He asks of you. His grace is sufficient, and with His power at work within you...you can do all things He asks you to do!

Hold tight to the truth-it's a lamp to your feet and a light to your path, giving you a clear view of the new things God wants to show you!

PS. 119:105, 139:5; COL. 2:12; 2 COR. 5:7, 12:9; EPH. 2:6, 3:20; PHIL. 2:13

December 8

"I spread out my hands to you; I thirst for you like a parched land."
PS. 143:6

Make your mission to seek your Father's face first thing each morning. Run to Him...His love is your power, giving you hope for the day; a confident expectation that He's in control of it all. Put your trust in Him; His love holds you and your life together; all that you see and don't see! He will direct you in the way to go. The more revelation you have of God's love for you...the more at peace you can be, trusting that the One Who gave you life can take care of you and handle anything you're up against!

HEB. 11:1; MATT. 6:33; COL. 1:16-17; PROV. 3:5

December 9

"Submit yourselves, then, to God.
Resist the devil, and he will flee from you."
JAMES 4:7

Desperation will try to lure you off the course God's called you to...don't take the bait! A mind led by emotions leads to death... a mind led by the Spirit leads to life and peace! *"Where the Spirit of the Lord is there is freedom"* (SEE 2 COR. 3:17). Don't settle for believing the lies of desperation. Your mind is being tormented! You feel it's impossible to turn your mind around, *and it is apart from Christ*, but nothing is impossible for God! His truth will calibrate your thoughts, so continue to think on His Word...over and over and over!

You can do all things when He strengthens you to, and He *will* strengthen you in His Word! His power is perfected in your weakness! Your feelings will change, your thoughts will get distorted and your hope will fail at times, but your Father God will never change. His Word is true all of the time and most of all...He will never fail you! Let His truth set you free. Don't let desperation lure you off course. God will finish the good work He started in you until the day Jesus Christ returns.

2 COR. 3:17; PHIL. 1:6, 4:13; JAMES 4:7

December 10

"May you be strengthened with all power, according to his glorious might, for all endurance and patience with joy..."
COL. 1:11 (ESV)

You are divinely designed to do great things, not because of what you can or can't do, but because of *Who you belong to*...you are a child of the Great I AM! God will carry out His great plans through those who believe and love Him. Many want to debate this truth as if it's open for modification. A consistent comment I hear in counseling sessions and in "church" conversations is, "I sure hope God can use me." We don't have to *hope*, as in "maybe God will" or "maybe He won't." You can count on God working through you because His Word says so.

We all experience feelings of unworthiness when we look at our abilities and wonder how God can use us, but *what we feel doesn't change God's truth*; our feelings and abilities don't exempt God from fulfilling His plans through us! Can somebody say, "thank you, Jesus!" So stop hoping in what you can or can't do and start hoping in Who God is. Don't lean on your reasoning, but seek God's spiritual discernment in all you do and He will show you the way you're to go!

You are divinely designed by God-uniquely knitted together to do good works and make an impact in this world for His glory! Are you ready?

PHIL. 4:13; 2 COR. 12:9; EPH. 3:16; COL. 1:11 (ESV)

December 11

"But blessed are those who trust in the Lord and have made the Lord their hope and confidence."
JER. 17:7 (NLT)

It's not the trials in life that mess us up...it's how we *respond* to those trials that mess us up! Trials are part of life and we have two choices every time we face one: seek spiritual discernment from God, or seek human reasoning from man. The mind doesn't naturally seek God's discernment, it has to be "led," or it will seek what it "reasons" to be right. The mind prefers reasoning of man versus reliance on Christ. It's a false sense of hope and confidence. And the people who default to their reasoning during trials are the ones who get messed up!

Their response is natural because our limited mind can't wrap around our unlimited God. God knows this, and that's why He gives us the Holy Spirit as our Helper. He will give us the power and desire to do what's pleasing to God. Our part is to *ask* for His help. God's Word works and when we apply it to our life...it works! Will you trust God and put your hope and confidence in Him when you face a trial?

JER. 17:7 (NLT); PS. 34:8; PROV. 16:20; ISAIAH 61:3

December 12

*"But as for me, I watch in hope for the LORD,
I wait for God my Savior; my God will hear me."*
MICAH 7:7

Keep your focus when problems sideswipe you...remember Who lives in you, Who loves you and Who's bigger than what you're up against! Then breathe and focus your mind on God's Word; be armed and ready at all times. Always have a few memorized scriptures ready to speak against the problems that want to paralyze you! One of my favorites is ROMANS 8:31: *"if God is for me-who can be against me!"* Sometimes I say this over and over when a problem sideswipes me, and each time I say it, the power of God is released to sustain me and move me through! God's Word is full of power. Each time you "think on" God, you open the door to the Holy Spirit. His help enables you to push back on the problem. Likewise, "thinking on" the problem closes the door to the Holy Spirit!

We're not exempt from life sideswiping us, but when it does...God's power is released through us to deal with it. When you know the power of God's love, the problems you face lose their power!

MICAH 7:7; ROM. 8:31; PS. 130:5; ISAIAH 45:22

December 13

"Before a downfall the heart is haughty, but humility comes before honor."
PROV. 18:12

Every trial presents a fork in the road of life...you can resent what's imposed on you or you can embrace what God will do through you! Resentment opens the door to pride, which fuels an indignant and arrogant spirit, which in turn demands to know the "reason" for the trial and then "why" God is letting it happen...as if some people are exempt from trials of life.

There's a way that appears right in the mind but that leads to death. Embracing the trial opens the door to humility, enabling your faith to be tested and tried, producing character in perseverance and patience! These character qualities are the rich soil needed to bring God's plans to fruition through us! Although the trials are tiring, God's strength will sustain and carry you through. What will you do at the next fork in the road of life?

PROV. 14:12, 18:12; 2 COR. 12:9; JAMES 1:25

December 14

"O taste and see that the LORD [our God] is good! Blessed (happy,
fortunate, to be envied) is the man who trusts and
takes refuge in Him."
PS. 34:8 (AMP)

Get the revelation...*you can't do anything on your own, unless God
equips you to do it*! We're called...God equips; follow His ways,
not yours and you will fulfill your call. Purpose to know Him.
Knowing Him is *not facts about Him*, but intimately seeking His
face, praising Him, finding your identity in Him, believing Him
when your life is falling apart around you...believing He's for
you and not against you.

Believing isn't a culmination of your feelings...your feelings
change moment by moment, but believing God is based on
Who He is; God is love! Receiving God's love daily is essential
for you to carry out your call; the fuel to sustain and move you
forward. Are you ready to move forward?

PS. 34:8 (AMP); PS. 119:103; PROV. 16:20; JER. 17:7

December 15

"I will say to the prisoners, 'Come out in freedom,'
and to those in darkness, 'Come into the light.'
ISAIAH 49:9 (NLT)

You can't separate from your past...but you can completely heal
from it! You must give all of yourself to Jesus. What you hold
back...He can't heal. Allow the love of Jesus to pour in and
through you, tenderly binding up every part of your broken
heart. Jesus will gently cleanse every wound with His Word...
whether it was imposed on you or if you brought it on
yourself.

This is a promise to you but...you have to release your heart to
Him. Only the love of Jesus can satisfy you. Don't waste one
more day looking back or trying to erase the past. The past is
not who you are...it's what you went through; God's love approves of all of you. Bring everything before Him. He works

your past mistakes into His glorious plan! The question is...will you let Him?

Isaiah 49:9 (NLT); Luke 4:8; Micah 5:4

December 16

"Forget the former things; do not dwell on the past."
Isaiah 43:18

Letting go of what was...the former familiar. You're in a new season, and to say you feel vulnerable, insecure and awkward is an understatement! The past is gone. There's nothing to hold onto there; you can't stay in a place that no longer exists. Trust God and reach forward to what lies in front of you. God wants to show you new things, but you won't see them if you're still looking back!

Life is constant. It continues whether you choose to move with it or not. God's made a way for you to move forward...will you say "yes" to the life He wants to show you?

Isaiah 43:18-19, 65:17; 2 Cor. 5:17; 1 Cor. 2:9

December 17

"The LORD had said to Abram, "Go from your country, your people and your father's household to the land I will show you."
Gen. 12:1

God does His best work in us when we've left our familiar but have not arrived in our new season. We're uncertain, unfamiliar, unsettled...pride purged, false confidence knocked out and beliefs challenged! This is the middle part of believing where we're undone and come to know first-hand God's love for us like never before. It's the season we'd never volunteer for, but once we experience the hope that it gives, we wouldn't trade it for anything...because God's hope never disappoints!

We come to know without a shadow of doubt the revelation that God's love accepts and approves us, and we know that we are known by Him. His love is the reason we do what we do...it is the sustenance of our existence! Don't pass on believing God through the middle and into the next season He's calling you to...it's where you experience His love that approves you not for what you do or don't do, but for who you are in Him!

GEN. 12:1; ACTS 7:3; HEB. 11:8; ROM. 12:12

December 18

"So don't worry about tomorrow, for tomorrow will bring its own worries. Today's trouble is enough for today."
MATT. 6:34 (NLT)

Are you in a waiting season? Did you think you would be through it by now? Do you find yourself a little anxious and wondering when God's going to make things normal again? First, you have to let go of your idea of normal-if not, you will forgo the destiny God's planned for you. Next, you have to decide if you believe God; He promises two outcomes for every trial: He will either remove it or bring you through it. But if you're waiting on the outcome of "when" before you enjoy your life "now," you're in for one long miserable ride.

God promises to bring us through every trial and do exceedingly and abundantly more than we can imagine, but we'll miss His provisions if...we're focused on the outcome versus relying on Him during the process leading up to the outcome.

Focusing on the resolution keeps us in an emotional limbo; we're forever waiting for...tomorrow. But, tomorrow never comes. We have to be purposed in relying on God *today*. As we seek God's hope for today, He gives us a supernatural ability to go through the season full of hope while we're pushing back on the adversity that wants to kill us emotionally. This is how we build our trust muscles and learn to persevere; perseverance builds character and character builds hope! This wait season will overflow with God's hope if we trust Him!

MATT. 6:34 (NLT); EPH. 3:20-21; 1 THESS. 5:24; PS. 27:14; ISAIAH 40:31

December 19

"Be joyful in hope, patient in affliction, faithful in prayer."
ROM. 12:12

Following Jesus can bring isolation, resistance and ridicule from many; it's the enemy's plan to abort the dream God put in your heart. If the enemy can distract you, he can get you off course. Going through these fires of persecution isn't in vain. God uses every part of your persecution for His glory! The full impact won't be known until you're in Heaven, but what you *do know* on this side of Heaven is that your spiritual tenacity is developed during persecution; every time you're pressed on, Jesus presses back through you and you're made stronger!

Cling tightly to Jesus, He's the Lover of your soul. It's His love that will nourish you when fatigue overwhelms you. When you're tired and just want to lie on the floor and cry because you can't see a way-*call out to Jesus*! His love will recharge and revive you to get up and go at it again! Be confident in His ability. You *will* overcome because He's overcome this world and gone before you to make a way!

And, He won't give up on you until He walks you across the finish line! Keep moving friend...you're making a difference in this world!

ROM. 12:12, 15:4; HEB. 10:32; PS. 119:50

December 20

"Peace I leave with you; my peace I give you. I do not give to you as the world gives. Do not let your hearts be troubled and do not be afraid."
JOHN 14:27

Jesus tells us to not let our hearts be troubled; He promises us peace, *despite* the problems we encounter in life. Most profess to believe this truth, but their lives don't reflect it. So why do so many people have troubled hearts? The answer is *fear*; none of us are exempt from experiencing fear, but we don't have to settle for it and let it dominate our thoughts by stealing the peace Jesus promises! Here's what you need to know about fear, so it doesn't trouble your heart.

Thoughts come into your mind from two sources: God's truth or the enemy's lies. Both operate on the same principle: they produce an emotional response that triggers thought patterns that determine how you perceive the problem in your mind. Every time you face a problem and choose to focus on God's truth, you appropriate His power from within you, which enables feelings of security; this response reinforces thought patterns rooted in a confident expectation. Likewise, when you focus on the enemy's lies, you appropriate emotions that produce fear; this response reinforces thought patterns rooted in doubt and insecurity! So, your *focus* determines the dominant thought patterns that grow the stronger roots.

Keeping the mind focused on God's Word is hard work, but it promises a great reward of peace. You have a choice. Don't forfeit your promise of peace and default to thinking on the enemy's lies, which will always leave you with a troubled heart!

JOHN 14:27, 16:33, PHIL. 4:7; COL. 3:15; 2 COR. 10:5

December 21

"Have I not commanded you? Be strong and courageous. Do not be afraid; do not be discouraged, for the LORD your God will be with you wherever you go."
JOSHUA 1:9

Confidence...do you have it? The world teaches a person to be confident in one's own ability and strength. Books and magazines promise and profess the best course. The truth is, we are promised confidence, but not as the world teaches; it's the confidence of Christ, His very own that He will flow through us! That's right: Lord God Almighty, Creator of the Universe will flow His power through you and me to accomplish His great and mighty plans like He did in Abraham, Deborah, David, Rahab and many others in the Bible who gave themselves to God for His glory! They knew they were unable to carry out what God asked but they laid down their plans for His, making themselves available, and God poured His "able" through them, giving them His confidence to walk out His plans! Confidence...you do have it, but you have to make yourself available to receive it. Are you available?

JOSHUA 1:9; PS. 18:29; ISAIAH 26:3 (AMP)

December 22

"But if you remain in me and my words remain in you, you may ask for anything you want, and it will be granted!"
JOHN 15:7 (NLT)

God's promises aren't like the arm of a slot machine: sometimes you get a win and sometimes you don't. God always delivers what He promises! But if you're looking to the hand of man to give what only the hand of God can deliver, you will knowingly settle to live in spiritual poverty...a life less than what God has promised. Oh, you've got to open up your eyes, ears and heart for more in life. Stop putting God in a little bitty box along with your little bitty dreams! He is big. His love is big and He loves you with all of His big love!

Listen closely: nothing gives us relief like the love of God. All else pales in comparison. When you renew your mind with God's truth and embrace His grace, you will know He's for you and not against you, and His truth will set you free to be the authentic person He designed you to be! Will you put your hope in God?

Until you do, you will seek from the hand of man what only the hand of God can deliver!

JOHN 8:31-32; EPH. 2:10; 1 COR. 2:5; ROM. 8:31; JOHN 15:7 (NLT)

December 23

"Stand firm, and you will win life."
LUKE 21:19

It's risky to lay down what you thought you'd be involved in for seasons to come, but disobedience will forfeit the next season God's leading you into. Many will ask you to reconsider and reminisce old times; don't let your mind go there! Doubt whispers, "You're a quitter," and you feel like you are giving up, but what you're giving up is...your plans in exchange for God's plans! Don't open the door to reasoning. Rely on faith. Faith sees what the mind can't comprehend, being certain of God's direction despite the evidence in your hands!

You won't miss God when you're seeking to obey; He goes before you and follows behind you, placing His hand of blessing on you. God's Word is your confidence in *all* matters, developing you in *every* season so you lack *nothing*. He gives wisdom generously and without finding fault. There's nothing holy about staying where God's called you from. Move forward in faith-He's got some things He wants to show you. Are you ready?

2 COR. 5:7; PS. 139:5; JAMES 1:4-5

December 24

"The virgin will conceive and give birth to a son, and they will call him Immanuel" (which means "God with us")."
MATT. 1:23

Don't let anyone take your joy during the Christmas season; recall the reason for the season...it's Jesus, our Savior! At Christmas, most want to be with their families, make memories, and be with those they love. This is not always the picture for many people for various reasons, but the theme is the same...it always centers around hurt. Understand this: you need to acknowledge your hurt-then celebrate Jesus. He knows all about your feelings-He experienced each one of them when He walked as a man. He leaned into His Father to get through-you do the same.

If you lean into your hurt, that is what you will have....hurt. Lean into Jesus-celebrate Him; move through with Him versus moving through alone and hurting. I don't know how He will handle what you're going through, but I do know He will go through with you and get you to other side of whatever you're facing. A Savior has been born to you, He is Christ the Lord! Will you let Jesus be your Savior? Merry Christmas!

Luke 2:11 (ESV); Isaiah 9:6-7; Matt. 1:23

December 25

"For unto you is born this day in the city of David a Savior,
who is Christ the Lord."
Luke 2:11 (ESV)

Merry Christmas! Here we are after months of activity: decorating, gift-buying, parties, candy and cookies, family gatherings and opening presents...the day is coming to a close, but the reason we celebrate isn't. As Christians, we should celebrate Christmas every day. We have a Savior, and His name is Jesus...because of Him we are free from the bondage of sin, and have a purpose and hope for today...and forever!

As you get ready to box up Christmas don't box up Jesus too...celebrate your privilege as a Christian and have yourself a very Merry Christmas every day of the year!

Luke 2:11 (ESV); Isaiah 9:6

December 26

"Then you will find favor with both God and people,
and you will earn a good reputation."
Prov. 3:4 (NLT)

Vulnerability-opening up the doors to the parts of your heart that you've hidden, and taking a risk to be known and accepted. When you take the risk to believe God at His Word and begin to embrace His love, He will give you the courage to confront what fear convinced you to hide! *What you bring into the light loses it's power*...God's love casts out all fear and destroys the lies of the enemy! The enemy wants you to believe you will lose credibility if you're vulnerable and let others see your struggle. But, he's a liar; people actually *gain* respect when they are real about struggles-people connect with struggles, not perfection.

There might be some who can't handle your story, but that's their issue, not yours. Others will accept the good and bad parts of you just as they have (or should have) accepted the good and bad parts of themselves. If you only present what you believe will be accepted, you remain a prisoner to self-imposed (and unrealistic) perfection. But when you embrace God's truth, you know that where the Spirit of the Lord is, there is freedom...if you're saved-you're free!

God has accepted and approved every part of you, and He will bring to completion the good work He started in you until the day Jesus Christ returns. See yourself as God sees you. His arms are wide open and waiting to love you into Jesus' likeness. His love will encourage and soothe you, and give you a hope and a future! Will you open up the doors to your heart to be known and accepted by others?

PROV. 3:4 (NLT); ROM. 14:18; PS. 27:1; ISAIAH 41:10

December 27

*"And God raised us up with Christ and seated us with him
in the heavenly realms in Christ Jesus..."*
EPH. 2:6

Many are excited about the new beginnings of each new year, but bring their old ways of thinking forward-so not much ever changes and they end each year with few accomplishments and many disappointments. To live the abundant life Jesus promises, you have to renew your mind constantly with God's truth..your end-is where Jesus begins. This is the sweet spot-where life is lived as God planned for all who believe in Him.

Jesus offers the ride of a lifetime to all who will let Him drive! God has not missed one tiny detail; He's included every mistake you've made (past, present and future), every wrong done to you and all your weaknesses. He even gives you the desire and power to obey him! Your part is to put your faith in Him... constantly. When you're ready to give the first of your last, believe without seeing, and risk leaving your comfort zone...*then* buckle up, baby, because you're going places! Riding with Jesus doesn't exempt you from heartaches and hardships, but He promises to deliver you from each one. Doubt will always loom-waiting to steal the destiny God has promised you. Don't allow these difficult and unknown seasons to interfere with your ride.

God is faithful and will give you the ability to endure and a way out...*every time!* Many leave the ride at this point, opting to believe what they feel instead of...believe what they know. Listen closely: *faith only grows in unknown and unfamiliar places.* You don't have to know *how* God will carry out what He's promised to choose to...*believe* what He's promised! I pray you won't opt out of the ride of your lifetime...will you follow Jesus in the coming year, and live the life He's promised you?

JOHN 10:10,16:29; ROM. 12:2; 2 COR. 12:9; EPH. 2:10, 3:20; EPH. 2:6

December 28

"Do not be afraid. Stand firm and you will see the deliverance the LORD will bring you today"
EX. 14:13

Life impacts you, how you respond...defines you! Trials are part of life-don't let them steal God's promises or be your identity. Take ownership of your life...repair what you've broken, return what you've stolen, stop blaming, quit wishing-take steps, make amends, finish what you've started, be real-stop faking, stop being stingy-it's not yours anyway, be a giver, keep your word, hold your words, let go of guilt-be full of joy, break off toxic relationships, bless others with words of life-not death, receive grace, give grace, be an overcomer.

Our Father promises to strengthen and harden you to difficulties: *"Yes, I will help you; yes, I will hold you up & retain you with My [victorious] right hand of rightness & justice."* (SEE ISAIAH 41:10 AMP). God promises His help to you; His Word is your confidence for anything and everything you need or have to take care of. Spend time in the Word daily and ask the Holy Spirit for revelation of how you're to walk it out. You're more than a conqueror-if God's for you, who can be against you? Don't waste another good day wishing...get moving!

ISAIAH 41:10 (AMP); ROM. 8:31,37; EX. 14:13

December 29

"Search me, O God, and know my heart! Try me and know my thoughts!"
PS. 139:23 (ESV)

If you find yourself consistently agitated with someone...usually it's because they have something you want, are stirring up unresolved issues, or they're having the boldness to go after a dream like God's prompted you to do, but which you've resisted out of fear. Ask the Holy Spirit to search what's going on inside of your heart and give you revelation regarding the reason for your irritation with this person.

The bottom line is that no person has the power to make you feel something, but their behavior can "irritate" an issue in you that you've not dealt with. Don't dumb-down your response and dismiss it. The Holy Spirit will give you insight if you're willing to receive it. Don't cheat yourself out of the wisdom He will give you by minimizing your feelings as, "I just don't like them-that's all." That's not all...there's more to it, and you won't know until you look into your heart with the Holy Spirit's wisdom!

PS. 139:23; JOHN 14:26; PROV. 14:8

December 30

"For the Spirit God gave us does not make us timid,
but gives us power, love and self-discipline."
2 TIM. 1:7

God uses adversity to test and deepen our faith-don't run from it...you will miss the work He wants to do through you! For years I prayed to just get through adversity-I would white-knuckle the ride and hope I would be able to hold on; this left me anxious and uncertain! Then the Holy Spirit gave me revelation: *I was relying on my ability to hold on instead of relying on His hope to flow through me!* This subtle but powerful shift in my thinking made a huge difference in my living! Anxiety and uncertainty no longer overwhelmed me because I was no longer relying on my ability to hope I could get through, but I was relying on the power of the Holy Spirit to flow His hope through me to bring me through! This allowed me to have a confident hope in God and rest in His provisions while following Him.

I still get off course at times even though I'm renewing my mind-no person is exempt, but immediately I adjust my thinking and remember where my hope comes from! My hope comes from the Lord...*and so does yours!* Will you let Him flow His hope through you so that He can carry out His work through you?

2 TIM. 1:7; ISAIAH 11:2; ROM. 8:15

December 31

"Yes, I am the vine; you are the branches. Those who remain in me, and I in them, will produce much fruit. For apart from me you can do nothing."
JOHN 15:5 (NLT)

Wow! Another year behind you! Whatever you do, don't begin to criticize what you didn't accomplish. Instead, look at the changes God made through you. God convicts us into victory; He never uses condemnation to get us there! Here are four steps to keep in mind as you move forward into next year:

1) Seek God first. Nothing lasting happens apart from His power working through you.
2) Accept where you are without making excuses, even if the excuses seem valid. Looking at the "why" instead of the "Who" puts the focus on the reasons for your undesired behavior instead of Who can empower you to overcome the undesired behavior. It's hard for us to compute. After all, we must be responsible, right? Our responsibility for change isn't based on what *we* can do-it's founded in what *Jesus* has already done for us!
3) Freedom is found in Christ-*exclusively*. What you seek is what you serve!
4) Wait on the Lord. Authentic change only happens from the inside out, but it's not in your strength. Christ's power is perfected in your weakness. When you're weak you're strong!

248

Well, that's a wrap for renewing your mind for *this* year. Remember that our *spirit* was saved once, but our *mind* has to be saved *every day of the year*! God bless you. I'm sure our paths will cross again!

Matt. 6:33; John 15:5 (NLT); 2 Cor. 3:17, 12:9-10

†

CHRISTIAN INSIGHT FOR LIFE...
FOR EVERY DAY

A DAILY DEVOTIONAL

The devotional *Christian Insight for Life*
includes over 100 powerful devotions taken from the popular blog of
the same name, authored by Laura Mangin McDonald.

Here you'll find daily readings offering just what you need for the day:
comfort for a weary heart, strength for walking out faith, encouragement in the face of adversity, the promises of a loving Father, sustenance for the spirit, freedom from anger, regret and doubt, and
Scripturally-sound insight for living a courageous life of faith.

Softcover: 1 4839 6576 7
Digital: B00E98RA8Y

Also available in Portuguese.
Softcover: 1 5003 9821 7
Digital: B00LXN072O

To order, visit:
www.christianinsightforlife.com, or

www.createspace.com/4222339 (English)
www.createspace.com/886033 (Portuguese)

or amazon.com

CHRISTIAN INSIGHT FOR LIFE

Christian Insight for Life is a non-profit teaching and discipling ministry founded by Rod and Laura McDonald, based in Garland, Texas.

The ministry is dedicated to fulfilling the call of Matthew 5:16, to shine the light of God's truth around the world. Through speaking and teaching, publications, outreach and social media, we provide practical, powerful and Spirit-led tools and insight to help people know who they are in Christ, enabling them to confidently put faith into action in daily life.

Over almost 30 years as a Christian counselor and therapist, and as a writer and Bible teacher, Laura has developed a practical, Bible-centered approach to seeing ourselves as God does, renewing our minds and sustaining change in the way we view ourselves, our relationships, our circumstances, and in our connection to God.

Bring Laura and Christian Insight for Life to your church or organization. She is available for:
• Speaking
•Group facilitating and team training
•Conferences and seminars

For resources, scheduling and other information, visit:
www.christianinsightforlife.com

Or write to:
Christian Insight for Life,
P.O. Box 452796, Garland, TX 75045-2796

Like us on Facebook:
www.facebook.com/christianinsightforlife
Follow us on Twitter:
@ItsLMM

This book is available in softcover and for Kindle e-reader.
To order copies, visit our website or go to:

www.createspace.com/5213518